African American Literacies

"Elaine Richardson's *African American Literacies* is a profoundly powerful and moving book. Though much has been written on Richardson's themes, her book is full of fresh ideas."

James Paul Gee, University of Wisconsin at Madison, USA

"Elaine Richardson has brought an energizing, critical Black voice into the conversation on African American literacy by grounding this book in African American ways of speaking and knowing. The daughter of an African American community where reading and writing failure often shortcircuited academic success, she is well equipped to confront attempted culture-cide in the writing classroom."

Arthur K. Spears, The City University of New York, USA

"Richardson has created an African American-centred composition curriculum that takes her students on the journey from 'slaveship to scholarship' . . . Ultimately, her book too will save somebody's life."

Geneva Smitherman, Michigan State University, USA

African American Literacies is a personal, public and political exploration of literacy education from the points of view of students from the African American Vernacular English (AAVE) culture.

Drawing on personal experience, Elaine Richardson provides a compelling account of the language and literacy practices of African American students. The book offers teachers new ways of thinking about and incorporating linguistic diversity into their theories and pedagogical methods of addressing students from AAVE cultures. Richardson builds on recent research to argue that teachers need not only to recognize the value and importance of African American culture, but also to use African American English when teaching AAVE speakers standard English.

African American Literacies offers a holistic and culturally relevant approach to literacy education, and is essential reading for anyone with an interest in the literacy practices of African American students.

Elaine Richardson is Assistant Professor of English and by courtesy Applied Linguistics at Pennsylvania State University.

LITERACIES

Series Editor: David Barton

Lancaster University

Literacy practices are changing rapidly in contemporary society in response to broad social, economic and technological changes: in education, the workplace, the media and in everyday life. The *Literacies* series has been developed to reflect the burgeoning research and scholarship in the field of literacy studies and its increasingly interdisciplinary nature. The series aims to situate reading and writing within its broader institutional contexts where literacy is considered as a social practice. Work in this field has been developed and drawn together to provide books which are accessible, interdisciplinary and international in scope, covering a wide range of social and institutional contexts.

CITY LITERACIES
Learning to Read Across Generations and Cultures
Eve Gregory and Ann Williams

LITERACY AND DEVELOPMENT
Ethnographic Perspectives
Edited by Brian V. Street

SITUATED LITERACIES
Theorising Reading and Writing in Context
Edited by David Barton, Mary Hamilton and Roz Ivanic

MULTILITERACIES
Literacy Learning and the Design of Social Futures
Edited by Bill Cope and Mary Kalantzis

GLOBAL LITERACIES AND THE WORLD-WIDE WEB
Edited by Gail E. Hawisher and Cynthia L. Selfe

STUDENT WRITING
Access, Regulation, Desire
Theresa M. Lillis

SILICON LITERACIES
Communication, Innovation and Education in the Electronic Age
Edited by Ilana Snyder

AFRICAN AMERICAN LITERACIES
Elaine Richardson

African American Literacies

Elaine Richardson

Routledge
Taylor & Francis Group

LONDON AND NEW YORK

First published 2003
by Routledge
11 New Fetter Lane, London EC4P 4EE

Simultaneously published in the USA and Canada
by Routledge
29 West 35th Street, New York, NY 10001

Routledge is an imprint of the Taylor & Francis Group

© 2003 Elaine Richardson

Typeset in Baskerville by
The Running Head Limited, Cambridge
Printed and bound in Great Britain by
St Edmundsbury Press, Bury St Edmunds, Suffolk

British Library Cataloguing in Publication Data
A catalogue record for this book is available from the British Library

Library of Congress Cataloging in Publication Data
A catalog record for this book has been requested

ISBN 0–415–26882–6 (hbk)
ISBN 0–415–26883–4 (pbk)

Contents

Figures and tables

Foreword

In essays and speeches contained in the collection, *The Education of Black People*, edited by Herbert Aptheker and published by the University of Massachusetts Press in 1973, W. E. B. DuBois laid out his grand vision for the education of Negroes (to use the terminology of that era). Focusing on higher education under US-style apartheid of the 1930s, DuBois argued that the role of education was not simply to teach Negroes how to make a living but how to make a life. He thus called for a curriculum and philosophical pedagogy grounded in their culture and real world needs.

In the same way, a Negro university in the United States of America begins with Negroes. It uses that variety of the English idiom which they understand; and above all, it is founded, or it should be founded on a knowledge of the history of their people in Africa and in the United States, and their present condition (DuBois, 1973: 93). College teachers cannot follow the medieval tradition of detached withdrawal from the world . . . The teacher . . . has got to be something far more than a master of a branch of human knowledge . . . the possibilities and advancement of [a Black man/woman] . . . in the world where [he/she] is to live and earn a living is of just as much importance in the teaching process as the content of the knowledge taught (DuBois, 1973: 78).

It is now more than seven decades since DuBois wrote these words. The US-style apartheid laws have been abolished. We have witnessed the emergence of a voluminous body of research on the language and culture of African Americans. Yet we find ourselves still engaged in struggle: how to implement pedagogical practices that will effectively and successfully address the continuing educational crises of Black students.

Elaine Richardson's work is a major contribution to that struggle. Her book brings together composition, African American language and the Black tradition of literacy. Seeking to do "right in a wrong world," Richardson has created an African American-centered composition curriculum that takes her students on the journey from "slaveship to scholarship." Along the way, they analyze literacy practices in Hip Hop and "discover" Black female literacies. For the first time, the students are exposed to a conception of the vernacular that goes far beyond phonemes, morphemes, and Black slang to encompass an Africanized worldview and what DuBois called the "wild sweet melodies" of African American rhetorical and cultural practices. Richardson argues, and quite rightly so, that African American discourses and rhetorics constitute a "survival culture" that transforms Black people while simultaneously enriching and enlarging mainstream White American discourses. Thus, the vernacular is a crucial resource that often goes untapped as African American literacy failure rates continue to rise.

With clever, creative topic titles (my favorite: "Freestylin' or lookin' for a style that's free"), Richardson methodically builds her case for an African American-centered composition curriculum. At this late hour in the history of the African-centered Educational Movement, pedagogical justification for this kind of curriculum should not be necessary, with some schools boasting a successful track record coming up on three decades—e.g., New Concept Development Center, founded in Chicago in 1972, Aisha Shule/W. E. B. DuBois Preparatory Academy, founded in Detroit in 1974. Nonetheless, Richardson early on takes pains to explain that such a composition course is not separatist or intellectually deficient. Rather, it is what Richardson describes as the "course of study of subjects" such as "English language usage, literacy acquisition, rhetoric, writing, and education from the point of view of African American experiences." Displaying her own "heightened consciousness" of the rhetorical situation presented by a book on African American-centered composition, she presents critical interpretive readings and creative rhetorical analyses of early Black writers such as Phillis Wheatley and Lucy Terry; enslavement narratives, such as those of Harriet Jacobs and James Gronniosaw; Hip Hop artists; Black women rhetors. With stark clarity, we are reminded of the richness of "speakerly" texts and the Black Vernacular tradition, a reservoir of cultural productions more than sufficient to comprise the curriculum in a composition course.

Bringing together theory and practice in her ongoing literacy work with African American students in Big Ten university writing courses, Richardson offers quantitative and qualitative analyses of numerous student essays to demonstrate the effectiveness of an African American-centered composition curriculum. Varying levels of critical literacy development occurred throughout the classrooms where she conducted her "experiment." In one class, three of the students had their work accepted for publication. Not bad for a classroom of "basic" writers.

Notwithstanding the success of such a curriculum, the African American-centered approach is fraught with complexity and the potential for high drama. Richardson lays it all on the line, exposing the problems and instructional challenges, e.g., the issue of authority and credibility presented by a Black woman instructor ("me against the world"), student perceptions of such a course as "less than" and not a worthwhile intellectual endeavor, student resistance in the form of the "bi-racial" and the "objective" rhetorical stances. Nevertheless, she clings to the "bloodstained banner," unequivocally advocating African American-centered literacy experiences to help Black students struggling to "define themselves in a high tech, materialistic, capitalistic society." In fact, Richardson concludes that the problems she has encountered in university and college classrooms excruciatingly demonstrate the need for African American-centered education all the way from Kindergarten through college. Word. Shonuff. Amen.

One of the most compelling aspects of Richardson's book is the interjection of her voice and personal herstory, in and outside of the Academy. We delight in reading about her Jamaican mother's ways of knowing and literacy practices that she has passed on to her daughter. We vicariously experience her Cleveland neighborhood, with its "number and reefah houses" and "stofront Churches galore." We suffer with her in her first experience in a college writing course where she wrote about that same neighborhood and its "nocturnal insects." We applaud her return to college several years and two babies later, as she struggles to stay afloat in a sea of redness in her "basic" writing class. We exult in her triumphant development of a strong sense of Intellectual Self in the face of societal and institutional messages to the contrary. Ultimately, her book too will save somebody's life.

Geneva Smitherman, PhD
University Distinguished Professor, Michigan State University
Author, *Talkin' that Talk: Language, Culture and Education in African America* (2000)
March 2002

Acknowledgments

First giving honor to God for making me and giving me the parents and fore-parents that I have. This book is dedicated to my momma and daddy, and to my beautiful daughters—Evelyn, Ebony, and Kaila. More love and good spirits. I want to thank my aunt, Hellen Vassel, who cleaned, cooked, washed, and prayed while I wrote the first draft of this manuscript. More fire! I have to thank my daughters again for being my best friends and understanding when momma ain't got time. Thanks also to my niece, Christina, and her father, my brother, Chris. Remember, the world is yours. I would like to thank all of the students with whom I have had the pleasure of working over the years. Don't forget to come back and see me before I get old. Power to the people! Thanks to all of my mentors who helped me with problems and for giving me much needed feedback: Keith Gilyard, Jim Gee, Bernard Bell, Jack Selzer, Cheryl Glenn, John Rickford, John Baugh. Thanks to the reviewers who made this book possible: Angela Rickford, Arthur Spears, and Jim Gee. Thanks to other colleagues in the profession for their work and guidance: Ted Lardner, Tom Fox, Walt Wolfram, Sonja Lanehart, Denise Troutman, Marcy Morgan, Arnetha Ball, Charles Debose, Walter Edwards, H. Samy Alim, Jackie Royster, Shirley Wilson Logan, Gwen Pough, Signithia Fordham, Rashidah Muham-mad, Vorris Nunley, the entire NCTE Black Caucus for hush harbor rhetoric. My church—Unity Church of Jesus Christ—for support and for understanding when I'm not able to attend services. Much love to all my colleagues and friends at the University of Minnesota especially Ezra Hyland, Terry Collins, Geoff Sirc, Lisa Albrecht, and all the supporters of The Real Deal on Ebonics Conference, especially Mahmoud El Kati. Most highest big up to my mentor, Geneva da Diva Smitherman. Thanks for helping me to stand on your shoulders. And finally, thanks to two of the best research assistants a sista could have. Thank you Aesha Adams, my sister, daughter, niece, cousin, friend! And, thank you to Adam "da bomb" Banks for your serious critiques and stimulating con-versations. I couldn't have done this without you. Many thanks to Christy Kirkpatrick, Louisa Semlyn, and David Barton. Early aspects of this work were supported by grants from the University of Minnesota, Minnesota Humanities Commission, the Pennsylvania State University Minority Faculty Development

Fund. Later stages of this work were supported by grants from the Research Graduate Studies Office and the Institute for Arts and Humanities of The Pennsylvania State University.

Permissions

Lyrics from Lauryn Hill/Poyser, "Superstar," © 1998/ATV Tunes LLC, Obverse Creation Music and Jajapo Music. All rights on behalf of Sony/ATV Tunes LLC and Obverse Creation Music administered by Sony/ATV Music Publishing, 8 Music Square West, Nashville, TN 37203. All rights reserved, used by permission.

Lyrics from Tupac Shakur, Joe Sample, Tony Pizarro, Joseph B. Jefferson, Charles Simmons and Bruce Hawes, "Dear Mama," © 1995 Songs of Universal, Inc., Joshua's Dream Music, Four Knights Music Co., WB Music Corp. and the Underground Connection.

Lyrics from Bessie Smith, "Poor Man Blues," reprinted with permission by Hal Leonard Corporation.

Phillis Wheatley, "'Twas Mercy" in "On Being Brought from Africa to America" from *The Collected Works of Phillis Wheatley*, reprinted by permission by Oxford University Press.

Excerpt from anonymous poem, "Shuck corn, shell corn," in the *Journal of American Folklore*, vol. 28, 1915. Reprinted by permission of the American Anthropological Association (or American Folklore Society). Not for sale or further reproduction.

"Mathematics" words and music by Dante Beze and Christopher Martin, © 1999 EMI Blackwood Music Inc., Empire International, Medina Sound Music, EMI April Music Inc. and Gifted Pearl Music. All rights for Empire International and Medina Sound Music controlled and administered by EMI Blackwood Music Inc. All rights for Gifted Pearl Music controlled and administered by EMI April Music Inc. All rights reserved. International copyright secured. Used by permission.

Introduction: don't we still have to prove our humanity?

The first time this prof humiliated me was when I used "nocturnal insects" in my paper on my neighborhood to describe my roaches. I had heard the word nocturnal and I thought I'd use it in my paper. My neighborhood was exciting to me, and I wrote about it. I thought he wanted us to tell the truth, from our own perspectives, and make it interesting. My neighborhood flourished in trade and industry with "the number house," "the reefah house," "the after hour joint," and other houses of ill repute. We also had churches galore. Lots of them right next door to each other—"sto fronts," we called them. Men and women went in and out of those houses 24/7/365. I couldn't wait until I got old enough to go into those joints, too. (That's another book though.) They shot dice on the side of the number house. Smoked reefah on the side of the reefah house. My Pal, the proprietor of the after hour joint, didn't let people hang around outside of his joint due to police heat. At about age 13, I could talk and shoot some mean dice. "Bet you don't barg." "Baby need a new pair a shoes." "7/11 is heaven." I thought he would like it, my English teacher. I laid it all out there. I remember talking about the kind of clothes people wore and being really descriptive. Okay, I didn't know how to use punctuation correctly, but was that any reason to give me a "D?"

We were from the same kind of place, Mike and me, and we were the only two Black people in the class. The assignment was to write about our neighborhoods and how they influenced us. Mike never let me read his paper, but he tripped the prof out, too. Mike was using stuff from *Manchild in the Promised Land* as his model. Neither Mike nor I liked how the prof would change the meaning of what we were writing about when he made us rearrange it and change our words. He did tell me that I was using dialectal variants. But that was the extent of any explicit instruction in negotiating different discourses and ideologies. When I went to his office for help, our twenty-minute sessions seemed to take a great toll on him. He seemed overwhelmed by the number of grammatical sins I had committed. Perhaps he pitied me, wondering why I was even attending the university. He did ask me what high school I attended. When I told him, he shook his head and directed me to further work in the writing center.

In my visits to the writing center, one teaching assistant would deal with my

1

paper for a while, but she would soon grow tired of asking me what I was trying to say. Quite frankly, I thought what I had written was plain and simple. When she would confer with her colleagues, I wondered: "Why don't they understand? They suppose to be smart." They were employed as college writing tutors, after all. It wasn't long before I figured out that I could succeed by relinquishing my language variety and my history, experience, culture, and perspective for theirs. All I had to do was let them Whitenize my papers. Though the images and reality of what I wanted to express were diminished on the page, their language could speak for me and "earn" me a grade of "C." And at that point in time, that was all I wanted. Ah, the price for a "C" was high, the subordination of my experience and the erasure of my voice paralleling the absence of Black voices and culturally relevant material and instruction in the curriculum and the classroom. There were instances when we read "I Have a Dream" by Dr King or "The Student as Nigger" by Jerry Farber. However, when we read "I Have a Dream," for example, no Afrocentric analysis was offered as a possible reading; no mention of the Black style in Dr King's speech. Unquestionably, Dr King's speeches and writings epitomize the Afro-Americanized rhetorical and literacy traditions. As for "the student as Nigger" both Mike and I were shocked that the professor offered this text unproblematically, as though we would accept that the average college student (who by the way is the White) has an experience that parallels the African American experience of dehumanizing slavery, rape, lynching, linguistic and cultural oppression, and continued structural inequality in the aftermath of legal segregation. He didn't and couldn't provide a context for which we could interpret that text and realistically identify with it. I'm not advocating that every course be about race, but if a professor chooses to include a piece of writing with the word "nigger" in it and then glosses over the significance of that concept in the lives and historical memory of African Americans, how could he lead us to a decent rhetorical analysis of the piece? On what grounds could we explore the ethos of the piece? The logos? Did he expect that Mike and I would just be joyful because the author chose to use a word that signaled some connection to the Black struggle? Any real discussions about the concept of race or racism were avoided. This is what I call the devoicing and disempowerment of African American students. The opportunity to see oneself in the curriculum is not encouraged in that type of composition classroom. Students want to learn standardized American English conventions, and to become skilled rhetors, but these are often presented as neutral practices, isolated from the history of power relations and the politics of literacy. Consequently, most African American Vernacular English speaking students become further indoctrinated in the precepts of White dominant discourse in the process. What the student brings to the classroom is not valued or recognized; no transcultural dialogism takes place. This is not to say that there are not educators dedicated to exploring these issues with their students, but far too often cultural conflict is decentralized even as it is significant in cross cultural written and oral communication.

After one of the regular trips to the prof's office for a one-on-one conference, Mike always said stuff like, "He got the power in here, but I'll kick his punk ass outside." That prof had a way of crossing all the life out of our papers with his red pen. I dreaded that. Of course, now I know that standardized American English is not the possession of any one group and can be used by any citizen as a tool of empowerment. It was not presented to me as something that strong conscious Black people could help to shape. I didn't see it as a tool of empowerment and nobody was showing me how I could make it my own. I wanted to know why the White kids that we sat next to (the niggers in Farber's words) didn't have the same kind of grades we had, Mike and me. Before I found out, I had some living to do. (That's the other book I mentioned.)

Now I was back and desperate to stay in school. I had two babies, and I was on welfare. I never liked the stigma attached to welfare, so my goal was to go to school, try the American way, and get a "good job." Maybe teach school or something—I didn't know for sure. I just felt that I was smart, and never really found out I was illiterate until I went to college and got placed into dummy English. And, yes, everybody knew it as dummy English. I didn't care. I just wanted to get a degree and a job. I was working in the school library on work-study, at the reserve desk. I had been in all the houses in my neighborhood now and came back to school for refuge. Dr P came into the library to put some books on reserve for his class when he bumped into me. I didn't remember him. He said, "I know you." I thought, "damn, I came to school to get away and this guy knows me." I wanted to keep looking away, but this man got in my face and kept going on and on about his knowing me from somewhere. He went away only to return a few weeks later saying, "You're the A/F girl, the one who sat directly in front and slept in my physics class. Where've you been?" I could say, but I wouldn't. That had been five years ago. I just put on my smile and vaguely remembered being in his class. I remembered almost flunking it, getting Fs on most all the quizzes and the midterm. He called me "the A/F girl" because I'd come to his class hungover and I'd sleep, but somehow I decided to learn the stuff. I got an A on the final so he gave me a C for the class. A plus F = C.

But now I was back, not just wanting Cs. I wanted to do school just as I had done the streets. Done it to death. I remembered that Dr P told me that he was glad that I had come back to school and that if I ever needed help, he would help me. He said they needed more bright Black students in Physics. He gave me his phone number and all. And once after a splash in the sea of redness, I decided to call him and see if he could help me with my papers.

Dr P looked at my paper and said, "you don't talk like this. Write like you talk." I was trying not to write like I really talked because I knew that would be rejected. The way I spoke with him was the speech reserved for strangers and White folks. I knew about style shifting from my home and the streets. When dealing with White folks you talked like them. But I didn't know how to translate that to the page. My problem was that I didn't know how to write standardized

3

English and I didn't know punctuation. Anyway, Dr P helped me with punctuation and organization. My tutor, a young African American woman, A, helped me, too. She worked for the developmental program, "Special Studies."

When I turned my paper in to this new prof, he asked me "Did you write this paper?" That was almost the last time I got humiliated about my writing. Well, that's an overstatement. Anyway, my tutor was so mad when I told her what he said. She said "Elaine you can't let him talk to you like that. He thinks you can't think. Ain't nothing wrong with your mind. You're smart. I'm gonna go over there and tell him something. Who does he think he is?" And she did. One day after class, A was there waiting in the hall. She beckoned for the prof to come over to her and they exchanged words. She felt it was her duty to protect my voice. I didn't hear their conversation. When they were done, she came over to me loudtalking saying, "You have good ideas and a nice way of expressing them. Don't let them kill your voice." I was on my way to figuring out one reason that the White kids that we sat next to didn't get the same grades as people like Mike and me. That problem is *waaaaay* bigger than us. I spent the rest of my undergraduate years becoming an English major, trying to find out the deal on Black folks, language, literacy, and schooling. On my journey, I met Geneva Smitherman's *Talkin and Testifyin*. In a sense, that book saved my life. It was the first time that I read or even heard somewhere that what Black people spoke was a treasure, that it had a history behind it—not just any old history either. I found out that African American language has rules. That African American language is a part of African American history, a part of African American cultural and intellectual heritage. I always thought deep inside that I was smart, or at the least, not dumb, and Smitherman's book confirmed it for me.

In Chapter 1, "Literacy, language, composition, rhetoric and (not) the African American student," I discuss social practices such as societal stratification and the ideologies that undergird the decades' long literacy underachievement of African American students. I also discuss how African American literacy has been worked with and around in the field of rhetoric and composition, evaluating new thinking there that led me to the exploration of African American-centered rhetorics and literacies. In Chapter 2, "The literacies of African American-centered rhetoric and composition: freestylin' or lookin' for a style that's free," I map the evolution of the Black Voice in America. Here, African American Vernacular English is presented as a part of the culture of African American survival and development from slave ship to scholarship. The complexity of this topic is explored from the view of rhetorical analyses of African American literature, folklore, and other vernacular expressive arts. Chapter 3, "'To protect and serve': African American female literacies," continues to explore the literacies that inform an African American-centered rhetoric, with a focus on the female contribution to African American literacies. In Chapter 4, "African American-centered rhetoric, composition, and literacy: theory and research," I report on a much more detailed study discussing theoretical

4

influences and moving on to analysis and interpretation of data. The central research question that my study sought to answer concerns the ability of African American methodology to enhance the literacy of African American students. In Chapter 5, "Composition in a fifth key: rhetorics and discourses in an African American-centered writing classroom," I discuss the actual curriculum that I taught and the thinking behind the curriculum, while Chapter 6, "Dukin' it out with 'the powers that be': centering African American-centered studies and students in the traditional curriculum," outlines the problems one can expect to incur when implementing such a course in predominantly traditional institutions. I hope this book helps someone the way Geneva Smitherman's book helped me.

1

Literacy, language, composition, rhetoric and (not) the African American student: sick and tired of being sick and tired

I was sitting here with a bad case of writer's block wondering how to arrange my arguments in the most persuasive manner. Hoping not to lose you, my K-12 language arts teachers, or you, my composition and rhetoric colleagues, or you, my fellow sociolinguists, or you, my new literacy studies family. And I sure couldn't stand to lose my African American generalists or anyone who is sick and tired of being sick and tired of the decades long struggle to stamp out our failure in the literacy education of African American students.

At first I started out with a chart that I replicated from the National Assessment of Educational Progress (NAEP), which detailed the disparate writing achievement of Black, Hispanic, White, and Asian students from fourth grade through twelfth grade. I decided to background that[1] when I, while rambling through a bookstore bag, saw this bookmark (see Figure 1.1). And that just got me burning. "He is in the eighth grade but he's reading at the fourth grade level. Will you change this?" The young Black male body is foregrounded in the picture of the bookmark—he symbolizes illiteracy—in need of only a helping hand. The target audience for the ad is recent college graduates. We realize that the founder of the organization intends to make a difference with her life and encourage others to do the same by encouraging young graduates to dedicate their time to a worthy cause. And to be fair, a small percentage of children might improve with the extra help, but we also know that this program cannot significantly stem the tide of literacy underachievement.

Recent college graduates are offered loan forgiveness in addition to salaries if they commit to teach in the public schools in urban and rural communities for two years, as if fresh graduates could actually change something rotten that's been going on for decades. We do the same thing at the university level by initiating teaching assistants into the freshman composition classroom and bidding them to learn on the job. The bookmark exhorts young graduates to "Teach for America." That's basically what we all are doing—Teaching for America. I want my student loans forgiven too!

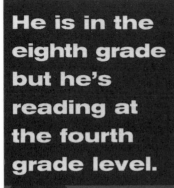

He is in the eighth grade but he's reading at the fourth grade level.

Will you change this?

Will you join the network of leaders committed to making our country a place where every child has an equal chance in life? Two-year commitment. No education coursework required. Full salary plus loan forgiveness.

TEACHFORAMERICA
www.tfanetwork.org/invite1.asp
1 800 TFA 1230 x410

Teach For America is the national corps of outstanding recent college graduates of all academic majors who commit two years to teach in public schools in our nation's lowest-income urban and rural communities.

Figure 1.1 Teach for America bookmark

For the most part, America continues to teach us to accept the status of lower achievement for Black students as the norm. Under the present system, we are set in motion to replicate the paradigm and the results. The old folks used to say, "If you keep doing what you always did, you gone keep gettin' what you always got."

Research has presented evidence which suggests that certain factors correlate with lower literacy achievement (and overall academic achievement) such as low parent educational level, low social economic status, poor school resources, no writing of successive drafts, or non use of portfolios, to name a few. Of course poverty and a host of other social problems hinder some students from coming to school every day and excelling in their work.

Community and family literacy programs have been instituted to counteract the problem of parents' educational level and family involvement to promote higher levels of literacy and to help "at risk" students of color to excel academically. To address the problem of low social economic status and poor school resources, movements such as school vouchers, charter schools, and school choice have become attractive to some. The theory behind these movements is that access to well funded schools, with lower teacher–pupil ratios and highly skilled teachers, will provide teachers with adequate resources to help students. In an effort to improve student writing, teaching writing as a process involving revision, audience accommodation, critical reflection, and portfolio evaluation are commonly thought of today as requirements in writing pedagogy.

Highly funded schools, highly trained teachers, Teach for America volunteer-paid teachers, community and family literacy programs, and open access to the latest technological advancements are a start in the right direction, yet these solutions evade a deeply rooted problem. We must face the facts. Most of us know that the majority of Black students are not cognitively deficient. So what's the real deal?

Background

One of the basic goals of the Civil Rights and Black Liberation Movements of the 1950s and 1960s was to gain access to institutions and begin the project of a multicultural America. I use the term multicultural to signify equal opportunity beyond the point of allowing people of color access to historically White studies and institutions. Multicultural in this usage means instituting Black, Latino/a, Native American, and Asian peoples, studies, and pedagogies into the center of the educational curriculum and traditional institutions, in a way that expands upon and critiques received knowledge. Yet, we are still replicating the unequal educational and literacy paradigm.

One of the major roots of African American literacy underachievement is the ideology of White supremacist and capitalistic-based literacy practices that undergird curriculum construction and reproduce stratified education and a stratified society, that reproduce the trend of African American literacy underachievement.

White supremacist ideology is insidious because it is entangled with the discourse of American meritocracy, which says that individuals are responsible for their own success. The value of individualism is consonant with White supremacy when large groups of students of color fail to achieve under its account. White supremacy in my usage refers to practices that confer privileges to white-skinned Anglo Americans at the expense of disprivileging people not of white skin, a form of racism. The percentage of students suffering under this paradigm is far beyond that of a smattering of lazy or cognitively deficient individuals who can't measure up. The failure is not individual, but ethnic and cultural groups are underachieving under the present (decades long) practices. This indicates that the problem is structural.

Characteristics of the ideology of White supremacist and capitalistic-based literacy include consumption, consent, obedience, fragmentation, singularity (as opposed to multiplicity), and positivism. The educational practices associated with this conception of literacy are naturalized in the system and taught to students as a set of isolated skills divorced from social context, politics, culture, and power (Street, 1993). Teaching standardized English, a narrowly conceived academic discourse, and their cousin, the "academic essay," are examples of the "neutral skills" needed to succeed in the corporate educational system and the market driven capitalistic society (J. Berlin, 1996). The viewpoint of official educational sites and institutions is that students/good citizens need these skills to function in society.

No matter how neutral the autonomous skills approach strives to be, many African American students detect the cultural bias early on in their school experiences, and many do not respond favorably. What many of these students see, and what many African Americans have seen down through the years is attempts to erase them culturally, word by word, from the literacy experience.

Writing on the mis-education of "the Negro," in 1933, Carter G. Woodson (1990: 3–4) articulated the problem like this:

> When a Negro has finished his education in our schools, then, he has been equipped to begin the life of an Americanized or Europeanized White man, but before he steps from the threshold of his alma mater he is told by his teachers that he must go back to his own people from whom he has been estranged by a vision of ideals which in his disillusionment he will realize that he cannot attain.

There is confusion in the literature on African American students and achievement concerning why some African American students reject their high-achieving African American peers as acting the role of a White supremacist. Carter G. Woodson identified this same phenomenon in the 1920s and 1930s. As discussed by Woodson, the culturally biased education that most African Americans experience trains them to sever ties with Black communities and cultural activities. It trains us to have no interest in making a commitment to the uplift of other African Americans less fortunate than ourselves for we have pulled ourselves up by our own bootstraps. Black community people see this as "thankin' that you betta than somebody." When this occurs, "the educated" Black person is ostracized from Black communities. This is the phenomenon of "sellin' out" or "acting white" as students in Fordham and Ogbu's 1986 work attest. It appears that many readers of Fordham and Ogbu's analysis overlook the concept of White supremacy. And that omission is crucial to understanding student rejection of so-called achievement. In this sense, achievement equals assimilating to something that is anti-Black. Students can't give us the critical historical explanation, that African Americans who have internalized White supremacist ideologies are those who have been "educated" away from the communities of their nurture. People are rejected in Black communities when their behaviors are seen as self-serving. We all have to play the game to some extent and are complicit or co-opted from jump street if we are to survive and if we need the system. The question is one of commitment to a community.

Woodson (1990: 37) noted that one of the problems with the educational system is that it teaches "too many [African Americans] to go to school to memorize certain facts to pass examinations for jobs. After they obtain these positions they pay little attention to humanity." This type of education trains students to fit into the status quo. It is a problem that is true across ethnic groups, and is supported by the ideology of American individualism. It is easy for people to buy into it as people are generally selfish; however, it really works against Black people, as lower-class White people, owing to skin privilege, are likely to have more opportunities for economic advancement.

Education that encourages students to reject the struggles of their cultures and their histories is what literacy theorist Donaldo Macedo (1994) has labeled "literacy for stupidefication." And as Fordham's (1999) work shows, this is still happening today. Research like Fordham's shows that it is not so much that academic achievement is despised but that standardized achievement qualifies one to become a sell out.

The African American struggle was always about getting education, bettering the condition of other African Americans, and changing society. That much was explicit and common knowledge in most African American families down through the years. But as we "progress" through the system many of us become inundated with ideas that those who are stuck in poverty or other urban traps deserve to be there. Let's look at the dominant literacy "success story" of an individual like Supreme Court Justice Clarence Thomas as an example. The struggle of African Americans of all class backgrounds afforded him the opportunity to reap the benefits of Civil Rights, Affirmative Action, and an American education. But his mind became so full of anti-Black propaganda in the process, that when he achieved a position within the dominant system in which he could be of service to the culture of his foremothers, he feels compelled to adopt positions that are anti-African American. He low-rates his own Gullah language background, silences himself, and perpetuates stereotypes about African Americans for self rather than community advancement.[2] This is the type of role model of educational achievement that many African American students reject.

Some people have run with the idea that African American students are anti-intellectual. Nothing could be further from the truth. Some young people manage to excel academically despite being disrespected (by the educational system) from Kindergarten through the college curriculum anyway, retaining a positive Afrocentric sense of self and still identifying with their home communities and peers (Spencer, Noll, Stoltzfus, and Harpalani, 2001).

Ogbu's work (1992) shows that the history of mistrust and dominance and subordination between European Americans and caste-like minorities such as African Americans produces oppositional attitudes and behaviors among African American students toward dominant literacy education. Other caste-like "minorities" such as Native Americans and Latino(a) heritage students also resist this type of education and their achievement trends are similar to African Americans' (see table in note 1).

Black noise

Through the early 1900s, the scholarly thinking about the language and culture of Black Americans reflected the common prejudices of the time: Blacks were inferior and culture-less and so was their speech. Since the 1940s, scholars such as Lorenzo D. Turner (1949) and Melville Herskovits (1941/1958) presented information confirming the systematicity, the West African background, the history and development of "African American Vernacular English." From an historical perspective, then, the study of the language and literacy education of African Americans has turned traditional thinking about this subject on its head. The African American tradition, that continuum ranging from oral—to literate—to post-literate creativity has been documented by many scholars of African American culture as being a rich reservoir of the cultural thought of African American people from field hollas to folksongs, to blues lyrics, to sermons, to poetry, to jazz, to treatises and on and on. African Americans have a valuable and significant world-class culture complete with its own language and literacy traditions.

African American language and culture at the crossroads of the educational system

Labov's (1972) groundbreaking investigations, reported in *Language in the Inner City*, investigated whether or not "dialect differences" had anything to do with reading failure: and if so, could educator knowledge of the differences between African American Vernacular English and standardized American English be useful in curricula design and delivery of services to AAVE speakers? Labov thought that teachers could be more effective with AAVE-speaking students if teachers used their knowledge about potential interference between "standard"

11

English and AAVE in their instruction. He concluded that the conflicts between AAVE and standardized American English were symbolic of the cultural conflict and racism that is inherent in the society at large, and played out in the classroom. Though Labov's work helped to validate AAVE as a rule-governed systematic manner of communication, it did not help to endorse the implementation of curricular strategies designed to improve literacy by applying comparative dialectology or comparative cultural studies (AAVE and standardized American English) to literacy education.

From the late 1970s, compositionists such as Shaughnessy (1977) began to think about culturally different writers and speakers differently, that is, in terms of the logic of their "errors." Shaughnessy's work, pioneering the field of basic writing, complemented Labov's work in language and literacy. She makes the following inferences about students who did not master a basic level of writing before college—"basic writers":

> [T]hey have never written much, in school or out . . . they have come from families and neighborhoods where people speak other languages or variant, non-prestigious forms of English and . . . while they have doubtless been sensitive to the differences between their ways of speaking and their teachers', they have never been able to sort out or develop attitudes toward the differences that did not put them in conflict, one way or another, with the key academic tasks of learning to read and write and talk in standard English.
>
> (Shaughnessy, 1987: 179)

This is Shaughnessy's definition of the basic writer. Basic writing is now a subfield of English studies. The crux of the phenomenon as she described it centers on difference, "differences between their ways of speaking and their teachers'," and the sorting out and development of "attitudes toward the differences" and "conflict." Shaughnessy also observes, and rightly so, that the closer one's mother tongue is to standardized Academic English or to academic discourse, the easier it is to develop the dominant code. Thus, Shaughnessy underscores the cultural conflict factor.

Shaughnessy (1987: 179) offers a description of so-called basic writers and their writing to illuminate the conflict:

> First, they tend to produce, whether in impromptu or home assignments, small numbers of words with large numbers of errors (roughly from 15 to 35 errors per 300 words) that puzzle and alarm college teachers when they see them for the first time, errors with the so-called regular features of standard English (the past tense of regular verbs, for example, or the plural inflections of nouns), misspellings that appear highly idiosyncratic, syntactic errors that reflect an unstable understanding of the conventions . . . Second, they seem to be restricted as

writers, but not necessarily as speakers, to a very narrow range of syntactic, semantic, and rhetorical options, which forces them into either a rudimentary style of discourse that belies their real maturity or a dense and tangled prose with which neither they nor their readers can cope.

Shaughnessy captured a critical aspect of the problem. The problem is (and was) that African American discourse is entangled with dominant and European American discourse. Shaughnessy saw this conflict as central, but her approach to the problem was to conflate the basic and culturally different writer and focus on error.

Shaughnessy's thinking was revolutionary in many ways and deserves the respected place that it has in the field of composition studies. However, other thinkers in language education, such as Smitherman (1977), put more weight on the language and cultural background of the learner than did those who followed Shaughnessy's error approach. In this respect, it appears that Shaughnessy took the path of least resistance. She helped to create a discipline, emphasizing logic rather than deficit, and my point here is not to discredit her in any way. In any case, the pattern of over-representation of African American students in basic writing courses (Rose, 1990; McNenny and Fitzgerald, 2001) and their general underachievement in literacy has not been resolved by the "error" approach or by other approaches that do not exploit the language and culture students bring with them to the classroom. I believe that Shaughnessy approached the situation in such a way as to deal with the middle ground and not single out any one cultural group, in order to service as many students as possible.

Smitherman's (1977) *Talkin and Testifyin: The Language of Black America* put more weight on the necessity of a culturally holistic approach to the language and literacy education of Black students. Her work on African American language and culture can be used as a resource for educators who want to centralize language diversity in their language teaching. Smitherman spelled out the cultural and historic background, and laid out the epistemological development of the language and its usage. Smitherman's work also described how the West African language background, along with music and cool talk, the traditional Black church, and the experience of servitude and oppression, influence Black language usage. She also gave us the linguistic rules along with the Black discourse modes, and rhetorical schemes and tropes. Smitherman's seminal work was out during the era of the errors approach, and though it received—and still receives—wide recognition, it is not sytematically centralized in literacy education.

In 1979, in the "Ann Arbor King School 'Black English' Case," a Michigan judge ruled that AAVE was a rule-governed, legitimate system of speech and that teachers needed to have knowledge of it in order to facilitate their students' literacy achievement. The Black parents brought suit against the school system. The common practice was that Black students were regarded as mentally retarded and in need of special education classes if they spoke African American Vernacular English. Judge Charles Joiner ruled that this was unfair and worked against the education of African American students. In their retrospective on that historic moment in language education, Ball and Lardner (1997) discuss how teachers have not taken up the charge of building on the language students bring to school, hindered by their dispositions toward Black language.

Linguistic diversity and African American approaches to literacy education

Although as far back as 1969, Smitherman suggested that teachers implement programs that expand on the Black student's existing linguistic abilities, only a few researchers dared to go where no one had boldly gone before. The College Conference on Composition and Communication (CCCC) in 1974 developed the "students' right to their own language." In theory, members of this influential and well-regarded language arts organization supported linguistic diversity and would develop theories and practices that upheld this policy. In practice, the profession is conflicted and full of contradiction as recent research has shown.[3] Some members of CCCC haven't even heard of the organization's policy and many that have are not sure of how to support it.

Among the researchers who have sought to develop a literacy curriculum using African American language as the basis of instruction were Baxter, Reed, *et al.* (1973) and Simpkins, Simpkins, and Holt (1977). These researchers came along at a time when Black educators and researchers wanted to define their language for themselves. Concomitantly, people such as Black psychologist, Dr Robert Williams who coined the term "Ebonics," in 1973, did so to redefine Black language from a Black perspective. From this perspective, labels such as Black English, Non-standard Negro English, Black dialect, slang, and Broken English, and such, further fragment the vastness, vitality, systematicity, and resiliency of the language and its speakers who exist throughout the African diaspora.

In similar fashion, Baxter and Reed and members of the Language Curriculum Researchers designed a holistic curriculum which consisted of instruction in the historical development of US Ebonics/AAVE, contrastive analysis of the grammatical systems of US Ebonics/AAVE and the standard language/variety, rhetorical sensibility, analysis of the speaking styles of African American communities and ways that these styles contrast with the written academic variety of English, and the values associated with US Ebonics/AAVE culture and those of the dominant culture as reflected in language use. Baxter and Reed contended that the US Ebonics/AAVE resource could be used as a scaffold for academic discourse. This instructional approach included use of African American literature, including the canonical, oral, folk, musical (sound and textual), and pieces from Black popular media. Another innovative aspect of the program was its use of computer-assisted instruction in the composing process. The curriculum also featured grammatical drill, textual analysis, and training in the modes of rhetoric.

According to Dr Carol Reed, researcher with the Language Curriculum Researchers and coordinator of the SEEK program at Brooklyn College, the approach was ESL ([standardized] English as a second language). The acronym SEEK stands for Search for Education and Elevation through Knowledge. The advantage of this approach was that students were credited for bringing a resource to the learning environment, and their language and culture was studied as a subject of worth. Reed notes that one of the myths held by teachers of AAVE-speaking students is that the grammar of the standard language variety is too hard for African American students to understand so they just don't teach it, hoping that their students will pick it up. Reed thinks that English teachers should be trained to teach the standard language variety as a language in their preparation as instructors. Not to be confused with the teaching of grammar out of context.

In 1969, the SEEK program applied for and received five years' funding, taking the program through the mid-1970s. The text and teacher's manual which came out of the extremely capable instructors' years of trial/error/success with program materials could not find a publisher. Dr Reed's personal opinion is that the book could not find a publisher because of the controversy surrounding the term "Black" in those days. Nevertheless, the SEEK curriculum received favorable reviews.

Another bold group of researchers were Simpkins, Simpkins, and Holt who came up with the *Bridge* reading program. This group of researchers developed a cross-cultural approach to reading instruction for middle-school students. This "bridge" approach involved beginning with students' home language variety, drawing heavily on the Black oral tradition and moving students to the standardized variety of English by the series' end. The series consisted of short books of stories that were relevant to the lives of Black students. The language use was authentic and not forced. In such an approach the teacher facilitates "small group, oral reading." The teacher acts as an "individual learning consultant." The series employed a teachers' manual which helped to explain the approach and make teachers comfortable using the materials. Straker (1985) notes that "The Bridge Program" was commendable on its content, its focus on a specific audience, its organization and underlying principles. But you know what happened. The politics of literacy for Black students made it such that Houghton Mifflin could hardly market the project as it was controversial to see Black language used in an educational context. You know the drill. Everybody said they were dumbing down standards, teaching kids Black English rather than standardized English.

The intermittent controversies that arise every other decade or so over use of African American language in the classroom point to the fact that educational institutions have not internalized and accepted systematic approaches that center African American discourse community students in the literacy experience. There have been attempts and exceptions to this such as the Dekalb County Georgia's home to school language arts programs. But even there, as I recall though from one of the CNN Talkback shows on the 1996 Ebonics "Controversy," the teachers were at pains to say that they didn't have to learn

African American English to implement the program. (How else could they teach contrastively if they don't know it?) Our American culture is so opposed to the idea of the rationality of African American ways of knowing that we are willing to accept the dismal literacy achievement rates rather than exploit the language and culture that students use as a technology.

African American literacies of survival

African American language and culture is seen as oppositional to achievement and is lumped in the category with poverty, lack of parental education, dysfunctional attitudes and values. Thus, we have most people who are products of the school system, including many middle-class and professional Black people who may themselves participate in Black Vernacular core cultural activities and rituals, who will dis the language and its users. The literacy education that most American students consume won't allow them to understand that African American language is more than grammar. It is a total system of living. It is a discourse. African Americans are a discourse community. This does not mean that only one discourse functions among 90 per cent of African Americans. It means that there are African American discourses (that exist among other discourses) that function as primary discourses among this population in significant ways. Following Gee (1996: viii) I understand discourse as a system of "behaving, interacting, valuing, thinking, believing, speaking, and often reading and writing that are accepted as instantiations of particular roles . . . by specific groups of people."

Basically, of their own devices, African American students train themselves to deal with the inequality of the educational experience and general societal conflicts. One option for school success for African American students lies in enduring the system and avoiding or masking vernacular literacies. I use the term literacies to signify opposition to the concept of monolithic autonomous literacy (Street, 1993: 9). "Literacies are social practices: ways of reading and writing and using written texts that are bound up in social processes which locate individual action within social and cultural processes" (Martin-Jones and Jones, 2000: 4–5). Further, African American literacies include vernacular resistance arts and cultural productions that are created to carve out free spaces in oppressive locations such as the classroom, the streets, or the airwaves to name a few. The epistemologies of these literacies are "precolonial in origin and modified by a racist system in which [Anglocentric] literacy is a privilege and the written word the signified of official . . . culture" (Chude-Sokei, 1997: 194). These survival literacies, like most aspects of African American life and culture, have been mis- and disunderstood. I develop this idea of African American literacies more fully in Chapters 2 and 3. It is important here to note the idea to show that students have been trying on their own to include these strategies to endure the system—but most of the time these literacies have not been encouraged or explored for maximum benefit of students and involve elements of self-denial. Students who won't play the survival games are stigmatized and sentenced to special education and the working and underworking class if they do not become successful entrepreneurs. This helps to perpetuate the myth that middle-class Blacks don't use African American language. African American Vernacular English is reduced to a set of phonological and grammatical patterns of poor Blacks. The school system and the media through misinformation and perpetuation of negative stereotypes train the public to believe this is correct. I must concede that it is estimated that only 90 per cent (not 100 per cent) of African Americans use and identify with this language and culture (Smitherman, 2000: 19).

Literacy work with African American students has shown that some successful students develop vernacular literacies to combat voice co-optation. One strategy that students use is the silent treatment. In this mode, students do not raise discussion of ideas that will not be appreciated or understood in official classroom talk (Fine, 1995). Another strategy that Black students have developed is code switching. As Fine notes (1995: 211):

> "Good students" . . . [manage] these dual/duel worlds by learning to speak standard English dialect, whether they originally spoke African American English . . . More poignant still, they trained themselves to produce two voices. One's "own" voice alternated with an "academic" voice. The latter denie[s] class, gender, and race conflict; repeat[s] the words of hard work, success, and their "natural" sequence; and stifle[s] any desire to disrupt.

Another strategy that students use is "fronting" (Canagarajah, 1997: 189). In this strategy students adopt White supremacist discourse against African Americans and use it in their essays or classroom talk because it is the privileged powerful discourse of the textbooks, curriculum, and sometimes the instructor. As in Canagarajah's study of college freshmen in a predominantly African American writing course, students used this style in their work to reap the rewards—to make the grade. This is also an offshoot of acting White. I call this filling the "academic essay" with emptiness. This is a dangerous literacy practice. As Canagarajah demonstrated, some students' work suffers because the writing comes off as flat, uncertain, and lacking confidence. Furthermore, this practice lends itself to permanent identity damage to the writer. Fronting is also akin to the raceless and colorblind literacy practices, wherein students feel they must deny their race or culture and divorce themselves from their heritage because it is seen as stigmatized. In this mode, students adopt a selfless persona and struggle (to their detriment) to have a neutral rhetorical stance. Our pedagogies and classroom environments must enable students to exploit fronting to the fullest (if they must) and flip the script on racelessness. I will demonstrate examples of these strategies through discussions of students' writing in Chapter 6.

Sociolinguistic ideas

William Labov's latest work on Black literacy still focuses on reading, but has extended beyond a straight linguistic knowledge model to include relevant and engaging reading materials, combining language and cultural knowledge and appreciation. While Labov still believes that teachers must have an understanding and appreciation of the linguistic system, he also emphasizes the fact that the reading materials must be engaging and relevant to the lives of students of color (see Labov and Baker, online).

Rickford (1998) argues for the use of AAVE in teaching academic English reading, as does Labov. Rickford's work shows that teachers can take advantage of the fact that AAVE is phonologically systematic and that knowing this system can help when teaching phonics. For example, in rhyming exercises, teachers may use words such as "pant" in which the final consonant is not lost by AAVE speakers as it is in words such as "past." The rule operating in such a linguistic environment holds that when consonants have heterogeneous voicing, such as the voiced /n/ sound and the voiceless /t/ sound (in "pant"), both sounds are obligatory; but if the sounds are both homogeneous, such as in the case of "past," where neither consonant is voiced, the /s/ sound nor the /t/ sound, the final consonant is not obligatory. Though this information may appear to be more useful to Kindergarten through twelfth grade teachers as they teach the basics, so to speak, it is also important for compositionists at the college level.

Despite the fact that compositionists don't need to teach phonics per se, having a knowledge and appreciation of the AAVE phonological system may be useful for college classrooms, especially when reading texts that employ orthographic representations of Black speech. Also some spelling which may appear to be idiosyncratic may be related to African American phonology. Further, many students of the Hip Hop orientation use spelling as ideology, discourse, and worldview markers. The possibilities for creativity increase if teachers become open to them.

Sociolinguists have offered concepts such as the "ethnography of speaking/communication" (Hymes, 1968; Kochman, 1981; Saville-Troike, 1982) that approach language more broadly emphasizing epistemology in communicative practices. Such concepts allow the language and literacy theorist to explore the relationship between language and knowledge making. In other words, what knowledge is created and exploited under certain conditions? How is this knowledge expressed and in reaction to what stimuli? How can we theorize about these experiences to stimulate learning in all of the interrelated domains of human experience including feeling (affective), knowing (cognitive), and acting (conative) (Locke, 1925/1968; Dubois, 1931/1973; Woodson, 1933)? Epistemology deals with the "general problems of how we can know something and what knowledge is" (Schweizer, 1998). In applying African American epistemology to literacy education the guiding principle comprises searching out the ways that Black folks have understood, believed, approached, and used the English lan-

NEW THINKING IN LITERACY AND COMPOSITION

guage to construct their identities and navigate their environments, using this information in a contemporary context to help students connect African American culture of struggle and subversion to literacy for social change.

Although Kochman's work (1981) on this topic was written in the 1980s, it nevertheless provides useful concepts to literacy education by demonstrating those areas in which Black and White styles conflict. Kochman observed differences in the participation styles of Anglos and African American college students, with Anglos viewing Black styles as emotional, personal, and interfering with rational thinking, while the Anglo style was viewed as objective and rational. However, from an African American epistemological perspective, the person-centered style heightens engagement with ideas. Using the "ethnography of Black American speech behavior," Kochman shows that the speech behavior of African Americans must be evaluated within the context of their culture, history, communities, and the context of the speaker's or writer's situation. All of this information may be helpful in the teaching of composition.

To summarize the concerns of the researchers discussed above, several observations can be made. Sociolinguists have laid the groundwork for researchers to investigate the ways in which we might employ AAVE in literacy education. They argue that differences in language varieties reflect cultural conflict, worldview, and racism in the larger society. We can glean from their works the general sentiment that educators should implement knowledge of cultural conflict/linguistic diversity into their teaching approaches. Another observation that can be culled from these sociolinguists is that effective language education deals with the total linguistic, cultural, and historical background of the learner. This background should be taken into account to more fully facilitate the acquisition of additional language registers and styles. The field of composition has come a long way and has done much to advance thought in terms of linguistic diversity and literacy education. A brief overview of the major theories and pedagogies of the field will show that it has struggled to come to terms with how to do right in a wrong world.

Composing and Black students: a rhetorical overview

Current composition scholarship suggests areas of reform in the teaching of writing. One way to look at the profession's movement is to observe the change in our thinking from product orientation, to process, to post-process. Traditionally and primarily, the composition classroom has been responsible for the literacy training of college students. However, from its inception, the teaching of composition functioned as a stratifying mechanism, helping to indoctrinate students into the values and thought of elite White culture. This indoctrination has been accomplished largely through autonomous literacy instruction involving imitation of standardized English grammar, form, style, structure, content, and focus on the "error-free" product. The product orientation is characterized by what some scholars call the current traditional paradigm. What rhetoric and composition scholars mean by "current" is that period around the eighteenth century, in a movement from the classical era around the fifth century BCE, to medieval, to Renaissance, to the current traditional.

- [This approach consists of] emphasis on the finished product. (Only finished products are considered, turned in, graded, and returned for optional revision.)
- [It analyzes] discourse into words, sentences, and paragraphs. (Commercial texts are used as models for drills and reference.)
- [It classifies] discourse into description, narration, exposition, and argument.
- [There is strong] concern with usage and correctness (syntax, spelling, punctuation) and with style (economy, clarity, emphasis, and the teacher is the sole authority and audience).
- [There is preoccupation] with the informal essay and the research paper.
  (Young quoted in Severino, Guerra, and Butler, 1997: 2)

Current traditional rhetoric is based in meritocratic rhetoric, which underlies many approaches to the teaching of writing. Though it has been demonized widely in the field of composition (Crowley, 1990) it has far from disappeared. It's a difficult notion to dispense with because American democratic rhetoric helps to reinforce it. The rhetoric of meritocracy stresses the potential of the individual to uplift himself/herself from his/her present condition. Its central tenet is that anyone can pull him/herself "up" by the bootstraps and get "a good job" through education and hard work. In other words, if students clean up their language and learn how to read and write, they can be successful. It is true that one's chances of being relegated to a life of poverty are higher if one is functionally illiterate; however, one's merit has never been solely based on the content of one's character(s). It has oft times been based on background, something that most people cannot change. As Villanueva (1993) notes individual encouragement is needed, but it must be balanced by identification of conditions that need to be changed. Recall Shaughnessy's resolve that culturally different speakers needed to make attitudinal adjustments in order to get their speech and writing in line with academic English conventions. What Shaughnessy and others may not have realized is that students' placement in basic writing classrooms for the most part is the result of their development of the "proper" non-conflictive attitude. This attitude includes rejecting one's own language and culture in the process of "pulling oneself up." In other words, people must prove themselves worthy by gaining more access to dominant institutional structures in which they may consume a dominant non-critical literacy. If the focus is on avoiding errors, when do people get to think beyond the surface level?

When students are not encouraged to think outside of formulas and accept traditions uncritically, their writing development suffers, even if it contains five paragraphs, with flawless topic sentences, punctuation, and standardized English grammar. The 1960s movements for access, equality, and justice led teachers and scholars to interrogate and critique current traditional or product oriented practices. These led to the process orientation. This era spawned other theories such as expressivist, cognitivist, and social constructionist. The 15 principles from research and implications for teaching writing articulated by Farr and Daniels (1986: 45–6) could be considered tenets of the process orientation to writing:

1 Teachers who understand and appreciate the basic linguistic competence that students bring with them to school, and who therefore have positive expectations for students' achievements in writing.
2 Regular and substantial practice in writing, aimed at developing fluency.
3 The opportunity to write for real, personally significant purposes.
4 Experience in writing for a wide range of audiences, both inside and outside of school.
5 Rich and continuous reading experience, including both published literature of acknowledged merit and the work of peers and instructors.
6 Exposure to models of writing in process and writers at work, including both teachers and classmates.
7 Instruction in the processes of writing; that is, learning to work at a given writing task in appropriate phases, including pre-writing, drafting, and revising.
8 Collaborative activities for students that provide ideas for writing and guidance for revising works in progress.
9 One-to-one writing conferences with the teacher.
10 Direct instruction in specific strategies and techniques for writing.
11 Reduced instruction in grammatical terminology and related drills, with increased use of sentence combining activities.
12 Teaching of writing mechanics and grammar in the context of students' actual compositions, rather than in separate drills or exercises.
13 Moderate marking of surface structure errors, focusing on sets or patterns of related errors.
14 Flexible and cumulative evaluation of student writing that stresses revision and is sensitive to variations in subject, audience, and purpose.
15 Practicing and using writing as a tool of learning in all subjects in the curriculum, not just in English.

The writing process movement found its beginnings in expressionistic rhetoric. Underlying expressionistic approaches is the rhetoric of liberal culture. It is no wonder then that some of the principles above point to access, valuing all students' backgrounds, direct instruction, practice, flexible and cumulative evaluation, etc. The ideals of liberal culture express the cultivation of the individual through the learning of literature, language, and art. A major premise of expressionistic rhetoric is that each individual has unique creative potentialities and that truth (knowledge) ultimately lies with the individual. As J. Berlin (1987: 74–5) informs us of expressionistic approaches:

> The writing teacher must therefore encourage the student to call on metaphor, to seek in sensory experience materials that can be used in suggesting the truths of the unconscious—the private, personal, visionary world of ultimate truth.

Expressionists understood that the conventional writing prescriptions associated with academic writing are rigid. They also understood that past emphasis on dissecting a "finished" product was counterproductive and that more attention should be paid to the writer and the process of writing itself. Process has its critics as well. Practitioners must be careful to be explicit about codes of power and formats that are expected in academic writing as scholars such as Delpit (1986) have pointed out. After all, you have to know the scripts in order to flip them. The authentic voice concept is at once useful and problematic. For students from stigmatized groups such as African Americans, it assumes that such students may find their primary voices in particular discourses. Furthermore, it could imply a conception of an Africanized English worldview. However, it is doubtful that expressionists are referring to voice in this way. Expressionistic proponents are to be commended because they recognize the personal dimension to writing and writing's political nature. Further they recognize that culturally different students have the potential to bring something new to established genres.

The problem for expressionists as I see it is lack of confrontation and specialization. There needs to be a concentrated effort to explore Black discourses and language styles. I recognize that applying this concept can be problematic for well-meaning instructors. They cannot misconstrue authentic voice to mean that Black students do not need to develop mastery in wider communication practices as long as they are sincerely engaged in inquiry and are in touch with their "authentic selves." There is a continuum of Englished African voices corresponding to the continuum of Black ideologies and selves. The continuum or aspects of it exist inside of many Black people. Black voices have ambiguous precarious positions in the mainstream and in the underground. They are tension filled, a predicament with which African American-centered composition and literacy theorists must struggle. This also raises other concerns. Do students from every cultural group need specialized rhetorics and specialists to teach them? Of course "separate but equal" practices should be shunned. They are a legacy of ignorance and shame. But at the same time, Black students deserve centered literacy experiences. Students have a right to know "When and where [they] enter." African Americans and other historically excluded groups have a history of struggling to expand the discourse to include their voices, experiences, and rights. This is a point that is often marginalized in the classroom rather than the center of inquiry for students, especially for students of African American heritage. Historically speaking, Black folks didn't get their rhetorical training through the basic writing classroom. Since Blacks have encountered Whites one of the main principles that governed Black/White discourse was power. Signifying and a host of literacy strategies were created in order to protect and advance the self and by extension African American culture. Investigation of Black folklore and African American ways of knowing is one way to get at the principles underlying successful Black communication strategies. However, folklore or African American epistemology is not often studied in connection with writing. For the most part, African American students receive an incoherent understanding of their language and literacy traditions.

Evans' (1997: 273–4) discussion of the Afrocentric Multicultural Writing Project is very instructive concerning this matter:

> United States elementary, secondary, and higher education is essentially fashioned so that European Americans receive an education [that insures the survival of their culture] and all other United States cultural groups do not. The frame of reference and the content of United States education are designed to promote knowledge and understanding of the European American by the European American. Other United States cultural groups are trained to support the European American cultural effort . . . Inclusion theory . . . marginalizes students when conceptualizations and curriculum do not offer concrete means for centering the student in his or her culture or means to an enabling and emancipating situated self. For example, any paradigmatic shift by theorists of curriculum transformation that moves beyond contribution approaches or add-ons but does not provide students with access to the classical origins of their cultures and with a systematic understanding of their culture's developments becomes truncated, privileging the students' extant access to European American classical cultures and these cultures' systematic development.

In this respect, African Americans' classical origins are rooted in the AAVE, the vernacular, partially developed on American soil for purposes of survival. Thus, expressionist composition theory has not expanded or narrowed itself to accommodate this purpose.

Composition theory influenced by cognitive psychology does not deal with many issues of cultural difference in its emphasis on understanding how the mind works as it is involved in the writing process. The theory holds that the mind has certain faculties that develop chronologically. Cognitive writing theorists study composing strategies involved in the writing process in order to facilitate students' problem-solving abilities. One way in which writing has been studied is by asking writers to compose aloud so that the written product may be examined in conjunction with the strategies or the ways in which it was composed. Cognitive theorists argue that experienced writers employ strategies that culminate in a satisfactory written product. For example, an experienced writer will go on to develop another idea if he or she is stuck. An AAVE speaker may employ a vernacular ideograph, as a way of saying a lot with fewer words. Horner (1994: 32) reminds us that cognitive theorists argue that inexperienced writers "are somehow stuck at a lower level of cognitive development, unable to engage at a 'formal-operational level of thought'."

It is problematic that cognitivist rhetoricians assume that beginning writers are "cognitively immature beginners." This approach is problematic because although students may not be familiar with college-level writing conventions, they are adults who make complex decisions in the everyday real world (Horner, 1994). Further, where an experienced mainstream writer may move on to another idea or draw on some recognized author's published writing to advance his/her work, a culturally different writer may shift to a narrative mode (which may lead to discussion of many loosely related points); Black writers may draw on experiences which are personally meaningful and culturally accepted from a Black perspective when they are stuck. This points up the fact that cognitive approaches are problematic because they universalize the psychology of learning. This approach is very valuable because it emphasizes the fact that all women and men are created equal. Nevertheless, cultural difference is not factored into the analysis of rhetorical approaches to problem solving. Students simply have not reached a sufficient level of cognitive development if they have not conceptualized or solved a problem in a conventional manner (Bizzell, 1982). Cognitive rhetoric simply does not focus on cultural difference.

Epistemic and borderlands theories are part of the post-process approaches to writing and literacy education. They are more inclusive and applicable to African American students than pre-process approaches. Epistemic approaches, like expressionist ones, see language at the core of truth-seeking. Truth is created through the interaction of the rhetorical elements: interlocutor, audience, reality, and language. In this view, language itself is the focus of writing instruction, while social aspects are minimized (Berlin, 1990). Epistemic rhetoric recognizes that knowledge is relative to different discourse communities and that there are diverse worldviews (J. Berlin, 1987: 170). In this respect, epistemic approaches complement linguistically diverse or African American approaches to literacy, rhetoric, and composition because they center on one's "ways with words" as a way of knowing. Further, epistemic oriented rhetorics underscore the point that meaning is co-constructed.

Borderlands rhetoric has as its emphasis the political and ethical relations involved in acquiring academic literacy. Horner (1994: 44) explains:

> This does not mean we ignore points of difference, problems we or other readers have with their writing. It means rather that both teachers and students need to focus on such points of contact, the borders

where different and shifting sets of conventions conflict, and to practice negotiating those differences.

The key to approaches based in both epistemic and borderlands writing theory is implementing strategies that allow students the chance at language exploration, locating and creating the self in Black/Anglo/African language, rhetorical, and literacy traditions, getting alternative language and views on the page. A related problem not addressed by borderlands rhetoric is the fact that students from oppressed cultures need to be immersed in aspects of their traditions in order to successfully cross back and forth between borders. Many students are not afforded the opportunity to experience a somewhat coherent understanding of Black "ways with words," Black subject matter, or Black history. Border crossing implies at the least a double exposure. Indeed, the African American experience, for example, epitomizes the struggle to reconcile Anglo and African identities. What traditionally happens though is that students concentrate on "passing," so that they might be successful in White supremacist and capitalistic based institutions. Again, the sooner a student "cleans up" her English, knows what every American should know, adopts received interpretations of texts, the sooner she is well on her way to "success." As Woodson (1933) showed, this most often occurs without students ever gaining an appreciation of their own classical culture, what they bring to the border. When this occurs students have been mis-educated into the "non-conflictive attitudes."

From the 1980s onward, overlapping with and complementary to the aforementioned reforms, the movement has been toward critical-multicultural-transcultural-democratic-literacy education in the post-process era. Critical literacy education posits that all education is value based and that students are members of cultural groups with competing values that are in constant negotiation. The critically literate student is one who can "read men and nations" in the words of Sojourner Truth (quoted in Royster, 1990); or in the words of Paulo Freire (Freire and Macedo, 1987), critical literacy is the ability to "read the word and the world." Cy Knoblauch argues that critical consciousness is the ability to identify oppression and counter it by speaking to power and contesting it. He writes that "definitions (of what literacy is) only tell what some person or group—motivated by political commitments—wants or needs literacy to be" (Knoblauch 1990: 79). This realization is critical for all students, but even more so for students from oppressed cultures. We learned from Freire that "A pedagogy will be that much more critical and radical, the more investigative and less certain of 'certainties' it is. The more 'unquiet' a pedagogy, the more critical it will become. A pedagogy preoccupied with the uncertainties rooted in the issues [of the politics of race, class, gender, culture, history] is by its nature, a pedagogy that requires investigation" (Freire, 1994: 102).

As defined by Severino (1997: 106), multicultural literacy is "the knowledge, beliefs, practices, and roots of the cultures in one's environment and the ability to communicate such knowledge in oral and written discourse." Multicultural literacy education involves the integration of content from students' cultures, perspectives, and ideas, including European American cultures, perspectives, and ideas, teacher facility with a wide array of culturally appropriate practices and attitudes, and the engagement of different ways of knowing and learning. Subsumed under multicultural literacies would be the concept of discourse communities. As defined by Gee (1998) a discourse is "a socially accepted association among ways of using language, of thinking, and of acting that can be used to identify oneself as a member of a socially meaningful group or 'social network' (Gee, 1998: 51). When we think of multicultural literacies that means that we have to be familiar with or open to learning about many different ways of thinking and various standpoints. We have to help students to identify and deal with conflictive and multiple discourses.

Arguing for literacy education for a transcultural democracy, Gilyard (2000: 262) asserts that "we need pedagogies to foster the development of the critical and astute citizenry that would pursue the task." This citizenry would be trained to interrogate discourses of race, ethnicity, gender, sexuality, disabilities, multiple subjectivities, contact zones, essentialism, social class, social constructionism, and post-modernism. Drawing from Gilyard then, a major aspect of literacy education deals with analyzing conflicts and problem solving.

Akin to transcultural democratic literacy is democratic literacy. Similar to Gilyard's argument, J. Berlin (1996: 102) asserts that:

> [A] group should be educated in the interest of the people as a whole to solve economic and social problems. This conception of literacy is the most committed to egalitarianism in matters of race, class, gender, age [and others]. Rhetoric [and composition] in college should prepare citizens for participation in a democracy.
>
> In teaching people to write and read, we are thus teaching them a way of experiencing the world. This realization requires that the writing classroom be dialogic.

The teacher is responsible to make certain that all the positions as represented by different members of the class are articulated and critiqued. Teachers must be able to question students and create scenarios that help students explore their consciousnesses, relating, for example, stereotypical ideas that are damaging to our relations with other social groups yet that influence how we make sense of the world.

Composing Black voices

Carter G. Woodson (1990) argues convincingly that education never sought to develop the existing ways of knowing of American slave descendants. As well meaning as they were, "the friends of the Negro" who helped us in our endeavors did not teach reading and writing according to the relevance of these to the lives of Black people. "Real education means to inspire people to live more abundantly, to learn to begin with life as they find it and make it better" (Woodson 1990: 20). To make literacy education relevant to the lives of Black students, an effort must be made to confront unethical educational practices, such as cutting Black students off from investigation and appreciation of their classical culture. When we cannot facilitate students' participation in investigating and exploring their literacy traditions, we're actually teaching them that the world cannot be changed and rhetoric ain't nuthin' but rhetoric.

Further, scholars of Black psychology argue that a healthy Black personality must be defined and affirmed in its own historical, philosophical, and socio-cultural context (Baldwin and Hopkins, 1990). In this view, people of African descent who are struggling to be healthy affirm an African American world-view. This does not mean that there is one authentic African self and that the discovery of that self is the answer to educational excellence. But viewing oneself through one's own heterogeneous cultural lens is an act of self-reaffirmation. It has had to be a conscious effort on the part of people of African descent because they have been trained to see African American ways of knowing as deficient or worthless. Thus, the folk saying "There's one mind for White folks and one for me" reveals this reality. Historically, many African American ways of knowing have been misunderstood or disregarded. Most scholars of Black cosmology invoke traditional African values and orientations, but I see no need to dig into the remote past, or to the diaspora, as the African American experience provides plenty of examples. When I say African American worldview, I am referring to knowledge that Black folks have about how to negotiate Blackness in everyday situations. For example, most Black folks have been taught that Black people have to be twice as good as a White person to be considered worthy. Another example of the African American perspective is that most Black people have been taught that most other ethnic groups think that they are better than Blacks, including other Black ethnic groups. Other examples can be found in Black idiomatic expressions such as "One thang is for sure. You don't have to do nothin' but stay Black and die." Some of these beliefs and ways of dealing with the world have come about through cultural and environmental conditioning, survival systems, and spiritual training. This kind of knowledge is common to most Black people of any socio-economic group, though socio-economic differences result in behavioral differences among African Americans as well as with all groups of people. This is not to say that all European American people are the same, or that all African American people are alike. What I am saying is that socially, historically, and politically, we can identify African American cultures and views of the world. As Gilyard (1999b: 187–8) notes: "It is not generally argued that nations do not exist, though there is much diversity within nations. Rare is the assertion that families do not exist, though there is obviously much variation among family members."

African American culture is complex and has many intersections; by the same token, it does have distinctive characteristics that change as African Americans adapt to new situations.

Once African American culture is understood as central to education, we may begin to use it to explore alternative ways that people have used language and literacy for their upliftment. This is the area most problematic for teachers who sincerely want to promote liberatory writing in the classroom. They want to let students be and write, and right, but they may not have the necessary understanding, such as a basic knowledge of Black language, cultural, and historical traditions or at least the willingness to lead students on a path of holistic self-discovery, to facilitate liberatory writing. Any approach that does not seek to facilitate liberatory literacy is detrimental as it is subtractive. Other scholars and researchers have been experimenting with multicultural and culture-centric approaches to literacy. For example, Mahiri (1998) and Camitta (1993) have introduced Hip Hop and vernacular writing curricula into their pedagogy demonstrating the ability of cultural knowledge to enhance the school literacy of their students of color. Mejia (2001) developed a Chicano/a sensitive pedagogy involving students in ethnographic research on their family histories. I don't want to imply that there hasn't been any work done on understanding African American language, literacy, and composition. There has. My point is that we have not sufficiently explored or encouraged the possibilities.

Overview of selected research on Black language in the composition classroom

In the study of Black rhetoric or discourse in the composition classroom, one school of studies has focused on describing the language patterns, students' preference for such language use, and the relationship between language use and assessment. Most of these studies were focused at the surface feature level. Noonan-Wagner (1981) and Visor (1987) looking at college-level writers, and Chaplin (1987) studying the writing of eighth graders, found several features that appeared more often in African American students' texts: "references to the Bible, redundancy, sermonizing and/or moralizing, use of quotations and word choice" (Noonan-Wagner); "repetition, indirection, shared knowledge, and fraternity of perspective" (Visor); "conversational tone, cultural vocabulary, and Black Vernacular English" (Chaplin). Ball (1992) working with adolescents found that students preferred orally based patterns—narrative interspersion and circumlocution—while Troutman-Robinson (1987) saw a heightened use of direct address in African American middle-school students' compositions.

Taylor (1991) developed an approach to teaching writing to AAVE students which was grounded in a bi-dialectal philosophy. She focused on acknowledgment of AAVE as a legitimate dialect, ethnosensitivity, trust building, the reduction of AAVE surface features in student writing, and attention to surface feature differences between AAVE and LWC (Language of Wider Communication). Taylor's goals (Taylor, 1991: xii) were:

1 to demonstrate the possibility of Black students' achievement in a predominantly White college environment;

2 to provide writing teachers, support professionals, and students with a tentative version of applicable techniques and attitudinal adjustments that proved to be successful enough to make a difference and lead to academic success rather than failure;

3 to convince . . . readers of the need for further exploration and expansion of [her] tentative approaches.

Taylor's bi-dialectal approach consists of identifying her students' use of AAVE in their writing, pattern practice drills, teaching students to recognize "high interference domains," "audio-lingual" repetition of LWC constructions, and translation of literary passages from AAVE to LWC. Taylor is to be commended for her endeavors to recognize the "value differentials" and complexities that exist between Black language and culture and the dominant culture. However, there is no evidence in Taylor's study that points to the promotion of her students' centeredness in their own culture, which is very important for students of African American heritage. Her acknowledgment of AAVE as a legitimate "dialect" is not backed up with classroom opportunities for her students to experiment with and discover the depth of knowledge stored in AAVE idioms. For this reason, Taylor's study/attempt was not fully bi-dialectal.

Redd's (1993) work focused on motivating students to read, write, and think using an Afrocentric approach to composition. Redd's Afrocentric approach involved the use of *Revelations: An Anthology of Expository Essays by and about Blacks* containing 41 expository writings by Blacks. It was her thinking that the Afrocentric reader in a composition class for Black students would promote more writing, thinking, and action on behalf of Black people. Redd found that 80 per cent of the student participants reported feeling better about writing, while 94 per cent reported that they read more than assigned. Redd also found that the majority of students who enjoyed writing, about the topics suggested in the reader, were the students who felt they had something authoritative to say about the issues. Writing about the Afrocentric topics made 89 per cent of the students think more carefully about issues of the Black experience. Redd cautioned, however, that interest in Afrocentric topics alone is not enough to help some students overcome their writing apprehension.

In further work in this area, Redd (1995) explored African American students' employment of African American rhetoric or "styling" and the role of audience in written composition. She found that when a Black audience is assigned, Black students may use Black rhetorical patterns in writing that they may not otherwise use. She recommended that students be afforded the opportunity to write for Black audiences in order to develop their full potential as writers. Redd also suggested that teachers may be able to help students style more effectively.

Ampadu (in press) studied the effects of "Modeling Orality" on the writing development of college students of multicultural backgrounds (including European American). In her study, students imitated the rhetorical strategies of African American oral texts as a means of improving their writing. Specifically, the students imitated the repetititon schemes of anaphora, antithesis, chiasmus, and parallelism. Ampadu drew on both the Greek classical rhetorical tradition and African American rhetorical tradition. She concluded that the students when drawing on the oral forms presented in speeches produced "more qualities associated with clarity and elegance."

To synthesize the research conducted on AAVE and composition, the several strands of research explore how AAVE has been used by students, and how it has been received and assessed in academia, and also how it may be used advantageously. It is important to note that many of the researchers of Black language traditions in the composition classroom suggested that the use of African American language is helpful in teaching composition as it helps to develop a more well-rounded writer, while showing that Black language usage is a worthwhile resource in the educational enterprise. Ball (1992) has suggested that there needs to be some bridge building between the discourse practices of African American culture and those of the academy. It appears that there have been more slippery slopes than bridges in the past. Theoretically, a culturally appropriate approach to teaching writing to African Americans would be based on an exploration of the ways in which African Americans have used English to better their condition in America. This includes an exploration of African American rhetorics, ideologies, and discourse practices.

In the next chapter, I trace the development of African American-centered rhetorics and literacies through analysis of African American oral and written texts and cultural productions from the eras of enslavement, Reconstruction, "separate but equal" racial segregation, Harlem Renaissance, Civil Rights Movement, Black Power Movement, and Hip Hop. In this way we may look to African American culture as a technology as African American people have created "a way outta no way" to negotiate their existence and to flourish in a hostile society. In the words of the old traditional Black church gospel song:

> Lord I want to thank you
> You made a way outta no way
> You made the blind to see
> The lame to walk
> You even made the dumb to talk
> And O Lord, I thank you Lord.

2

The literacies of African American-centered rhetoric and composition: freestylin' or lookin' for a style that's free

Work, culture, and liberty—all these we need, not singly, but together, each growing and aiding each, and all striving toward that vaster ideal that swims before the people [of African descent], the ideal of human brotherhood, gained through the unifying ideal of Race; the ideal of fostering and developing the traits and talents of [Black people], not in opposition to or contempt for other races, but rather in large conformity to the greater ideals of the American Republic, in order that some day on American soil two world-races may give each to each those characteristics both so sadly lack. We the darker ones come even now not altogether empty-handed: there are to-day no truer exponents of the pure human spirit of the Declaration of Independence than the American [Africans]; there is no true American music but the wild sweet melodies of the [Black] slave.

W. E. B. DuBois (1903/1997: 43)

I chose to begin this chapter with an excerpt from W. E. B. DuBois' (1903/1997) *Souls of Black Folk*. I can imagine some people understanding DuBois' words to represent Black separatism and Black supremacy, that Black people have certain characteristics because of their race, and that European Americans have made only evil contributions to world history. I understand DuBois differently. Because race has been used to justify the oppression of Black people, DuBois holds that "the Negroes" must prove themselves a world-class people by exploiting their talents—not racial talents, but cultural talents developed in response to their environment and through the continual interaction with "work" and "liberty" or working for freedom. By so doing, Black people will justify their right to exist in equality and be evaluated without suspicion as valuable members of the human race. Centering on race, racism, and culture as heuristic tools in rhetoric and composition and literacy education, I understand that the ground upon which I tread is dangerous, since race and racism are unpleasant topics and cultural diversity is in vogue. My arguments will perhaps be resisted and opposed even more because the approach that I have espoused has an African American-centered or Afrocentric orientation which generally has a negative popular reputation because of certain scholars' revisionist claims about African civilizations or theories that could be interpreted as separatist.[1] African American-centered is applied here to mean the course of study of subjects (i.e. English language usage, literacy acquisition, rhetoric, writing, and education, for example) from the point of view of African American experiences.

Like many other American linguistic minority groups, African American Vernacular English speakers who wish to become participants in mainstream institutions have to master spoken and written forms of elite White American languages of commerce. Unlike most other American groups, African Americans' experiences of slavery, fight for social equality, and self-determination have established a history of mistrust of American institutions. African American literacy scholars such as Ogbu (1992) discuss this condition in terms of caste-like minority status, whereby many African Americans develop oppositional attitudes and behaviors because their upward mobility in Anglo American society requires that they eradicate "their mother tongue, mother culture, mother wit—the feminized discourse of voice, identity and native knowledge" (Cooper, 1995: 3). These experiences are often left unexplored or are presented unsystematically in school settings even as their omission hinders healthy identity development, broader understanding of the human condition, and acquisition of empowering literacies for many African Americans and others. African American experiences of racism and cultural conflict are centralized in an African American-centered approach to literacy, rhetoric, and composition. These experiences are explored and negotiated alongside what DuBois calls "the greater ideals of the American Republic" to develop a broader understanding of rhetorical situatedness and invention or reinterpretation of strategies, to combat perpetuation of ineffective rhetorical practices and unequal access.

In such a course of study, rhetoric, composition, and literacy are engaged from the perspective of traditions that African Americans have created in their development of African American literacies, their historical and current usage of the English language to achieve their goals of making lives better. The seriousness of the effect and centrality of race and racism on the learning, literacy experiences, and sense of self of African American students warrants an examination of concepts in African American literacy acquisition and some major themes and motives that emerge from African American rhetorical conditions and epistemologies. It is from this examination that a rhetoric of African American-centered composition theory emerges.

African American discourse and rhetorical practices emanate from Black American people's social, economic, cultural, political, educational, and historical experiences. At the heart of these are African American epistemologies, ways that African Americans come to know and act in response to their environment. W. E. B. DuBois argued over one hundred years ago that each "race" has talents, which should be fostered to the benefit of the greater good, the ideal of human brother (and sista) hood. Dr DuBois held up "the wild sweet melodies of the [African]" as a talent, as a Black way of knowing, that could be used to uplift the status of Black people. He believed that the wild sweet melodies of the enslaved Black person were gifts that they could exploit and share with the world for the "unifying ideal of [the human] race." These wild sweet melodies of the African are more than cool, more than Black musics, and soulful beats, although they are all that. Expanding on Dr DuBois' metaphor, the wild sweet melodies refer to the vast array of free forms that African Americans created to struggle against oppressions—the Vernacular. This metaphor seems fitting for vernacular practices since so many remain undervalued or undertheorized—hence, "wild." The Vernacular represents the historical and current survival strategies including counterlinguistic practices and vernacular arts, African American-centered thought, literature, music, art, and religion that African Americans have used and continue to use to achieve their goals of making lives better. These strategies can be exploited for the purposes of understanding and developing literacy acquisition to the benefit of African Americans and by extension, the entire human family. I believe that exploiting and exploring the intellectual depth of African American Vernacular practices and their interaction with literacy acquisition is key in accelerating the literacy achievement of many African American students.

As argued by DuBois, African Americans need "work," "culture," and "liberty" together. The Black rhetorical condition, a condition in which Black life is both desired and devalued, behooves the interested to revisit, rethink, and redefine cacophonous discourses. Out of their creativity and their need, Black people create ways to both express and value themselves. African American Vernacular expression is created in part by resistance to oppression. This resistance is "an assertion of humanity . . . [C]ollectively [these acts express] a need for self-identification, for a reality apart from the one being foisted upon [African Americans] by" the dominant culture (Wideman, 1976: 34–7). I intend to argue that Black Vernacular discourses and rhetorics have helped to sustain and transform Black people themselves as well as enrich and change America and its discourses and deserve broader analysis and application in American rhetorical and literacy education.

In the present work, African American Vernacular English includes the broad repertoire of themes and cultural practices as well as narrowly conceived verbal surface features used by many historic and contemporary African Americans, which indicate an alternative worldview. In other words, AAVE represents the totality of vernacular expression. AAVE should be understood as African American survival culture. On the level of language, although the majority of the words are English in origin, their meanings are historically and contextually situated relevant to the experiences of African Americans. Further, a point that is often overlooked is that there is a standard African American English within the vernacular worldview. Scholars of AAVE argue for an expanded conception of AAVE, whereby African Americans can be located on different points on a continuum of post-creole, non-standard to standard forms of AAVE. Many speakers command a wide range of forms on the continuum from basiclectal to acrolectal. In this sense, "an educated, middle-class [B]lack person may express his or her identification with African American culture, free of the stigma attached to nonstandard speech [/grammar]" (Debose, 1992: 159; see also Rickford, 1980). AAVE discourse is often just under the surface of the rhetoric of African American standard English rhetors. Aspirations of Black people, their words and thoughts do not belong to any individual since the variant survival strategies and experiences of the group keep the discourse alive.[2]

To put it another way, African American standard English discourses are in dialectical relation to Black Vernaculars and other non-standard American discourses as well as mainstream American discourses. By extending the definition of African American language usage beyond (surface level) syntax, phonology, and vocabulary etc. into (deep level) speech acts, nonverbal behavior, and cultural production, the role of language as a major influence in reality construction and symbolic action is emphasized. The multiethnicity of symbols is more apparent in this view (Asante, 1974).

Debose (2001) reminds us that the everyday experiences of African Americans require heightened attention to language use and ritual performance. Uniquely Black usages of language occur in most domains of life including street life, church life, politics, and others. Thus, theorizing about African American language use requires emphasis on rhetorical context, the language users, their history, values, and their socio-cultural, political, and economic position.

In *Singing the Master: The Emergence of African American Culture in the Plantation South*, Roger Abrahams (1992) explores some aspects of this alternative worldview of the enslaved persons of African descent in the plantation South. Implicitly, the enslaved people negotiated the work of the "corn shucking," in Africanized fashion. Briefly, their year was organized around such festive occasions, which provided them with opportunities to eat better, shift power relations, and comment upon the world as they saw it. One proverb that illuminates the difference in the worldview of the enslaved and the master is: "Come day, go day,/God send Sunday" (Abrahams, 1992: 89). This statement gives a whole new understanding to the contemporary "Thank God It's Friday" (TGIF). In one sense, the performances involved in "corn shucking" helped the enslaved to organize and endure the work in a manner that quenched their spiritual and physical needs through song, dance, festivity, and community building. The lyrics and the sound creation fed their inner and outer needs for spiritual and self-upliftment. Inwardly, the music through its use of call-response and improvisation provided an individual and communal soul-liberating experience. Outwardly, the occasion of the corn shucking and its accompanying

34

festivity was an opportunity for the enslaved to be served by the house servants or sometimes even Ole Missus and Master, and to lyrically comment on life as they saw it. The lyrics below demonstrate such commentary:

> Shuck corn, shell corn,
> Carry corn to mill.
> Grind de meal, gimme de husk;
> Bake de bread, gimme de crus';
> Fry de meat, gimme de skin';
> And dat's de way to bring 'em in.
> (Perrow, 1915: 139)

I believe the verbal art of "shuckin' and jivin'" evolved from this survival strategy of performing the "corn shucking" during the 1800s. Clarence Major (1970/1994) defines shuckin' and jivin' as "originally, southern 'Negro' expression for clowning, lying, pretense," term originating around the 1870s. The lore of Black people in all of its manifestations provides a way to examine how Black people have negotiated the world as they experienced it.

This alternative reality or vernacularity of African American rhetoric is largely investigated in the study of speeches or informal activities of African Americans, not generally viewed as an aspect of the formation of African American intellectual thought. In Black traditions of literacy and rhetoric, there is a dialogic relation between vernacular and standard forms, which should be investigated with a view toward polysemy, give and take, and the implications of that multiplicity. There is always tension and multi-layeredness involved because of the complex rhetorical situation and worldviews of African Americans. The terms literacy, literacies, and rhetoric are essential to my analysis. For people of African descent, literacy is the ability to accurately read their experiences of being in the world with others and to act on this knowledge in a manner beneficial for self-preservation, economic, spiritual, and cultural uplift. African American literacies are ways of knowing and being in the world with others. When we think of African American cultural practices as literacy technologies or literacy practices, we see reading, writing, speaking, storytelling, listening, rhyming, rapping, dancing, singing, computing, phoning, mopping, ironing, cooking, cleaning, performing, and shuckin', jivin', signifyin' among other activities as vehicles for deciphering and applying knowledge of public transcripts to one's environment or situation in order to advance or protect the self. African American literacies influence African American rhetoric(s). Analysis of cultural artifacts and art in effect, argumentative strategies, and tropes will reveal that a major issue for African American literacy development is the negotiation between vernacular and standard forms. I will highlight various rhetorical situations in the works of African American rhetors, illuminating crucial tropes that they used to compose themselves, in their antagonistic relationships with Anglos beginning in the enslavement era.

35

Enslavement, African American vernacular English rhetoric and literacy

AAVE rhetorics and literacies are a direct result of African–European contact on the shores of West Africa and in what became the New World. The use of English by Africans originated for purposes of negotiation and trade, initiated by Europeans. In 1554, an Englishman, William Towerson, took five Africans from a British territory in West Africa known as the Gold Coast to England, to learn English, to become interpreters. Three of these Africans returned to the Gold Coast in 1557. Thus, 1557 is accepted as the beginning of the African use of English (Dalby, 1970). We could say that the Africans were already at a disadvantage because they were in the position of learning a language of trade and commerce while having no familiarity with its total system. In a language-learning situation like this one, critical and multiple consciousnesses are built into the language acquisition process. In other words, a group makes the new language fit, to the extent possible, its epistemological, ontological, and cosmological system. This is how we can say that there are uniquely Black versions of English, French, Dutch, and Portuguese, for which Robert Williams and associates coined "Ebonics." Other scholars, Africologists, consider all forms of Ebonics as new African languages, rather than Black versions of European languages.[3] People of African descent have evolved and contributed Ebonic and Pan African discourses to the world wherever they have found themselves on the continent and in the diaspora bringing with them that flava and spirit of survival. Most scholars of language agree that when Africans and Europeans "met," their languages mingled to create new African and European influenced language systems. Dalby (1970: 4) gives a useful outline of this phenomenon:

> "Black" enables us to group together a wide range of speech forms, on both sides of the Atlantic, in which a largely European vocabulary is coupled with grammatical and phonological features reminiscent of West African languages: . . . The clearest examples of ["Black Atlantic"] languages are what may be termed "creoles" or "creolized languages," in each of which the divergence from the original European language has been so great that one may consider a new language to have come into being, no longer inter-intelligible with its European counterpart.
>
> Examples of these creole languages are found on both sides of the Atlantic, especially in the Caribbean and along the West African coast. At the other end of the scale of Black Atlantic languages are the dialectal variants of European languages which, although directly identifiable with Black speakers, have remained largely intelligible to White speakers of the same languages. [African] American English and Jamaican English (as opposed to Jamaican Creole) may be cited as examples, in which the structural influence of West African languages—although very much reduced—may nevertheless be clearly traced.[4]

In any case, in 1619, a "Dutch man-o-war" sold 20 Africans, as indentured servants, to John Rolfe in Jamestown, Virginia (Berlin, 1998). Thus, 1619 marks the beginnings of African American Vernacular English on the western side of the Atlantic. Before race and color became determining factors in who could become free or remain enslaved, Africans worked for eventual freedom alongside White indentured servants. However, whatever the ingredients of the English spoken by Africans in the New World, it was no doubt lined with a strand of critical identity consciousness developed in the Old World. "Into the middle years of the seventeenth century [in the Chesapeake region of the colonies, for example] and perhaps later, slaves received the benefits extended to White servants in the mixed labor force" (Berlin, 1998: 32). The "benefits," however, of this complex system included abuse and exploitation, with Black people being brutalized and exploited far worse than Whites, their material and social situation one of degradation unimaginable. When race became the sole determinant of enslavement, the lives of Black people in the colonies were governed by slave codes denying them any rights. Black survival voices are tied to these experiences of subordination, dominance, cultural memories of Africa, and the desire to be free. These experiences are also factors in the double and multiple consciousnesses characteristic of the linguistic and cultural development of many African Americans. The world of freedom or the interior world of Africans, in which they sheltered their African ways of knowing, helped them to survive. They were in a situation where practicing their culture was seen as heathenistic, as justification for enslavement and race superiority, and most often outlawed. Despite the hostile environment that most people of African descent experienced in the enslavement era, scholars have identified retentions, reinterpretations, syncretisms, and creolizations in art, music, dance, religion, language, and folk customs.[5] Another way of thinking about multiple consciousnesses in many African Americans is to explore the ways of knowing that people of African descent had prior to the enslavement experience and how these influenced responses to the "New World" environment. An important example of this is reflected in African American language and literacy traditions, which are the foci of this book. The Africans took the English language that helped to dislocate them, to fragment their reality, and put it to use to invent lives that only they could envision for themselves.[6] African American literacies come out of this tradition of negotiating vernacular and standard epistemologies and ontologies.

The enslaved population developed alternative ways of creating knowledge and transmitting it to each other in hostile conditions.[7] For example, the enslaved Africans took the religious teachings of their enslavers and resisted Christian hegemony through their appropriation of Biblical stories, the intermingling of those with their own native beliefs, practices, cosmologies, and the creation of their own brand of spirituals that identified themselves with the oppressed Children of Israel.[8] According to historian Lawrence Levine (1977), the overwhelming image in Black spirituals is that of the chosen people. Further, Levine argues that: "not only did [the enslaved] believe that they would be chosen by the Lord, there is evidence that many of them felt their owners would be denied salvation" (Levine, 1977: 34). Although by the nineteenth century literacy was outlawed in every southern state, and in general, most of the North was opposed to the education of people of African descent (Woodson, 1919: 8–14; Engs, 1992: 13–17), it is clear that when Black people were able to gain European-oriented literacy, it too became colored with the epistemological and ontological issues of the culture. Autonomous and narrowly conceived conceptions of literacy, like most official or standard cultural productions, present tensions for people of African descent. In African American literacy traditions, Black people "place only limited value on the written word" (Smitherman, 1977/1986: 76) for it signifies oppressive and exclusive values. Consider the folk saying "Ain't nothin' worse than a educated fool." An educated fool is one who swallows the standard (written) word wholesale without question. Such a person fails to read the word in relation to what's going on in the world. Foreshadowing the theorist and activist, Paulo Freire, I think Sojourner Truth said it best when she signified and said, "I don't read such small stuff as letters, I read men and nations" (quoted in Royster, 1990: 103–12).

For Black writers, the written English word must be imbued with the ontological and epistemological projects of African American cultures. Thus, a major aspect of the Black literacy tradition is its rewriting of Anglo European conceptions of Black people. "This helps us to understand why so very much Anglo African writing—whether Phillis Wheatley's elegies, or Olaudah Equiano's autobiography, or Ignatius Sancho's epistles—directly addressed European fictions of the African in an attempt to voice or speak the African into existence in Western letters" (Gates, 1987: 403). Another African American tradition is that literacy should be used to change negative social conditions of African people. This does not mean that one has to become a missionary, but that one is a part of a tradition of struggling to make positive change, if only changing oneself. An equally important aspect of this tradition is emphasis on the power of the word or "Nommo." An element of African orature, Nommo plays an important role in African American literacies. African orature's "Nommo" addresses "the social, political, and religious moments in the history of a society" (Knowles-Borishade, 1991: 495). Nommo is "[t]he force, responsibility, and commitment of the word, and the awareness that the word alone alters the world" (Smitherman, 1977/1986: 78). To be in line with the experiences of the culture or Black folk wisdom of the culture, the word written by people of African descent should struggle to carry out the life force of Nommo. I say struggle because the realities of the world must be reconciled to the word.

In 1773 Phillis Wheatley, a native African, enslaved in what became America, was the first African American to have a book of poems published officially with the London publication of her internationally famous *Poems on Various Subjects, Religious and Moral.* Her benefactors and owners, the Wheatleys of Boston, supported Phillis in her learning to read and write, as part of an experiment of sorts, to see if Africans were the intellectual equals of their European counterparts. To ensure that she had indeed written the poems of her own mind, a group of well-respected citizens of Boston, John Hancock among them, examined Ms Wheatley and testified to the largely Anglo European audience/public that the teenage Phillis had written them. It is in such a climate that many African American literacies originated, a climate of mistrust. Anglo Europeans did not trust that people of African descent were fully human. People of African descent set out to counteract that belief, accommodating Anglo European needs, while also using the English language to develop an inner sense of self that only they had the vision to create, always at least doubly conscious. One of the poems of Phillis Wheatley that has often been viewed as a symbol of her renunciation of her cultural identity as an African woman and indifference to the plight of enslaved Black people is "On Being Brought from Africa to America":

> 'Twas mercy brought me from my Pagan land,
> Taught my benighted soul to understand
> That there's a God, that there's a Saviour too;
> Once I redemption neither sought nor knew.
> Some view our sable race with scornful eye,
> "Their colour is a diabolic die,"
> Remember, Christians, Negros, black as Cain,
> May be refin'd, and join th' angelic train.
> (Shields, 1988: 18)

This poem is popularly read and categorized as assimilationist/accommodationist. And of course, considering Ms Wheatley's audience, that reading is valid. However, that is a very reductive reading of the poem, which is at least double-voiced. Knowing that her audience consisted largely of hypocritical Christians who practiced enslavement while professing the universal brother and sisterhood of humanity, Ms Wheatley enters the conversation where she will be accepted. She begins with a warrant that all Christians can agree on: "'Twas mercy brought me from my Pagan land." Successful rhetoric is usually based in a warrant on which speaker/writer and audience can agree. The warrant for Wheatley's argument is: if one is a Christian one should not engage in pagan practices.[9] Anglo Europeans saw African religious practices such as ancestor or nature worship as paganism or savagism. Knowing this and being raised as a devout Christian by her owners, Ms Wheatley concedes that she has found solace in the mercy of God through Christianity. Ms Wheatley's purpose is to broaden the definition of paganism. This argument can be expressed as a syllogism: Christians practice universal brotherhood. Anglo Europeans are Christians. Therefore, Anglo Europeans should practice universal brotherhood. However, one practice in which Anglo European Christians participated was pagan—tyranny.

The line "Remember, Christians, Negros, black as Cain" carries a lot of weight in the poem. What is Ms Wheatley asking her audience to remember? The Anglo Europeans should remember that they came to this land seeking

mercy and religious, political, and economic freedom, that they too were sub-
jects of the British crown (benighted as were Black slaves), lost in the darkness of
feudalism and serfdom. Furthermore, one signification of the phrase "black as
Cain" is murder. All devout Christians would know this to be a reference to
Cain as the murderer of his brother. Notice that the placement of the commas
after "Christians" and "Negros" suggests a list which puts Christians and
Negros on equal footing so that not only can Negros be "black as Cain" but
Christians who practice enslavement are murderers and are black in that sense.
Some would say that Wheatley is using self-deprecating language by equating
black with murder. However, these are connotations that have been inherent in
the English language for centuries and Wheatley uses them to her advantage,
acknowledging her readership's thought patterns. Hence, Ms Wheatley, however implicitly, is admonishing her readers to reject the tyranny and
enslavement of their Black brothers (and sisters), the Negro. The hypocritical
Christians can also "be refin'd, and join th' angelic train." Wheatley turns the
language back on itself to voice her new world African perspective. This
double-voiced literacy practice is used by people of African descent to express
alternative or vernacular views of reality, or their doubleconsciousness. Students
of the vernacular tradition may wonder why a rhetor goes through all of the
trouble to embed implicit meaning in their texts, if only the surface meaning is
important to indifferent audiences. One answer is that especially in strong racist
climates if a rhetor only communicated this alternative reality to herself, that is
enough to sustain a sense of self and survival. Further, the rhetorical situation of
the rhetor, her audiences' views and power dynamics existing in the situation
determine the rhetorical strategies or conventions that the rhetor deems as
having a chance of reaching the hearts and minds of her audience. Throughout
the works of Phillis Wheatley one finds evidence of doublevoiced patterns com-
municating the desire for freedom of self and of African American people
(Levernier, 1993; Shields, 1988).

The African American rhetor repeats and revises themes of Black experiences
to fit his/her perception of reality. Repetition and revision or intertextuality is
not exclusive to Black writers/rhetors; however, the rhetorical situation and the
content of their texts can be traced throughout the Black experience. This repetition and revision of themes is what Henry Louis Gates Jr has termed
Signifyin(g). Briefly, Signifyin(g) involves indirection, double-voicedness, and language ritual. For Gates, Signifyin(g) encompasses all other African American
Vernacular English/US Ebonics rhetorical patterns (rappin', snappin', namin'
etc.) (Gates, 1998: 52). The major preoccupation of Signifyin(g) is redefinition
and revision. Gates uses the "(g)" to indicate that African American language
usage can have at least two referents—one standard, and one vernacular. In
accordance with Smitherman's "forms of things unknown," the rhetor is challenged to do they own thing within the traditional mold. And again, coincidental
with Baker, "the already said" lays preconditions for the production of African
American narrative. AAVE rhetors critique or comment on vernacular scripts as

well as standard ones. In the case of standard critique, AAVE rhetors take concepts and change their meaning, representing the tension between received truths or realities and non-official ones. There are two divisions of Signifyin(g): Signifyin(g) as the all-encompassing trope of Black experience and signifying as a Black mode of discourse, along with "call/response," "tonal semantics," and "narrative sequencing" as defined by Smitherman (1977/1986). The subcategory of signifying refers to the deployment of indirection or irony as a way of making a point on more than one level.[10] The all-encompassing or structural Signifyin(g) is employed to revise themes pertinent to the Black experience. In the Phillis Wheatley example above, Wheatley revised an Anglo European fiction of Africans as pagans and Anglo Europeans as faultless Christians.

I offer another example of an AAVE rhetor from the enslavement era in Olaudah Equiano's *The Interesting Narrative of the Life of Olaudah Equiano, or Gustavus Vassa, The African: Written by Himself*, first published in 1789. The structure of Equiano's narrative, beginning with his African birth, the recounting of his African culture, his acculturation of European manners and customs, his uncommon sufferings at the hands of most of the Europeans that he encounters, his manumission, underscores Equiano's rhetorical stance—a logic of progress, reflected in the title of the text and mirroring stages of the author's developing consciousness—from essential African consciousness, to colonized Afro-European, to free-thinking American African. It is interesting to notice Equiano's use of vernacular literacy and rhetorical practices, especially signifying.

The first hint of doublevoicedness is presented to us in the title *Olaudah Equiano or Gustavus Vassa, the African, Written by Himself*. This title invites its readers to consider the identity structures of its author. He gives first his African name, then his European name, and seemingly finishes it off with the name of his race, the African. But he adds that this production is "Written by Himself." On one level, the author is giving his readers the names of his "interesting" lives. But later, Equiano tells us that after leaving Africa he was not called Olaudah [Equiano] ("one fortunate," "favoured," "having a loud voice and well spoken" [Equiano 1789: 20]) again by anyone, but Jacob, then Michael, and then the European name that stuck, Gustavus Vassa, after being sold to Captain Pascal on board a ship. He began life as the African, Olaudah Equiano, and it appears that after all of his life-changing events and the writing of this book, he has come to realize that he is both African and European, and that this negotiated self composes his life. But he is careful to add "the African" and "Written by Himself" to his title to signify these important aspects of his identity.

In order to engage his audience, Equiano begins by seeming to use self-deprecating descriptions of his literacy and ways of knowing as an African, a common rhetorical convention for rhetors in his position. In the following passage, Equiano seems to use a strategy similar to Wheatley's:

> I am sensible I ought to entreat your pardon for addressing to you a
> work so wholly devoid of literary merit; but, as the production of an

unlettered African, who is actuated by the hope of becoming an instrument towards the relief of his suffering countrymen, I trust that such a man, pleading in such a cause, will be acquitted of boldness and presumption.

(Equiano, 1789: 3, Dedication)

Just as Wheatley illuminated the stereotype of the pagan African, Equiano illuminates that of the illiterate African. His readership would agree that he is out of his place to present himself as an advanced critical thinker and writer in civilized thought, freedoms largely designated to Europeans in this time. The writer of Equiano's Preface cites a former editor who holds this popular belief. This editor spoke thus of Equiano's narrative (7):

> The rational and thinking of our race, when they discover the traces of [superstition and God's (in)action on the part of some individuals and not others] such a system,—a system so dishonorable to God, and so disgraceful to man, in the narrative before us, will do well to remember, that it is the production of the *"untutored mind"* of an African.

However, Equiano is well versed in the ways of European supremacist thought and writes on and underneath the lines. On the surface is a man at the mercy of sympathetic but somewhat racist Europeans, in whom he hopes to cultivate the feeling of equality; and underneath the lines is an Anglo African, bold enough to describe not only the "third" world, but also the underworld, the present world, and the future world that he envisions for other Anglo Africans.

One scholar argues that the dominant discourse of *The Life of Olaudah Equiano (or Gustavus Vassa?)*, as she titles it, is that of the "conversion as acculturation" discourse. She writes:

> The narrative authority in Equiano's narrative, for instance, can be classified as a teleological authority, as opposed to Douglass's original generic authority or Jacobs' acquired personal authority. A specific choice of discourse is naturally influenced by the time period, which largely determines what discourses are available (or printable) and by many other historical and personal factors, including the author's geographical and social mobility and, quite significantly, his or her gender.

(Orban, 1993: 656–7)

It is partly true that Equiano uses the discourse of Christianity to persuade his Anglo European audience since that is one of the dominant discourses that they could relate to; but this discourse does not appear unanimously dominant for Equiano. If this discourse were solely dominant, Equiano would have no use for vernacularity after his conversion, which he presents significantly in several ways. Further, although Equiano refers to God's Providence and purpose often, rarely does he make explicit reference to Christianity. In fact, most of the time, when he refers to Christians, it is in an indirect signifyin' way. Equiano's text itself redefines or signifies on the concept of literacy since it is "Written by Himself," a self composed by African and European consciousnesses. Finally, Equiano invents arguments that are not a part of the dominant European discourse, especially his truth argument: Blacks are not inferior.

Equiano states well after his conversion and baptism that he "was from early years a predestinarian" (Equiano 1789: 87). This claim coincides with Orban's assertion that Equiano's narrative authority is teleological. If this is the case, then whatever rhetorical strategies Equiano employs, including his use of Christianity as a persuasive strategy, are means to an end. That end for Equiano and those for whom he speaks is freedom, freedom to pursue life as one sees fit so long as it doesn't involve tyranny, dishonesty, rape, and oppression. Equiano sees no contradiction between his belief as a predestinarian and his belief in Christianity. As history shows, early Africans infused their religious beliefs with Christianity to make it work for them. Thus, Equiano (1789: 87) writes:

> I thought whatever fate had determined must ever come to pass; and therefore, if ever it were my lot to be freed, nothing could prevent me, although I should at present see no means or hope to obtain my freedom; on the other hand, if it were my fate not to be freed, I never should be so; and all my endeavours for that purpose would be fruitless. In the midst of these thoughts I therefore looked up with prayers anxiously to God for my liberty; and at the same time used every honest means, and did all that was possible on my part, to obtain it.

Equiano's outlook coincides with my mother's folklore: "if you born fi hang, you kya drown." Translation: if one is born to hang, he/she can't drown.

Another instance of Equiano's sustaining himself through vernacular thought and practice is evinced in one of his poems. In it, he "recall'd those pleasing scenes [he] left behind." "Scenes where fair Liberty in bright array / Makes darkness bright, and e'en illumines day." It appears that he is most certainly referring to scenes from Essaka, Africa, though his closest hope of better treatment was Old England. Early in the narrative when he discusses the customs of his people, he describes their clothing and its color which he describes as a blue, "brighter and richer than any . . . in Europe," the uniform of the women of Essaka consisting of "golden ornaments" (Equiano, 1789: 14). Further his reference to making "darkness bright" signifies his respect for many practices of his former culture. The penultimate and ultimate lines of the poem invite a comparison of European and African slavery: "Where nor complexion, wealth, nor station can / Protect the wretch who makes a slave of man." The practice of African slavery retained the humanity of the person. As Equiano explained earlier in the narrative, when African traders brought slaves through their country "the strictest account is exacted of their manner of procuring them." And when his countrymen sold slaves to these Africans "they were only prisoners of war, or such among us as had been convicted of kidnapping, or adultery, and some other crimes, which we esteemed heinous" (Equiano, 1789: 17). Equiano explains "with us they do no more work than other members of the community" (Equiano, 1789: 19). African slaves were permitted themselves to have property and slaves. However, this situation lies in stark contrast to the way Europeans dehumanized people of African descent enslaved in the West Indies and even in some parts of North America and England.

Equiano's reliance on vernacular practices to inform the making of himself in this world is also evident in his mixture of African and European religious practices as evidenced in the induction of the vision and the mystic scene. Previous to his conversion, he relates his native African belief system in which "priests and magicians, or wise men" "foretold events" and were also magicians and doctors who were powerfully effective because of the culture's base in superstition (Equiano, 1789: 21). After his conversion, Equiano struggles to live his life as a pious servant of God, he is overcome by a vision of a wise woman who tells him the truth of his past and his future freedom. Someone had told Equiano of a "wise woman" and that night he dreamt of her, even before he met her, which compelled him to go to see her, and at such time she appeared to him as she did in the dream. Just as could the priests of Essaka, this wise woman saw into his past and future. Equiano assures his audience that since his conversion, he believes in only the revelation of "the Holy Scriptures," while at the same time throughout his narrative he insists that one must look to God's Providence in all events. Though acculturated to the ways of Europeans, this "extraordinary occurrence," as he calls it, demonstrates Equiano's juxtaposition of native epistemologies with other knowledges, which help him to sustain a sense of self in the world.

Toni Morrison's "Rootedness" discusses the blending of African belief in the supernatural and the "rootedness in the real world" as a characteristic distinguishing African American culture. She writes:

> It is indicative of the cosmology, the way in which Black people looked at the world. We are very practical people, very down-to-earth, even shrewd people. But within that practicality we also accepted what I suppose could be called superstition and magic, which is another way of knowing things. But to blend those two worlds together at the same time was enhancing, not limiting. And some of those things were "discredited knowledge" that Black people had; discredited only because Black people were discredited therefore what they *knew* was "discredited."
>
> (Morrison, 1984: 342)

In Equiano's narrative, the struggle to negotiate these two worlds is apparent. For him the choice is not between European and African, but making the best of both worlds work for him. And he employs what he has learned of both to compose and represent himself to others.

Equiano's use of signifyin' (as a mode of discourse as opposed to the structural level) represents his rejection of European customs that are harmful to his conception of truth. Equiano litters the text with Black styled signifyin' references to various hypocritical Christians. Although he uses several instances of signifyin' before his conversion in the narrative, it is important to note that he employs this vernacular practice well after his conversion as well. "My captain afterwards frequently used to take my part, and get me my right, when I had been plundered or used ill by these tender christian depredators" (Equiano, 1789: 86). In another instance in which Equiano is robbed and seeks to recover his wares he says: "I lost some time in seeking after this Christian" (Equiano, 1789: 94). When discussing the resolution of the "poor negro-man" who saved his money and purchased a boat only to be robbed of it by his master, Equiano writes: "The last war favoured [him], and he found some means to escape from his christian master" (Equiano, 1789: 72).

This alternative view of Christianity is exemplified in the folk poetry of the Spiritual, "Go Tell It on de Mountain:"

He made me a watchman
Upon a city wall,
And if I am a Christian
I am de least of all.
(Hill, 1998: 561)

Equiano's structural signifying represents his revised conception of the truth of what it means to be Anglo African. In an early section of the narrative, he discusses African customs, their manners, religion, and economy. Some of his descriptions, for example, language usage in Essaka, foreshadow his rejection of some of the European customs he encounters and his reverence for some of the African ways. As mentioned earlier, his name Olaudah, which in his mother tongue meant "fortunate," "one having a loud voice," holds true. In his discussion of swearing and the irreverent use of language, he says: "[W]e are totally unacquainted with swearing, and all those terms of abuse and reproach which find their way so readily and copiously into the language of *more civilized people*" (Equiano, 1789: 20). Further, he details several characteristics of his people which are attractive to both Africans and Europeans: "The West India planters prefer the slaves of Benin or Eboe, to those of any part of Guinea, for their hardiness, intelligence, integrity, and zeal.—The benefits are felt by us in the general healthiness of the people, and in their vigour and activity . . . their comeliness" (Equiano, 1789: 17). Toward the later stages of his developing consciousness (post-mental colonization), he refers to these African characteristics as "the African Metal" (Equiano, 1789: 93). "Metal" signifies that Equiano sees these characteristics as essential or substantive to his being. However, at an early point in Equiano's developing consciousness, his mind is colonized. In his early interactions with Europeans and observations of their customs, he sees them as gods of a sort, "men superior to us." He "had the stronger desire to resemble them, to imbibe their spirit, and imitate their manners" (Equiano, 1789: 51–2). But Equiano later realizes that the Europeans are only humans, humans who have faults as do all humans. He also realizes that not all Europeans "were of the same disposition" (Equiano, 1789: 40). Thus, we can see in the writer's narrative different levels of self-conception. He starts out as Olaudah Equiano, the African. After many decentering and dehumanizing experiences that cause him to question everything he knows and his own self-worth, he becomes Gustavus Vassa, the mentally colonized slave. After developing ways to negotiate African ways of knowing with European ones, he is the writer Olaudah Equiano or Gustavus Vassa, the free-thinking Anglo African.

His acquisition of literacy and the writing of his text revises the received concept of literacy. At the time of the writing of his text, literacy was very narrowly defined and was seen as something innately European. In contrast, Europeans thought illiteracy native to Africans.[11] To revise this concept, Equiano and other Anglo Africans took the European letters and developed their own spin on them. Equiano's text represents an example of that tradition. At an early stage in his development of Anglo African literacy, he desires that books would speak to him. Afterwards, he learns to decode texts. This decoding entails the knowledge that he brings to the text and what he makes of what he finds in a text. We know that one of his first books was the Bible. No doubt, this text representing Christianity did not equal its human representatives in the persons of slaveholders. His consciousness is heightened between what he reads in the world and in The Book. The other book that Equiano owned was one on Native Americans. This book perhaps contributed greatly to his development of reading the word in relation to his experiences in the world. Although Equiano reminds us that he was "fortunate," one of the few to achieve his level of consciousness, he sees the potential of all enslaved persons to be literate and offer different insights into the expanding world.

Equiano uses appeals based in arguments of ethos, which worked well for him in enslavement and which he uses in his text as well. His presentation of himself as honest works on the levels of pathos and ethos. On becoming free he muses (Equiano, 1789: 92):

> [B]ut as I thought that if it were God's will I ever should be freed it would be so, and, on the contrary, if it was not his will it would not happen; so I hoped if ever I were freed, whilst I was used well, it should be by honest means; but as I could not help myself, he [God] must do as he pleased; I could only hope and trust in the God of Heaven; *and at that instant my mind was filled with inventions, and full of schemes to escape* [my emphasis].

A literal reading of this passage relates Equiano's situation of having only a faith in God and his own ability to think of ways to escape, a version of faith with honest works. Equiano only needs to think of himself as a free man, envisioning himself in this way would escalate his freedom. Throughout the narrative, Equiano proves to us that his lot was most fortunate considering the treatment of other enslaved persons he encountered. His being only a boy when first enslaved left his mind more impressionable and more easily manipulated, therefore, less physical abuse was used in controlling him. He basically operated off of trust, so to speak. He trusted that if he performed well for his masters, they would treat him well.

Equiano relies heavily on the truth argument as one of his schemes of invention mentioned in the above passage. Truth arguments are those that require interpretation, when facts are questionable. From the viewpoint of European philosophy and science, the African's full humanity was questionable. In Equiano's view, Europeans just deemed Africans as such because of cultural and racial differences and the disadvantaged position of the Blacks (slaves) that the Europeans created. Hence, the truth claim: Black men are not inferior, or X is not a Y. Equiano relies on a treatise "Essay on the Slavery and Commerce of the Human Species" that he hopes will be perceived as a reliable source to support his argument. He also employs his knowledge of other parts of Africa and the world. Further, he discusses hybridity and miscegenation to support his view that Africans and Europeans are equal (Equiano, 1789: 23):

> The Spaniards, who have inhabited America under the torrid zone, for any time, are become as dark coloured as our native Indians of Virginia.

> There is another instance of a Portuguese settlement at Mitomba, a river in Sierra Leona, where the inhabitants are bred from a mixture of the first Portuguese discoverers with the natives, and are now become in their complexion, and in the woolly quality of their hair perfect negroes. . . . Surely the minds of the Spaniards did not change with their complexions!

Not only does he liken Spaniards to Africans, but Africans to Jews (Equiano, 1789: 23):

> Like the Israelites in their primitive state, our (Essakan) government was conducted by our chiefs or judges, our wisemen, and our elders; and the head of a family . . . enjoyed a similar authority over his household with that which is ascribed to Abraham and the other Patriarchs.

To demonstrate that he is a brother to the Europeans and that Black men are not inferior, Equiano uses logical arguments as well (Equiano, 1789: 80–1):

47

Are slaves more useful by being thus humbled to the condition of brutes, than they would be if suffered to enjoy the privileges of men? The freedom which diffuses health and prosperity throughout Britain answers you—"No." When you make men slaves, you deprive them of half their virtue, you set them, in your own conduct, an example of fraud, rapine, and cruelty, and compel them to live with you in a state of war; and yet you complain that they are not honest or faithful! You stupify them with stripes, and think it necessary to keep them in a state of ignorance; and yet you assert that they are incapable of learning; that their minds are such a barren soil or moor that culture would be lost on them.

It can be said that Equiano's premise is that slaves are not born; they are made. The Africans were brutalized, terrorized, not allowed to think or feel and left in a state of constant hunger and terror. Under these circumstances, slaveholders are in no moral or ethical position to enumerate the shortcomings of the Black people, since they bear the burden of most of them. Equiano argues that it is the Anglo Europeans' refusal to offer the Africans sufficient opportunities to learn their language and customs and their dehumanizing treatment of Africans which make them inferior, not Africans' natural characteristics.

Another proof that Equiano offers of African and European equality is his own ability to acquire European customs—assimilation. Early in the narrative, Equiano is distressed about his inability to interact with other African countrymen, but later when he has become familiar with the Englishmen and their customs, he is no longer fearful of them and respects their power and conventions. He says, in speaking of his first church experience (Equiano, 1789: 43):

And from what I could understand by him of this God, and in seeing that these White people did not sell one another as we [Africans] did, I was much pleased: and in this I thought they were much happier than we Africans. I was astonished at the wisdom of the White people in all things which I beheld.

He tells his audience of his love of the Bible and learning of its teachings. He is baptized and called "the black Christian." He is eager to learn reading and writing, to improve himself.

Equiano's discussion of his experiences of the seafaring life "naturalizes" him in the European environment. In his youthful wonder and ignorance, Equiano sees the captain as a brave and righteous hero, a role model. Equiano aspires to the status of captain and chief navigator. Why not? After learning the ways of the sea and White folks, he has all of the characteristics. He tells us that after a while, he is no longer fearful of the White man's ways "and was so far from being afraid of any thing new which I saw, that after I had been some time in this ship, I even began to long for an engagement" (Equiano, 1789: 45). He was encouraged by the ship's company to fight "White boys" for money and sport. His use of pronouns "my," "our," and "us" to signify his thinking of himself as a brother to the European demonstrates his youthful perception of himself as insider. He doesn't discuss battles as those of the Europeans but as "our" engagements, the company men as "our men," "our killed and wounded." He is careful to note his devotion to his master and every kind White person who befriends him. Speaking of his master (Captain Pascal) he writes: "I was much alarmed for him, and longed to assist him" (Equiano, 1789: 56). "[M]y master treated me always extremely well; and my attachment and gratitude to him were very great" (Equiano, 1789: 51).

Equiano is so naturalized in the Anglo European environment that he almost forgets the Black plight. When he sees a young Black boy who runs over to him on sight, he relates (Equiano, 1789: 58):

> [T]his boy having observed me from his master's house, was transported at the sight of one of his own countrymen, and ran to meet me with the utmost haste. *I, not knowing what he was about, turned a little out of his way at first,* but to no purpose; he soon came close to me, and caught me in his arms as if I had been his brother, though we had never seen each other before [my emphasis].

One of the main purposes of Equiano's text was to promote humanity and brotherhood. This brotherhood is not only of Africans and Europeans, but of African and African. Though many of his experiences sought to distance him emotionally and culturally from other Africans, Equiano's strategic placement in the text of his encounter with the Black boy points to his developing Black consciousness. He has moved mentally from African, to European, to Anglo African; or African free-thinker, to colonized European, to free-thinking Anglo African. In other words, his being pro African or Black is not in conflict with his being a brother to Europeans.

Just as Equiano's autobiography employs vernacular rhetorical strategies that reflect the development of his identity and consciousness, David Walker's treatise reflects his struggle to define what it meant to be a "free" born, God-fearing, African man, born amid a land of enslaved Africans and threatened White society. *David Walker's Appeal to the Coloured Citizens of the World, but in Particular, and Very Expressly, to Those of the United States of America* first published in 1829, was the first sustained critique of slavery by a person of African descent (Turner, 1993: 9). Though the writings of Phillis Wheatley and Olaudah Equiano were inherently political and critical, even if sometimes indirect and multivocal, David Walker's text was overtly political. Though Ms Wheatley and Mr Equiano imagined their works to be read by some people of African descent, they were also aware of the primary purpose of their texts: to convince Whites that Blacks deserved freedom. Coming along a generation or two behind these freedom writers, Walker took a decidedly different approach. His rhetoric is designed to directly address the oppressed people, whom he sees as in danger of relinquishing all control of their humanity and cultural identity. His purpose is to unify them under the premise that God is on their side. He draws his authority from God and from his knowledge of himself as a free African American. Although many would dismiss Walker as angry and working against progress for the pointedness of his language, some of his major arguments are based in Biblical teachings and values of the Protestant ilk, in which many Anglo Europeans and Anglo Africans believed. However, religion had been used to justify the poor treatment and enslavement of people of African descent.

Thus, Walker's rhetorical task was that of redefining and reinterpreting the meaning and role of religion for the benefit of Africans in America. For example, Walker renames or redefines the Anglo European slaveholders as natural enemies of Africans:

> [T]hey know that they have done us so much injury, they are afraid that we, being men, and not brutes, will retaliate, and woe will be to them; therefore, that dreadful fear, together with an avaricious spirit, and the natural love in them, to be called masters, . . . bring them to the resolve that they will keep us in ignorance and wretchedness, as long as they possibly can . . . Consequently they, themselves, (and not us) render themselves our natural enemies, by treating us so cruel.
>
> (Turner, 1993: 81)

Walker also articulated hatred while preaching Christianity and God's judgment:

> You may do your best to keep us in wretchedness and misery, to enrich you and your children, but God will deliver us from under you. And wo, wo, will be, to you if we have to obtain our freedom by fighting. Throw away your fears and prejudices then, and enlighten us and treat us like men, and we will like you more than we do now hate you . . . and tell us now no more about colonization, for America is as much our country, as it is yours.
>
> Treat us like men, and there is no danger but we will all live in peace and happiness together. For we are not like you, hard hearted, unmerciful, and unforgiving. What a happy country this will be, if the Whites will listen.
>
> (Turner, 1993: 89)

From the dominant Eurocentric Protestant perspective of that time, slaves ought to do nothing but obey their masters and love them that curse and spitefully use them. Interpreted from that perspective, Anglos are inherently superior to Africans and the two groups can never live together as equals. From this point of view, Walker's rhetoric is a worse social crime than the racist acts themselves. However, Walker explains that Whites are the natural enemies of African people because of their appalling treatment of them, not because Africans are superior to the Anglos. Just as the oppressor group had used religion to enslave the African, for Walker, the Africans must appropriate religion for freedom. From an African American perspective, Walker has a right to strongly denounce racism, White supremacy, and inhumane treatment and admit hatred of Anglos for their actions while preaching God's judgment or the fall of America.

David Howard-Pitney's (1990: 12) discussion of the *Afro-American Jeremiads* illuminates the context for Walker's rhetorical strategy:

> Messianic themes of coming social liberation and redemption have deep roots in black culture. The biblical motif of the Exodus of the chosen people from Egyptian slavery to a Promised Land of freedom was central to the black socio-religious imagination. Afro-Americans, by virtue of their unjust bondage, felt that they had a messianic role in achieving their own and others' redemption. Similarly themes of messianic purpose and identity and of a historical Exodus figured prominently in both Black and White antebellum culture.

Walker's stance that Black people should obtain their rights by means of violence if necessary, and also his conviction that America belongs as much to Black people as White, shed light on the need for African people to develop an organized abolition movement and the problem of African and Anglo American alliances over the tactics and direction of the movement (Turner, 1993, "Introduction," *David Walker's Appeal*).[12]

I offer here an example from *Narrative of the Life of Frederick Douglass* to illuminate the differential in meaning of the English language for African Americans. Young Frederick Douglass had made a habit of reading the *Columbian Orator* at every opportunity. In it, he read Sheridan's speeches on Catholic emancipation. As a youth, Douglass writes, these speeches spoke to his condition of "slave for life." His reading caused him to ponder deeply how he could escape that condition:

> While in this state of mind, I was eager to hear any one speak of slavery. I was a ready listener. Every little while, I could hear something about the abolitionists. It was some time before I found what the word meant . . . If a slave ran away and succeeded in getting clear, or if a slave killed his master, set fire to a barn, or did any thing very wrong in the mind of a slaveholder, it was spoken of as the fruit of *abolition*. Hearing the word in this connection very often, I set about learning what it meant. The dictionary afforded me little or no help. I found it was "the act of abolishing;" but then I did not know what was to be abolished . . . I did not dare to ask any one about its meaning, for I

was satisfied that it was something they wanted me to know very little about.

(Douglass, 1845: 279–80).

Douglass goes on to say that after reading a newspaper article about abolishing slavery in Washington D. C., he finally understood the meaning of "abolitionist" and "abolition." He was able to make sense of these concepts after hearing the words used from the perspective of the enslaved or ex-enslaved person—setting fire to a barn, killing a master, etc. Douglass could not relate the standardized dictionary definition to himself or his brethren and sistren. The word or the concept was not a part of his experience. It only pointed to other words—"the act of abolishing." Certainly, the standardized definition of abolition did not include killing masters and burning down barns. In the sense that the book (dictionary) does not speak to the experience of the Black person, Douglass' example is a revision of the talking book trope.[13] This is also an example of structural signifying, revision with a difference signalling individual experience within a tradition.

Douglass' example demonstrates that until English words, concepts, and even events are infused with lived experiences and ideas that can be applied personally, they are not a part of the Black lexicon. The famous rhetorical question that Frederick Douglass (1852) asks in his "Fourth of July Oration" makes this point plain: "What to the American slave, is your Fourth of July?" (cf. Hill, 1964: 26).

The importance of worldview and experience is crucial in grasping the development of African American language and literacy practices. The American African use of the English language is fitted to their particular rhetorical situations.

Reconstruction era literacies and African American vernacular English rhetoric

During that period in American history known as the Reconstruction era, around 1862 through 1880, Black people sought to reconstruct democracy, revise the Constitution, and further their struggle for freedom. People of African descent were at the forefront of the abolition of slavery as evinced by their continual escapes, fighting in the Civil War, and movement on the part of free Black people to speak, write, and petition against slavery. Landmark events took place during this period. The thirteenth amendment of 1865 outlawed slavery. The fourteenth amendment of 1868 allowed citizenship for Black people born or naturalized in the United States. By 1870, the fifteenth amendment guaranteed African American men the right to vote. "In a sense, the amendments, as well as the Civil Rights Acts of 1866–75, were vindications of words and deeds that had characterized the Afro-American freedom movement before, during, and after the Civil War" (Harding, 1987: 724). After the Civil War, the general thrust was for integration, though racial solidarity among Black people, along with support from some sympathetic Whites, helped them to elevate the race politically and economically (Meier, 1964: 8). Black legislators and officeholders became a reality, and Black men could participate in the official political process. (Black women did so unofficially.) Just as Black people were fighting for power and access, White southerners were fighting against them.

The masses of Black people during the Reconstruction era were interested in landownership, while those who had some kind of economic security were more interested in civil and political rights (Meier, 1964: 16). This is not to suggest an essentialist or undifferentiated group in thought and deed. No, wrote W. E. B. DuBois (1935/1962: 125):

> There was no one kind of Negro who was freed from slavery. The freedmen were not an undifferentiated group; there were those among them who were cowed and altogether bitter. There were the cowed who were humble; there were those openly bitter and defiant, but whipped into submission, or ready to run away. There were the debauched and the furtive, petty thieves and licentious scoundrels. There were the few who could read and write, and some even educated beyond that. There were the children and grandchildren of white masters; there were the house servants, trained in manners, and in servile respect for the upper classes. There were the ambitious, who sought by means of slavery to gain favor or even freedom; there were the artisans, who had a certain modicum of freedom in their work, were often hired out, and worked practically as free laborers. The impact of legal freedom upon these various classes differed in all sorts of ways.

I would like to underscore two important points brought out in the DuBois excerpt. First, people cope differently with their experiences of being Black in White dominated and oppressive societies, yet there are broadly conceived behaviour patterns. Second, various literacies are developed according to values, situatedness, and environment. Several historical Black discourses can be traced to these dispositions.

An excerpt from the Oklahoma slave narrative of Alice Alexander bears this point out as it embodies characteristics of several Black discourses. I want to highlight the themes of liberation, literacy, and economic empowerment. Mrs Alexander was 88 years old in 1937, at the time of her interview. She was born in 1849 and lived through the Reconstruction era.

> We had a overseer back on Colonel Threff's plantation and my mother said he was the meanest man on earth. He'd jest go out in de fields and beat dem niggers, and my mother told me one day he come out in de field beating her sister and she jumped on him and nearly beat him half to death and old Master come up jest in time to see it all and fired

dat overseer. Said he didn't want no man working fer him dat a woman could whip.

After de war set us free my pappy moved us away and I stayed round down there till I got to be a grown woman and married. You know I had a pretty fine wedding 'cause my pappy had worked hard and commenced to be prosperous. He had cattle, hogs, chickens and those things like that.

A college of dem niggers got together and packed up to leave Louisiana. Me and my husband went with them. We had covered wagons, and let me tell you I walked nearly all the way from Louisiana to Oklahoma. We left in March but didn't git here till May. We came in search of education. I got a pretty fair education down there but didn't take care of it. We come to Oklahoma looking for de same thing then that darkies go North looking fer now. But we got disappointed. What little I learned I quit taking care of it and seeing after it and lost it all.

I love to fish. I've worked hard in my days. Washed and ironed for 30 years, and paid for dis home that way. Yes sir, dis is my home. My mother died right here in dis house. She was 111 yeahs old. She is been dead 'bout 20 yeahs.

(Baker and Baker, 1996: 24)[14]

Reading Mrs Alexander's narrative of her slavery experience according to W. E. B. Dubois' categories of Negroes freed from slavery, I classify her as "ambitious, who sought by means of slavery to gain favor or even freedom; [and as an artisan], who had a certain modicum of freedom in [her] work, . . . often hired out, and worked practically as [a] free [laborer]." I say this because Mrs Alexander experienced slavery as a child, as opposed to an adult. Slavery ended when she was around the age of 14. She learned most of what she knew of slavery's harshness from her mother, as evinced in her mother's story of beating the overseer down, because of his whipping of her sister. Alice probably began to gain her expertise in ironing before the age of puberty. She probably discerned early on that she should perfect this chore, as it was a means of freedom. It probably kept her out of the fields, got her off the plantation for a while and maybe even allowed her to envision other lives for herself as she became such an expert ironer that she could do it with her eyes closed.

Her parents planted the seeds of liberation, literacy, and ambition in her from an early age. As mentioned previously, her mother taught her to resist oppression with her story of how she beat the overseer down. "After de war . . . [her] pappy moved [them] away . . . worked hard and commenced to be prosperous." Thus, her father also was an example of liberation and economic freedom. As a married woman, Mrs Alexander "walked nearly all the way from Louisiana to Oklahoma . . . in search of education . . . looking for de same thing then that darkies go North looking fer". But Oklahoma didn't turn out to be the land flowing with milk and honey. Mrs Alexander says she was disappointed when she got there. She was no doubt disappointed by discrimination, lack of educational and job opportunities, and racism. She says she was unable to take care of her education and lost it all. I would argue that Mrs Alexander was at a critical moment of negotiation between standard and vernacular practices when she realized her predicament. She applied her knowledge of the world to her situation and composed her life with the help of vernacular knowledge and an iron. "I've worked hard in my days. Washed and ironed for 30 years, and paid for dis home that way." Fully aware of the values that count in African American and American culture, such as education, literacy, and acquisition of property, Mrs Alexander used the vernacular literacy practices available to her to acquire land and build a home for herself. In this way, she demonstrates an African American literacy practice—vernacular—makin a way out of no way—and standard—doing it the American way.

Literacies of the post-Reconstruction period and Harlem Renaissance

It is important to note that before, during, and immediately after the Civil War, 95 per cent of the Black population lived in the openly hostile South. Southern Whites "with much active and passive cooperation from official and unofficial forces in the North . . . mounted a harsh campaign that severely contained, restricted, and often overturned the results of the black movement toward the re-construction of the Constitution" (Harding, 1987: 724–5). As historian Melvin Drimmer (1987: 90–4) noted, "race and violence, not ineffectual black leadership" thwarted Black reconstruction. The Democratic Party and the Klan were practically one in the same. Lynching, legal segregation, economic exploitation, and discrimination were the sequel to slavery. People such as Ida B. Wells launched anti-lynching campaigns. Between 1892 and 1900, using her writing, speaking, and journalistic skills, Wells "put mob violence on the American agenda and established a pathway to change" (Royster, 1997: 41).

As noted by John Hope Franklin (1957/1994), despite hostility and the fear of lynching, Black people were still voting during the period 1876–90, though their voting strength had been cut considerably in some areas. Black voters made it possible for Blacks to still hold offices.

> In Mississippi there were seven Negroes in the legislature in 1888. In the same year there were eight Negroes in the Virginia General Assembly. They held numerous minor offices in many parts of the South; and in 1890 there were three Negroes in the federal Congress.
> (Franklin 1957/1994: 119)

I have often heard, as a child and since, the phrase "Sweatin like a nigga goin to Election." Now I know what it means.

As expressed in the Black gospel song, "We Are Soldiers in the Army":

Chorus
We are soldiers, in the army
We have to fight although we have to cry
We have to hold up the bloodstained banner
We have to hold it up until we die.

Verse
My mother was a soldier
She placed her hand on the gospel plow
One day she got old
She couldn't fight anymore
But she just stood there and fought on anyhow.
(traditional Black church song)[15]

The choir would come marching in on this song at the Cedar Avenue Church of my youth, Holy Grove Baptist, on Sunday mornings in Cleveland, Ohio, in the 1960s. I didn't understand the meaning of the song then, but I have come to understand its function in the formation of African American literacies and consciousnesses.

Still searching for full citizenship and economic freedom, many African Americans needed and wanted education and literacy. But the "separate but equal" doctrine, which was made law in 1896 with the Supreme Court decision of Plessy *vs.* Ferguson, along with poverty, and shortage of qualified teachers, made it difficult for the masses to obtain quality education, though many strides were made. Grandfather clauses, literacy laws, and such worked to disenfranchise people of African descent. Born in Jamaica, British West Indies, in 1887, the rhetoric and discourse of Marcus Garvey came along in this type of environment.

Garvey can be linked ideologically to Nat Turner, David Walker, Malcolm X, Kwame Ture, and perhaps to those classes of enslaved folk DuBois referred to as the defiant, or the educated African ancestors.[16] Garvey's rhetoric, classified as Pan African and Black Nationalist by many scholars, was directed toward re-educating the masses of Black people for the purposes of racial, cultural, educational, economic, social, and political uplift. Arriving in North America in 1918 too late to meet Booker T. Washington and start a school in Jamaica on the Tuskegee Institute Model,[17] Garvey wrote and spoke on behalf of himself or the Universal Negro Improvement Association (UNIA) during the period from about 1914 through the late 1930s. During this time, there had been few public texts designed to instruct the masses of people of African descent from a Black nationalist perspective, *David Walker's Appeal to the Coloured Citizens of the World* notwithstanding. Garvey's teachings exemplify the Anglo African tradition of multiple literacies. In his writings such as *Message to the People: The Course of African Philosophy*, Garvey taught his followers to master the

English language, study its grammar and rules, and to read avidly. In addition to these directives, Garvey also taught that "[The white man's] school books in the elementary and high schools, colleges and universities are all fixed up to suit his own purposes; to put him on top and to keep him on top of other people" (Garvey, 1986: 11–12). He thus advised his people to read these texts critically.

Written in the mid-1930s, to be read as a script reflecting two voices, Garvey's (1987) "Dialogues" are an attempt to translate his ideas and philosophies into a Black discourse pattern, call-response, for the benefit of community literacy. As Smitherman (1977/1986) explains, call-response works to create a unified movement and understanding among Black people. The "Dialogues" are styled on a Father/Son dialogue or a call/response structure, a structure that Garvey knew would be attractive to those members of the Black community who might have had little in the way of formal education, but had been raised in the Black oral tradition (Garvey, 1987: 144–5):

Father: The lack of this knowledge, my boy, is the great disadvantage of the race as a whole. Most of our people born to modern environments in our civilization seem to think that they were destined to be an inferior people. Their school and education was based upon this assumption.

Son: But why so father?

Father: Because under our present civilization the Negro was forced to accept his educational code from other peoples who were not disposed to give him credit for anything. They wrote books quite disparaging to the Negro. Their literature was intended to bolster up their particular race and civilization and down that of the Black man . . . The Black man has not written recently his own history, neither has he yet engaged himself in writing his own literature; and so, for the last hundred years, he has been learning out of the White man's book, thereby developing the White man's psychology.

Son: I can see, father, that is why at school I wanted to be a White man, because the books I read all told me about the great deeds of White men. I wanted to be like Abraham Lincoln and George Washington and Napoleon, but I thought I could only be that by being White.

In Garvey's rhetorical strategies, the pattern of vernacular and standard negotiation is apparent in his consciousnesses—vernacular consciousness—reading against the grain and exploiting vernacular patterns (call/response dialogues)—standard consciousness—learn and memorize how the (standard) English language works.

The mass movement of Garvey is one of the catalysts for the "New Negro" cultural awakening of the 1920s through the 1930s (and some scholars mark it through the end of the 1940s). (See Spencer, 1997: xviii.) Popularly known as the Harlem Renaissance, this period of Black experiences represents a classical movement in literature and music—"that is, a Renaissance of black vernacular sources but classical forms. Ragtime, blues, and jazz were the wells to which the Renaissance artists went for the substance—the themes, rhythms, and 'feel'—of their 'high' art. This is true whether we are speaking of the musical composition or the novel, painting, or anthology of poetry or folklore" (Spencer, 1997: xx). One of the main purposes of the Harlem Renaissance was to reverse the stereotype that Black people had no social or cultural life worthy of admiration by the mainstream. Alain Locke, the first African American Rhodes scholar and professor of Philosophy at Howard University, was one of the major movers and shakers in this movement. In essence, Black people strove to redefine what it meant to be Black in a White-dominated society. Other significant events in Black history that enkindled the Renaissance included the following: Booker T. Washington's (1895) Atlanta Exposition Speech, emphasizing an economic (rather than political) approach to uplifting Black people with a focus on industrial education and compromise between the races (see Cummings, 1977); W. E. B. DuBois' formal statement of his concept "The Talented Tenth" in 1903 (emphasizing an educational and cultural approach to uplift);[18] The Niagara Movement started in 1905, which became the National Association for the Advancement of Colored People (NAACP) in 1909; The National Urban League started in 1910; The Association for the Study of Negro Life and History in 1915; The Great Migration of African Americans from the South to the North beginning around 1915; the return of Black soldiers from World War I in 1919 with greater literacy, fighting for first class citizenship as they had been exposed to the world outside of America's brand of racism.[19] Harlem, with the largest Northern concentration of African Americans, symbolized Black urban life, poverty, underemployment, mis-education, discrimination, second-class citizenship, patterns that were occurring in Chicago, Philadelphia, Detroit, Cleveland, and other major metropolitan cities. (See Wintz, 1996: 3.)

The main objective of the period, in the eyes of most Black Americans, was uplifting the Black segment of American society, the means of which came to be identified with Booker T. Washington and W. E. B. DuBois. Booker T. Washington's strategy came to be identified with separation though that is not what he actually said. Washington advocated Black economic nationalism, with Black people controlling certain businesses and industries, having mastery over certain skilled and semi-skilled trades. He thought that Black people would progress most expediently through the economic rather than the political route. He also thought Black people should be educated in business or trades and such, rather than Latin or Greek, and that they should exploit their education to build up their communities, which would command respect and economic independence for African American people. W. E. B. DuBois' strategy of political agitation and liberal education came to be identified with integration. DuBois felt that a group of Black people should be groomed and educated as leaders to uplift the Black masses. Further, DuBois believed that Black people would garner respect for their cultural contributions to American civilization and that the leadership would help to guide the masses in this way. Of course both DuBois and Washington advocated self-reliance and self-help.

The city of my birth, Cleveland, Ohio, provides a local example, in the person of Jane Edna Hunter, of the African American upliftment experience of the period. Ms Hunter migrated from the South to Cleveland in 1905, seeking housing and employment as she was a skilled nurse, but she soon realized that racial discrimination would prevent this from being a smooth transition. White medical institutions would not hire her. Housing was available to her only in poverty stricken neighborhoods (designated for Black people) that had few spaces for wholesome recreation. These places generally put women at risk of harm and sexual exploitation. Boarding house owners denied certain privileges to Black women—the right to entertain guests, for example. The YWCA was closed to Black women. Though Ms Hunter was able to slowly build a clientele of White patients as a private duty nurse, she at first began work in Cleveland as a domestic and at several odd jobs beneath her educational level, while becoming a member of Cleveland's Black community.[20]

The standard situation in Cleveland was that the White community was used to dealing with a small group of elite Northern Blacks. This relationship was problematic as the racial climate made dependence on White patronage essential for Black elite businesses to succeed. Because Ohio was one of the first states to pass an anti-lynching law and there had been 12 civil rights court cases against White proprietors for discrimination in the late nineteenth century, the early twentieth-century group of Black Clevelanders lived under the illusion of racial harmony. But as European ethnic groups arrived in Cleveland and began rivaling Black workers for jobs and businesses, the façade of racial harmony became a reality of disillusionment. This situation pushed more and more Blacks into racially segregated neighborhoods and schools.[21] More and more Black workers were denied access to semi-skilled and professional trades and Blacks were excluded from white-collar and skilled municipal and industrial jobs. European immigrants came over and moved into positions unavailable to persons of African descent, putting Black people at the bottom of the social ladder.

In comes Jane Edna Hunter with her idea of a home for Black working women. She, along with a group of women, pledged to raise funds, give concerts, bake goods, put on all types of events, and to donate 0.05 cents a week of their own money to create a home. Based on her own experience of the struggles of Black females migrating to the North, Ms Hunter wanted to create a space that would shelter Black women from the wiles of immorality and degradation, support Christian values, and that would also train Black women in industrial and domestic skills. According to a pamphlet on the Home, the "Work of the Association" was:

> To protect young colored women and others who come to Cleveland
> as strangers; to help them make friends; to secure suitable boarding
> places for them if there is not room with the Home; to help develop

true womanhood; to conduct classes, educational and gymnastic, in the evenings to better fit them for earning their living, and to develop wholesome Christian character.[22]

In trying to generate support for this home, Ms Hunter had to advocate on behalf of the situation at hand—the needs of the Black female. Some of the Black elite subscribed to the DuBoisian view of racial uplift, and others to the Washingtonian view. Thus, Ms Hunter, herself a Washingtonian, had to carefully choose her words to gain support from all factions of the Black community. In any case, her appeal to the Black leaders of the community met with hostility. The Cleveland Black elite felt that Ms Hunter came up North with these Southern Black Jim Crow ideas. They, in fact, felt that they'd had more exposure to integration and that they knew how to best deal with the local scene. There was this intraracial divide thing happening: Northern Blacks *vs.* Southern Blacks, with the Northerners seeing the Southerners as backward. Furthermore, some of the elite who depended on White patronage didn't want to upset their White customers on whom they depended for financial security and political favors. Eventually, Ms Hunter was able to garner the support of the Black leadership; however, she had to depend on White philanthropists to generate the funds needed. Drawing on contacts she had gathered from private White patients, she appealed to rich Whites who agreed to support the effort if they could control the board of the home. It is important to note that Ms Hunter agreed to let the Whites be board advisors as a survival strategy. She negotiated with Whites on their terms, a standard arrangement. She did what she felt she had to do. She struck a compromise, something that many Black people have to deal with. The present generation regards this phenomenon as "Keepin' it real *vs.* Sellin' out." However, Ms Hunter would not be categorized as a sell out since she compromised in order to advance the Black community, rather than for personal gain. Carter G. Woodson (1933/1990: 29) discusses this type of situation as "The Negroes do[ing] the 'coing' and the whites the 'operating.'" In other words, the fact is, oftentimes, Whites see themselves as participating in interracial cooperation when in actuality it is the Black person working to carry out interracial effort.

Talking about being a masterful rhetorician! This woman had to please many factions to achieve her goal. When Ms Hunter wrote to potential White donors, she emphasized that the women would be trained as good domestic help. When she appealed to the Black ministers, who were staunch integrationists, she emphasized the good Christian atmosphere and the fact that White institutions would not provide space for Black women. Similarly, when dealing with the old guard Black elites she emphasized the fact that the White institutions would not accept the Black females. She had to further assure them that the home would "protect colored women and *others*." When dealing with newer Black leadership who themselves had migrated to the North, she emphasized the self-help philosophy. When all was said and done, Jane Edna Hunter real-

Figure 2.1 The Working Girls' Home Association, Cleveland, Ohio, 1911

ized her goal. In 1911, The Working Girls' Home Association became a reality (see Figure 2.1).[23]

The name was later changed to the Phillis Wheatley Association in 1913 (see Figure 2.2, next page). The renaming of the institution signals that Hunter and her associates understood the depth of what it means to be a literate African American, including: the ability to earn an honest living and commensurate wages, a commitment to physical, spiritual, and cultural development, in short, the freedom to realize one's full potential.

It is also interesting to note that as a Cleveland Public School student, I'd

Figure 2.2 The Phillis Wheatley Association, Cleveland, Ohio, 2001

walked past this great art-in-effect/artifact of Black literacies on my way to Central Junior high school for years, and never appreciated its full worth. Yes, I spent a summer at a camp sponsored by the Association, but the depth of Jane Edna Hunter's contribution to the Cleveland Black community was never emphasized to me in my education as a student, nor at the camp. As a matter of fact, as I got older, I recollect the Phillis Wheatley building as a place where hos (prostitutes) worked in front and on the side of the building for years.

The struggles of the majority of Black people in this country during the period are captured vividly in the lyrics of a Bessie Smith post-World War I blues tune "Poor Man Blues":

> Please listen to my pleading, 'cause I can't stand these hard times long.
> Please listen to my pleading, 'cause I can't stand these hard times long.
> They'll make an honest man do things you know is wrong.
> Now the war is over, poor man must live the same as you,
> Now the war is over, poor man must live the same as you,
> If it wasn't for the poor man, Mr. Rich man what would you do?
>
> (Harrison, 1988: 70–1)

The rhetorical effect of this blues lyric is a text of social critique of classism and poverty, representing the voice and rhetorical situation of Black communities. The structure of the song reinforces the semantics. The first line repeated in each stanza emphasizes the urgency of the situation—"Please listen to my pleading, 'cause I can't stand these hard times long." That line speaks volumes concerning the Black experience from slavery to sharecropping to segregation to ghettoization. The lives sung about in this music, of these communities, influenced literature, scholarship, and activism.

It has been argued that from the Harlem Renaissance onward, folklore was no longer seen as simple or something to be looked down upon, but that it, especially Black music, shaped the literary imagination of Black writers (and some White ones). (See Raussert, 2000: 13.) I would argue that from the enslavement narratives onward, Black folk thought and cultural productions can be shown as a major influence and that vernacular epistemologies inform African American literacies. Here is a rhyme of my youth that I believe was passed down from the New Negro era:

> I'm not a nigga
> I'm a nigga ro
> When I become a nigga
> I'll let you know.

You will recognize the vernacular pronunciation of "nigger" which is "nigga"— signifying its reappropriation. Similarly, the term "nigga ro," a play on the term "Negro," has been Blackenized to indicate on one level of meaning, that the entity conventionally referred to as "nigger" is so far opposite of being a "nigger" that s/he is in fact a "nigga." A "nigga" is someone who cannot be controlled or defined from without. A "nigga" defines him/herself. And, this is so much the case and even more than that, that a real "nigga" can take it upon him/herself to add an extra syllable at will—"ro." Of course, I didn't know any of this when I was growing up. It was just something kids said to each other when grown ups weren't around to tell us that we shouldn't repeat the word "nigga." I remember people saying, "That kinda talk make White folks think we ignorant." Now that I think about it, I guess the grown ups thought we were saying "nigger."

Literacies for access, equality, civil rights, and Black power

The African American struggle for equality and access has been simultaneously foremost and multivarious as can be evidenced through the numerous social movements and organizations among Black people. First in date came the Black women's clubs, begun in the mid-1800s, yet active as the National Association of Colored Women (NACW), concerned with cultural, political, social, educational, and economic uplift. Next were the Black labor unions, such as the Brotherhood of Sleeping Car Porters, begun in 1925 in Chicago, led by A. Philip Randolph, focusing on economic access, working conditions, and political consciousness raising. There followed the Future Outlook League of Cleveland, Ohio, begun in 1935, pursuing better working and economic conditions for Black workers. Next came the Southern Christian Leadership Conference (SCLC) begun in 1954, led by Dr Martin Luther King and dedicated to eradicating segregation and creating economic and social equality via nonviolent direct action. The sequence continued with the Student Nonviolent Coordinating Committee (SNCC), organized by Black college students in 1960 to fight against segregation through civil disobedience. Most recent in date is the Black Panther Party for Self-defense, founded in 1966 by Huey Newton and Bobby Seale, focusing on "Black self-determination, freedom, employment, decent housing, exemption from military service and an end to police brutality and murder in Black communities" (Pough, in press). All the while, many Black churches and Black mosques have demonstrated an understanding that Black religion and social and political activism go hand in hand; Black social movements and organizations have worked to address the needs of African Americans and in the process have helped to transform the concepts of equality and democracy. To quote the eloquent scholar Dr Vincent Harding (1990: 6):

> At its deepest and best levels, what we so often call the civil rights movement (the post-World War II phase of the African American freedom movement) was in fact a powerful outcropping of the continuing struggle for the expansion of democracy in the United States, a struggle in which African Americans have always been integrally engaged, but one in which we provided major leadership from the mid-1950s at least to the 1970s.

The call for change sounded through every possible medium, employing a diversity of rhetorical strategies and ideological formations, spawned from the same rhetorical situation. Black writers and poets such as Gwendolyn Brooks,

Haki Madhubuti, Sonia Sanchez, Mari Evans; Black entertainers, for example, Billie Holliday, Nina Simone, Josephine Baker, Duke Ellington, Miles Davis, James Brown, Charlie Parker; Black intellectuals for instance Malcolm X, Stokely Carmichael (Kwame Ture), Dr Martin Luther King, W. E. B. DuBois and many others sought to flip the public script of segregation, dehumanization, and poverty for Black and poor people.

The writer Gwendolyn Brooks argues for social equality very creatively in her novel *Maud Martha* (1993). In it, Brooks deploys, as one of the novel's central discourses, the impregnation of the sign "gray" with a wealth of meanings, which signal her concern with the Black condition. Brooks' novel was published in 1953, near the end of the legal segregation era plagued by public devaluation of Black life, Black education, Black creativity, Black beauty, and discrimination in housing, employment, and wage practices. Brooks is concerned with Black assimilation to White cultural values. For Brooks, the melting pot metaphor of American racial, cultural, and ethnic blending does not describe the American struggle as aptly as the sign gray. In *Maud Martha*, gray signifies death, powerlessness, and ambiguity, as Black cultural values become filtered through White ones. From Brooks' vantage point "It all came down to gray clay" (Brooks, 1993: 25). This metaphor signified, among other things, that American society was socially constructed, molded, and controlled.

Brooks plays with White on Black images to symbolize the American struggle for co-equal lifestyles among Blacks and Whites as illustrated through the south-side Chicago story of Maud Martha. Brooks shows that both segregation and integration are problematic in a fundamentally racist society. Briefly, Paul and Martha's night out to a segregated theater illustrates this point. Martha talks her husband (Paul) into taking her to the World Playhouse, a White theater house, where Black persons were not welcomed. In this scene, Brooks shows the unsettling nature of the whole situation. The White tickethandler gazes in amazement on the Black people. The Black people are uncertain of their fate because they want to experience the theater. Martha is angered by Paul's reticence as he approaches the ticket seller. In some ways she feels her husband is emasculated because of his (dis)position. On the way to the theater, Martha wonders what people think of her, a dark Black female, with long wavy hair, who is not considered particularly attractive by European standards, accompanied by a lightskinned (high yellow) Black male. These are concerns that don't even enter into the everyday consciousnesses of White folks, much less White theater goers! In this way, Brooks demonstrates the everyday hassles of being Black in an environment where White supremacist values dictate societal behavior. This scene evinces Maud Martha's desire for equal access to American institutions, the right to be free to be self-determined and self-defined. But it also demonstrates the long-standing legacies of Black devaluation that must be eradicated. Nevertheless, the experience of theater, showing that Black persons appreciate artistry and culture, just as any other American ethnic group does, made one feel good, as though one would return home to a nice "sweet-smelling apartment with flowers on gleaming tables" afterward, rather than to the "kit'n't apt., . . . with narrow complaining stairs." Paul enjoyed the experience, telling Maud Martha that they "oughta do this more often" (Brooks, 1993: 77). Her ability to fulfill her inner desires and have Paul to share in them demonstrates Maud Martha's agency, and by extension Black people's power to overturn discriminatory practices and bring about social equality. Maud Martha and Paul's integration of the theater turns out to be a harbinger for the situation in American public schooling in the year that follows Brooks' novel.

When challenged by Justice Frankfurter in both the 1952 and 1953 oral arguments of the Brown *vs.* Board of Education Supreme Court case, Thurgood Marshall unwaveringly and consistently held that "any segregation, which is for the purpose of setting up either class or caste legislation, is in and of itself a violation of the Fourteenth Amendment" (Rowan, 1993: 213). The rhetorical task of the NAACP's Legal Defense Team (LDT) led by Thurgood Marshall was to persuade the Court that the purpose of the Fourteenth amendment was to guarantee complete *equality* to African Americans.

Thurgood Marshall's (and the LDT's) claim was that: "Any segregation for class or caste legislation is a violation of the 14th amendment." In Section 1 of the 14th amendment of 1868 America's claim was that:

> *All persons born or naturalized in the United States* and subject to the jurisdiction thereof, *are citizens of the United States* and of the State wherein they reside. No State shall make or enforce any law which shall abridge the privileges or immunities of citizens of the United States; nor shall any State deprive any person of life, liberty, or property, without due process of law; nor deny to any person within its jurisdiction the equal protection of the laws.[24]

It is very important to note that the LDT chose to use the terms class and caste. African American communities were stratified by material wealth, social attitudes, educational level, and values, yet bound by Black cultural institutions (the traditional Black church), the shared historical experience of slavery, and its legacy, the continued practices of Jim Crow and White racism and supremacy, and political and economic exploitation. This made American Africans triply a class-based group, a cultural group, and a castelike group. Under such conditions, access to equal educational facilities or relevant education was impossible. Thus, the LDT held that legislation that upheld segregation denied Black folks the opportunity of their right to a quality education (and social uplift—life liberty, property), and denied them equal protection under the law.

In May of 1954, the Supreme Court revised the dominant discourse when it agreed that "separate educational facilities are inherently unequal" (Martin, 1998: 174).[25]

Black rhetors continued to push for the vernacular concept of equality, in order to change American dominant discourse and society and gain access to

rights and privileges accorded to Whites. What I mean by the vernacular concept of equality is that though Black rhetors and Black people wanted the same
opportunities and human rights as any other cultural or racial group, this aspi-
ration does not include the desire to be White for the sake of being White. The
Black Power Movement of the 1960s and 1970s represented another transformational moment in Black Experiences. This new era, led by many Black
organizations, most popularly identified with the Black Panthers, encouraged a
renewed sense of power, a new psyche, new artistry, and new (more soulful)
music.[26] Remember? James Brown encouraged Black people, not just in America, to "Say It Loud" (I'm Black and I'm Proud). Thus, equality does not
necessarily mean the desire to be integrated. Being Black and being equal is not
merely a matter of feeling good about one's African features or African American heritage; it is that, coupled with self-conscious practices of culture building.
Nevertheless, even when Black persons align their rhetoric with religious discourses, political discourses, familial discourses, or any other discourses with
which Whites can identify, or even when Blacks perform Whiteness or pass for
White, it is a means to life, liberty, and the pursuit of happiness—equality.

In *The Autobiography of Malcolm X*, Malcolm X discusses the complexity of the
concept of equality from an African American perspective (Haley and Malcolm
X, 1964: 313):

> The truth is that "integration" is an image, it's a foxy Northern lib-
> eral's smokescreen that confuses the true wants of the American black
> man. Here in these fifty [two] racist and neo-racist states of North
> America, this word "integration" has millions of white people con-
> fused, and angry, believing wrongly that the black masses want to live
> mixed up with the white man. That is the case only with the relative
> handful of these "integration"-mad Negroes.
>
> Human rights! Respect as *human beings*! That's what America's black
> masses want. That's the true problem. The black masses want not to
> be shrunk from as though they are plague-ridden. They want not to be
> walled up in slums, in the ghettoes, like animals. They want to live in
> open, **free society where they can walk with their heads up,
> like men, and women!** (Bold emphasis mine.)

Of course some would interpret Malcolm X's language as separatist, because he
also endorsed Black self-determination, and (what I would call) African American-centered education, and Black economic self-help through support of Black
entrepreneurship. However, shoving these culture-building ideas under the rug
as Black supremacist or separatist is a very narrow read, and a misread.

Malcolm's rhetoric called attention to the fact that merely making it legal for
Blacks and Whites to interact in public spaces would not bring about the opportunity for Black people to become full citizens and to reach their fullest

potential. For Malcolm X, Black nationalist strategies were a means to an end—"free society where [African Americans] can walk with their heads up, like men, and women!" He saw these strategies as practical, considering the blatant social inequities of American society.

Speaking to Local 1199, a labor group of hospital and nursing home workers in 1968, Dr Martin Luther King discussed the inequalities that existed even after Brown *vs*. Board, in the midst of the Civil Rights and Black Power eras:

> In this other America, thousands, yea even, millions of young people are forced to attend inadequate, substandard, inferior, qualityless schools. And year after year, thousands of young people in this other America finish our high schools reading at an eighth and a ninth grade level sometimes. Not because they are dumb, not because they don't have innate intelligence, but because the schools are so inadequate, so overcrowded, so devoid of quality, so segregated, if you will, that the best in these minds can never come out.
>
> (King, 1968)

What Dr King's observations revealed was that though "separate but (un)equal" had been revised in the discourse, it was still operating in practice, and thus the vernacular concept of equality was (and is) yet to be realized. In this context, segregation means "devoid of quality," not devoid of Whites, or devoid of qualified Black students, but devoid of economic resources and quality education. Can legislation root out institutional racism?

Hip Hop literacies and consciousness

> [W]ith the continuum from the Burrus to the beat-boxes, the griots to the DJs (or MCs), we find not simply the resilience of the African oral tradition; certainly this is the case, yet all too often a monolithic "African oral tradition" is evoked as a crude and romantic answer to diasporan complexities. Also at work here is a conscious attempt on the part of sound culture to force new technologies to address forms of knowledge that are precolonial in origin but continually produced and modified by a racist system in which [Anglocentric] literacy is a privilege and the written word the signified of official (white or elite) culture.
>
> (Chude-Sokei, 1997: 194)

As referred to in the above quotation, Hip Hop is an example of African American creativity, a merger of African American oral tradition and "stray technological parts intended for cultural and industrial trash heaps," transformed "into sources of pleasure and power" (Rose, 1994a: 71). The American version of Hip Hop mixes Anglo American literacies with Afro-American literacies to create the dynamic literacies of Hip Hop. Black American, Caribbean, and Latino/a youth of 1970s New York City found themselves in the pre-dawn of the Reagan–Bush era, in a nearly bankrupt city, in the poorest neighborhoods, in the poorest funded school districts, yet in a land of plenty. Hip Hop ideology is a response to Reagan–Bush era ideologies of social and civic abandonment of inner city communities (J. Morgan 2000). This rhetorical situation shaped the production and creation of Hip Hop. Hip Hop is itself a product of all the musics that preceded it: spirituals, Blues, Be bop, Jazz, Gospel, R&B/Soul, dancehall reggae, Rock & Roll and others through sampling and mixing. Though Hip Hop is conventionally defined as rapping, deejaying, graffiti writing, and break dancing, Hip Hop veteran MC KRS One (1999) defines it as "a behavior that frees the mind of inner city people." In his poll of 800,000 people around the world, KRS One collected nine elements of Hip Hop: "(1) graffiti art, (2) Djaying (Emceeing/Rapping), (3) break beat, (4) break dancing, (5) beat boxing, (6) street fashion, (7) street language, (8) street knowledge, and (9) street entrepreneurism."

It is important to view Hip Hop as a total culture (a subculture within larger African American culture). The American version of Hip Hop[27] emanates from African American literacies. I find the definition of Jones and Jones (2000: 4–5) helpful: "Literacies are social practices: ways of reading and writing and using written texts that are bound up in social processes which locate individual action within social and cultural processes." The social processes have everything to do with the dialogic interaction of American discourse communities. The communicative styles and ways of knowing of the performers can be traced to Black Vernacular expressive arts developed and constantly modified by African Americans as resistance and survival strategies. Many of the experiences such as police brutality, racial profiling, inequality, and sexual issues, for example, are consequences which are fundamental to the American social system and are apparent in various cultural expressions. Thus, the music and lyrics must be considered in relation to beliefs, values, mores, and complex ideologies that underlie the street apparel, hard body imagery, and the sometimes seeming celebration of misogyny, thuggishness, and larger than life personas narrated in the music. One way to look at the celebration of gangsta practices, thuggishness, rampant materialism, and seeming disrespect for law and mainstream values in Hip Hop is in relation to Black vernacular folk epic story and song tradition. In African American culture, there are two character types in particular that appear in rap music—the "bad nigger" and the badman. The "bad nigger" is a type of trickster that defies dominant mainstream values and those of traditional Afro-American culture. He "threatens the solidarity and harmony of the group" and may bring potential harm to everyone (Roberts, 1989: 199). Conversely, the badman is an amalgamation of the trickster and the conjurer and is associated with a secular lifestyle that appeals to some segments of the Black community for badmanism offered an alternative route to success through gambling or some other illegal activities

(Roberts, 1989: 206). The badman often resorted to gun violence in an act of self-defense or victimization.

Another way to explore the cultural form known as Hip Hop is to look at it as a site of struggle to reconcile vernacular and standard knowledges, beliefs, and practices. The vernacular is based on the African American cultural matrix including the West African background of oral traditions and their reinterpretation in the American context. The concept of the power of the word or Nommo is ever present in Hip Hop. The manipulation of sounds is important not only to word delivery and creativity but in its connection to aesthetics, visual imagery, polyrhythmic beats, technologies, and vibrations. The Black American experience of fictive kinship, for example, provides an example of reinterpretation of the West African community based clan model for purposes of protection and advancement. In Hip Hop the most significant and core unit is the family or crew (Morgan, 2000).

On the other hand, the standard ingredients of Hip Hop are brought about by Hip Hoppers' socialization in American society. The weight American society places on the acquisition of wealth and material possessions, patriarchy and the social construction of maleness, as a means of power and prestige, are also factors in the production of the music, lyrics, expressive behaviors and its focus on materiality, sex, and power by many artists. Currently, Hip Hop is the most popular and biggest selling music. Music conglomerates largely control the distribution of the music. The genres of the music that are aggressively promoted by the industry and pitched to the mainstream public are those that mainly depict sex, violence, and materialism. Yes, many of the artists are rapping about life as they have seen or experienced it at some level. Yet, much of it is also fantasy and fiction and many rappers are helping the industry to cash in on racist and sexist stereotypes. Cinema has also cashed in on rap music and Hip Hop culture. Films like *Boyz N the Hood*, *Baby Boy* and many many others are promoting a "ghettocentric" imagination, which some see as pimping the struggles of the Black underclass who have been abandoned in urban centers. Another problem raised by the onslaught of gangsta themed Black films is that they tend to overly represent distorted images of Black people and fail to show the complexity, heterogeneity, and vastness of Black experiences. The dilemma for African Americans has always been one of "keepin' it real vs. sellin' out." Contemporarily, an important dilemma for popular rappers is the commodification of their narratives in the global economy of rap music and Hip Hop culture, which leaves them in the popular imagination as agentless narrators stripped from their cultural and historical contexts. Given that rap music and rappers are seen as commodities globally marketed largely by exploitation of stereotypical images of "niggas," "pimps," "gangstas," "militants," "hos," and "bucks," how do rappers display on the one hand, an orientation to their situated, public role as performing products, and on the other, that their performance is connected to discourses of authenticity and resistance?

This struggle to define reality from a Black perspective is a major aspect of the ideological matrix of Hip Hop: the imperative—"keep it real." Though violence and sexism does not represent THE Black experience, it is true that many economically impoverished African Americans are stuck in urban centers and have to deal face to face with societal ills rapped about by many of the artists. Thus, artists are revered for speaking the truth or representin' which is a Hip Hop literacy practice. A rap is "wack" (lame, uncool) if the story ain't good, does not *move* the crowd. Being a commercial success and making songs that are not explicitly critical of the state does not necessarily make one wack, non-political, or unconscious, although there are a lot of wack rappers out there. The delivery of the lyrics, the personal style of the performer, the beat, and the sonic quality of the music are equally important. In fact, the audacity of this performer to command attention, to invent a life for herself or himself, to wield signs of power, to attract a large market share and fill auditoriums and stadiums is in and of itself political. Hip hoppers continue to flip the public script on undervalued Black life by making their aesthetics the overwhelming standard by which popular music and style are evaluated.

As advanced by Tricia Rose, Hip Hop's "flow, layering and rupture simultaneously reflect and contest the social roles open to urban inner city youth at the end of the twentieth century" (Rose, 1994a: 72). For example, in Lauryn Hill's "Superstar" (from L. Hill, 1998), she raps about those who want to reach a level of success through MCing/rapping as opposed to dead end jobs:

> All I wanted was to sell like 500
> And be a ghetto superstar since my first album, Blunted
> I used to work at Foot Locker, they fired me and fronted
> Or I quitted, now I spit it—however do you want it?
> Now you get it.

Tupac's "Dear Mama" also illustrates a redefinition of the role the dominant society created for his mom:

> And even as a crack fiend, Mama, You always was a black queen, Mama.
> I finally understand, For a woman it ain't easy tryin' ta raise a man.
> You always was committed. A poor single mother on welfare
> Tell me how ya did it. There's no way I can pay ya back, But
> The plan is ta show ya that I understand. You are appreciated.
> (From T. Shakur, 1995, cf. the album *Me Against the World*, original CD
> released by Jive/Interscope)

Drawing heavily on the African American language tradition, Hip Hoppers consciously reclaim and restructure the language (in recreolization mode) to signal the intense tension between African American discourse and dominant discourse and to connect with their core culture audience members (Alim, 2001).

Being an MC, beat boxer, graffiti artist, or street entrepreneur, in Hip Hop, offers youth a different way of doing, seeing, living, and being in the world and offers alternative ways of achieving, such as getting "props" which is another literacy practice of Hip Hop. Props are achieved by skills and street credibility.

Hip Hop is more than the surface appearance of vernacular speech and style. It is borne from a culture of underground struggle and survival on a deep level, no matter if the surface appears to comply with official dominant discourses. Historical memory, deep cultural practices along with resistance to current oppressions plays a major role in maintaining, developing, and creating worldviews, identities, and means of survival.

Literally, in the African American tradition, rap and rappers "made a way outta no way" when they took elements of their pain and struggle "along with stray technological parts" and brought into being a subculture of resistance and creativity that has commanded global respect. A deeper level of investigation of African American cultural forms is needed in order to get at the broad range of African American literacies.[28]

In this chapter, I have demonstrated the situated yet evolving literacies and rhetorical practices of African America through the analysis of its literature, folklore, and vernacular expressive arts, from the eras of Enslavement, Reconstruction, Jim Crow, Harlem Renaissance, Civil Rights, Black Power, and Hip Hop. Central to the rhetorical history of African Americans is the fact that the rhetorical context for Black women and men has not changed all that much in terms of power relations. The struggle has been about liberty, equal access to resources, and self-determination. Thus, Black rhetors of earlier eras such as Phillis Wheatley or Gwendolyn Brooks live in the same universe and have concerns similar to contemporary rhetors such as Lauryn Hill and Tupac. Though this is not an essential interpretation of the study of African American rhetoric(s), it is a unique aspect, which helps to distinguish it. The omission of African American literacies and rhetorics from traditional English curricula has rendered the African American contribution to the rhetorical project of democracy in America obscure and aids in disconnecting Black youth from the classroom.

3

"To protect and serve": African American female literacies

All I claim is that there is a feminine as well as masculine side to truth, that these are related, not as inferior or superior, not as better or worse, not as weaker or stronger, but as complements—complements in one necessary and symmetric whole.

Anna Julia Cooper (1892: 60)

No matter how backward and negative the mainstream view and image of Black people, I feel compelled to reshape the image and to explore our many positive angles because I love my own people. Perhaps this is because I have been blessed with spiritual African eyes at a time when most Africans have had their eyes poked out. . . . So, like most ghetto girls who haven't yet been turned into money-hungry heartless bitches by a godless money centered world, I have a problem: I love hard. Maybe too hard. Or maybe it's too hard for a people without structure—structure in the sense of knowing what African womanhood is. What does it mean? What is it supposed to do to you and for you?

Sister Souljah (1994: x)

Twisted images of Black womanhood have always been a pivotal element of the American economy. That system of brutal patriarchy and chattel slavery has been reduced and metamorphosed into present day forms of structural racism, sexism, and cultural hegemony and still powerfully influences the lives and futures of Black females, their families, and people around the world. Sister Souljah laments the obstruction of African womanhood from the African American worldview. Though many Black females were not born into literal American ghettoes, as were Souljah and I, most nevertheless struggle for self-determination and self-definition against the world's ghettoized image of them. Young Black females often struggle to invent themselves against the distorted images of "money hungry heartless bitch," "Jezebel," and good ole "Mammy" among others, many of which were created during slavery. Patricia Hill Collins (1991: 71) explains:

The first controlling image applied to African American women is that of mammy—the faithful, obedient domestic servant. Created to justify the economic exploitation of house slaves and sustained to explain Black women's long-standing restriction to domestic service, the mammy image represents the normative yardstick used to evaluate all Black women's behavior.

Mammy tended to the every need of White families often at the expense of her own, even though the White people she worked for may have been very fond of her. She is also asexual.

The stereotype of the Black female as "heartless Nigger bitch" is another controlling image. A synonym for this stereotype is "wench" which was used to refer to an enslaved (and sometimes a free) female, "as a woman whose sexual behavior [was] loose and immoral."[1] The basic idea here was that Black females were subhuman. From the White supremacist point of view, they could not love—not even their children. They could be used for sexual exploitation and they enjoyed it. They served at the pleasure of their master in order to maximize his profit. They were ignorant, and good only for working—outside the home, unless it was the "Big House." The Jezebel stereotype is closely related to the wench.

Slaveowners operating under the ideologies of White supremacy and the economic system of capitalism foisted onto Black women these images during chattel slavery, and they are still going strong as many many television shows and movies will confirm. There is hardly a media outlet to which a Black woman can turn and not see a negative image of herself. When I plugged the terms "Black girls" and "young Black girls" into a Yahoo search engine, for example, the sites "Black pussy" and other pornography sites came up for my consideration. The search "Black Woman" yielded the webpage "Pink Chocolate," which featured "lovely dark ladies" complete with pop ups of graphic sex acts and links to more hard core sex sites. Similarly, I didn't have to search too far with the term "Black Women" before the sites "World of Black Women," "Hot Nude Black Women," "Black Women Exposed" popped up. Thankfully, there were other sites to counter those images such as "Beautiful Black Women Online," "Black Women in the Arts," "Black Career Women," and "Sistahspace," and other sites sharing cultural, spiritual, and uplifting information. Music videos, television talk shows, news shows, newspapers, and tabloids show us one-sided and oft times disfigured representations of African American females: pulsating genitals, hood rats, "successful" professional sisters alienated in Corporate America or the academy, low-income single mothers, falling stars.

With an aura so critical to the personhood of the Black female, her literacies have, by necessity, developed to fulfill a quest for a better world. And so, Black females, Sojourners and Souljahs, have special knowledges and develop language and literacy practices to resist White supremacist and economically motivated stereotypes conveying subhuman or immoral images.

Woman is the child's first teacher, who protects it even in her womb and begins to socialize it. In Geneva Smitherman's words, "when you lambast the home language that kids bring to school, you ain' just dissin' dem, you talkin' 'bout they mommas! Check out the concept of 'Mother Tongue'" (1997a: 28). The term "mother tongue" can be understood on several levels. Most obviously, mothers transmit their language into their children who develop facility with it. In this sense we all inherit the condition/ing of our mothers if she has a word in our socialization. But more basically, our language, our mother tongue, is at least partly how we know what we know. Every language represents a particular way of making sense of the world. As contextual factors in our realities change, our language changes to accommodate our world/view. Non-standard languages typically change faster than standard ones because they are not authorized in the larger society or carefully written down (Gee, 1996). Nevertheless, various nuances and ideas are descended in those languages that reflect a past and help to shape the future of the language users. An aspect of the argument which I wish to make about African American literacy as indicated by Anna Julia Cooper's words that open this chapter is that the female contribution to knowledge-making must be recognized to give a fuller understanding of the world in which we live. I will argue here for the significance of mother tongue literacies in African American culture and literacy education.

The concept of mother tongue literacy is based on the premise that literacy acquisition is accelerated through exploiting the tongue of nurture in literacy education. Objections to the concept as it applies to African American discourse community speakers include shortage of qualified instructors, instructional materials, that AAVE itself is deficient, that it is a mostly unwritten code, and that exploitation of AAVE will stunt the acquisition of academic discourse. In the face of these objections, I hold that suppression of mother tongue literacy further subordinates African Americans in society and in educational institutions and is unhealthy for African American identity development in that it negates the lived experience of at least 90 per cent of African Americans, who are members of the African American discourse community. Smitherman estimates that 90 per cent of African Americans use some forms of AAVE (Smitherman, 2000: 19). We can assume that there are African American discourses (that exist among other discourses) functioning as primary discourses among this population in significant ways. Following James Gee (1996: viii), I understand discourse as a system of "behaving, interacting, valuing, thinking, believing, speaking, and often reading and writing that are accepted as instantiations of particular roles . . . by specific groups of people . . . Discourses are ways of being 'people like us'. They are 'ways of being in the world'; they are 'forms of life'. They are, thus, always and everywhere *social* and products of social histories."

Following Brian Street (1993), I use the term *literacies* to signify opposition to the concept of monolithic autonomous literacy (*Cross-Cultural* 9). Like Marilyn Martin-Jones and Kathryn Jones (2000: 4–5), I am working from the theory that "Literacies are social practices: ways of reading and writing and using written texts that are bound up in social processes which locate individual action within social and cultural processes." In particular, I see African American literacies as including vernacular resistance arts and cultural productions that are created to carve out free spaces in oppressive locations such as the classroom, the streets, the workplace, or the airwaves to name a few. The epistemologies of these literacies are "precolonial in origin and modified by a racist system in which [Anglocentric] literacy is a privilege and the written word the signified of official . . . culture" (Chude-Sokei, 1997: 194). African American language and literacy traditions are dynamic and fluid cultural matrixes from which revolutionary life and culture sustaining ideas and practices can be fashioned.

For many African American girls, various phenomena gnaw at our connection to knowing our language, this "how we be" and "who we be," this foundational element of our development. There has been a conflict, between our mothers and others, about what our language is and does for us. This conflict is so prevalent that many Black females at some time or another internalize it: Should we respect our language and ways of knowing as little girls, or in our homes as we develop into women? Or should we gradually have our minds (our mother wits) erased with each passing year of formal schooling? These conflicting views of reality create the need to verify and codify Black females' ways of knowing and acting to help us successfully and purposefully cross borders. Making explicit some of the literacies of Black females can help educators to build from that foundation.

To do this I will draw upon work concerning African American preschool girls, elementary school-aged girls, adolescent girls, high school girls, and college level females—Black women, period! I examine creative literature by African American females, my own experience, and other scholarly works.[2] My primary concern is to identify several important African American female literacies and how African American females exploit their sex, race, cultural, and class backgrounds to their advantage in their opposition to White supremacist stereotypes. I also strive to demonstrate how Black females linguistically navigate and convey this experience and unique understanding of themselves to others. I then sketch out some trials and educational issues of this population. Then I move on to point to new directions, showing areas wherein African American female literacies could be used in African American literacy education.

Toward a definition of African American female literacies

Concepts of literacy among African American females have been woefully undertheorized. An important departure is the work of Jacqueline Royster, who explores elite nineteenth-century African American women's subjective use of written literacy, particularly the essay, as a social, cultural, and political tool for social change. Royster's work is valuable as she understands written literacy and orality as parts of a continuum of language practices that converge in knowledge making. Another important aspect of Royster's study is that it underscores that African American women's consciousness, shaped by historical memory and social conditioning, informed their literacy and rhetorical practices. Other important work in the area of African American women's literacy practices is offered by Shirley Wilson Logan who charts "distinctive and recurring patterns of rhetorical practice" in the oratory of elite nineteenth-century women (Logan, 1999: xiii–xiv). Logan's work is instructive as it illuminates the continuity in the production of rhetorical forms and strategies that emerge from similarities of the rhetorical situations across historical Black women orators. Joycelyn Moody's work demonstrates African American women's manipulation of literacy even working from disadvantageous rhetorical situations—when they were supposedly "illiterate slaves" in the nineteenth century dictating their narratives to White male biographers.

The concept of African American female literacies as I explore it here refers to ways of knowing and acting and the development of skills, vernacular expressive arts and crafts that help females to advance and protect themselves and their loved ones in society. African cultural forms that are constantly adapted to meet the needs of navigating life in a racist society influence these practices and ways of knowing and coping. African American females communicate these literacies through storytelling, conscious manipulation of silence and speech, code/style shifting, and signifying, among other verbal and non-verbal practices. Performance arts such as singing, dancing, acting, steppin', and stylin', as well as crafts such as quilting and use of other technologies are also exploited to these purposes (e.g., pots, pans, rags, brooms, and mops); African American females' language and literacy practices reflect their socialization in a racialized, genderized, sexualized, and classed world in which they employ their language and literacy practices to protect and advance themselves. Working from this rhetorical situation, the Black female develops creative strategies to overcome her situation, to "make a way outa no way."

African American female socio-cultural conditioning is different than that of the Black male, though she shares with him the historical reality of a racially oppressed group, which has developed a distinctive culture of survival to deal with its position. It is the African American male who has been identified as an endangered species because of the profile that he has been given in the American social, political, economic, educational, and racial realms. African American males are almost half of the prison population (Woodley, 1999). Black males are often suspended from school for behaviors associated with their culture—expressive clothes, hats, and styles of wearing them, styles of speech (woofing, rapping, playing the dozens) (Majors and Billson, 1992). Their posturing is interpreted and stereotyped as more threatening than Black females. They are represented in higher percentages than White males in the categories of death, unemployment, poverty, AIDS, drug and alcohol abuse, health problems, lower incomes, lower educational achievement (Majors and Billson, 1992). Thus, it is not surprising that the Black male has been the focus of much research in language and literacy studies of African Americans (Labov, 1972; Gibbs, 1988; Watson and Smitherman, 1996; Campbell, 1993).

Sharing many similarities with the African American female, the most influential social constructions surrounding Black male literacies are procreator, provider, and protector of life. To say the least, slavery hindered the Black man's ability to control his role. Thus, the Black male has had to read the world from his perspective and devise ways to meet the needs of himself and his family in slavery and its aftermath of racism and oppression. One of the ways of knowing and acting exploited by Black males is being cool. Coolness has at once positive and dangerous consequences. The positive side of coolness is that it helps African American men to handle conflict in potentially life-threatening situations, enhances pride, and develops unique styles of expression (verbal, written, performance in all facets of life). The stereotypes associated with coolness are the bad N___r, the smart N___r, the outlaw, the womanizer, among others. Other ways of knowing and surviving related to cool employed by Black men are shucking, jiving, and others associated with being a "good non-threatening Negro." Stereotypes associated with these strategies are Uncle Tom and Sambo among others (Majors and Billson, 1992). Coolness is used by both males and females and has precolonial antecedents (Majors and Billson, 1992) as have the less threatening strategies. My point here is not to elaborately compare African American female and male literacies but to give a more holistic picture of African American literacies.

Literacies of Black womanhood, racism, and classism

A fundamental variable in the social cultural construction of African American female literacies is her role as nurturer and protector of life. Without her, African American culture would be no more. Influencing this construction, however removed, is her role in West African precolonial cultures, where woman was a highly valuable source of wealth, as she brought forth offspring to carry on the family clans and controlled and worked surplus crops (Robertson, 1996). Some women worked in the market and other professions, including the oldest. Although coming from a patriarchal society, African women controlled the domestic sphere. Because of her role as nurturer and agricultural head, child-rearing and nurturing was shared by women, including extended breastfeeding. The women took care of their own children as well as others. As women had childcare and labor responsibilities, they worked and mothered together. Hence, the proverb, "it takes a village." Though under drastically different and dehumanizing conditions, the enslaved Black woman also performed valuable labor, except not to benefit her or her community, but her master's. Despite these obstacles, in her quest to fulfill her role, even when in the field, she provided precious life-giving labor in the domestic sphere to her people. From a Black

78

perspective, it was perhaps the only meaningful work operating in the slave community. In the American slavery context, fictive kinship was devised as a way of surviving, achieving prestige and creating a Black human identity apart from dehumanized slave. Consonant with the fictive kinship ideology, Black people performed in a manner that protected the humanity of the collective enslaved community. As Signithia Fordham explains, "in contexts controlled by (an) Other, it was necessary to behave as a collective Black Self while suppressing the desire to promote the individual Self" (1966: 75). Through the drudgery of domestic work, the enslaved female was "essential to the survival of the community" (Davis, 1998: 116).

Though the precolonial experience was significantly different from the colonial one, Black women always had to work to survive. This African cultural tradition coupled with the subhuman slave status conflicted with White elite romantic ideas about the role of the feminine woman and mother. As a result, from a White supremacist perspective, Black women were seen as unladylike, unfit, and immoral.

The African American females' struggle included devising ways to protect and advance themselves and their families—to assert their humanity—against stereotypes and controlling images. Holtzclaw's autobiography includes details about his mother's role in his education in *The Black Man's Burden* (Holtzclaw, 1970: 30):

> As I grew older it became more and more difficult for me to go to school. When cotton first began to open,—early in the fall, it brought a higher price than at any other time of the year. At this time the landlord wanted us all to stop school and pick cotton. But Mother wanted me to remain in school, so, when the landlord came to the quarters early in the morning to stir up the cotton pickers, she used to outgeneral him by hiding me behind the skillets, ovens, and pots, throwing some old rags over me until he was gone. Then she would slip me off to school through the back way. I can see her now with her hands upon my shoulder shoving me along through the woods and underbrush, in a roundabout way, keeping me all the time out of sight of the great plantation.

Notice Holtzclaw draws attention to the domestic items that his mother used to protect his schooling, as she hoped schooling would guarantee him a life better than cotton picking. Working from her position, she hid her son behind "skillets, ovens, and pots" and covered him with "old rags."

As expressed by Souljah in one of the opening quotes to this chapter, love of self and others is the Black woman's charge. What's love got to do with it? Everything, as we realize that Black females are programmed to love, support, and protect our children, brothers, sisters, lovers, friends: Our family! Sethe, the main character in Toni Morrison's *Beloved*, exemplifies the ultimate dilemma as she is deemed an animal for killing her female child rather than allowing her to endure slavery. Equiano's *The Interesting Narrative of the Life of Olaudah Equiano* tells of captured African women who jump ship during the middle passage when they find out they are pregnant by White sailors. Similarly, in Georgia Douglass Johnson's play *Safe* a mother strangles her boy child after witnessing a lynching. Examples abound. What is important to note is that Black females' experiences drove them to use whatever they had to protect their children by any means necessary.

Stevenson offers another significant, yet much less horrific, example of the Black woman using her knowledge of her place and role to protect life. This information comes from the narrative of a Black woman, Fannie Berry, who was interviewed in the 1930s about her recollection of slavery (Stevenson, 1996: 169):

> There wuz an ol' lady patching a quilt an' de paddyroolers wuz looking fo' a slave named John. John wuz dar funnin' an' carrying on. All at once we herd a rap on de door. John took an' runned between Mamy Lou's legs. She hid him by spreading a quilt across her lap and kept on sewing an', do you kno', dem pattyrollers never found him?

From a White supremacist perspective, Mamy Lou's quilt symbolizes her lowly status as domestic worker, and her legs symbolize her position as sexual object. However, it is clear that Ms Berry sees Mamy Lou as the epitome of Black womanhood. Mamy Lou's action is heroic, a gesture of love, as she uses her quilt and her legs to save this young man's life. The ultimate struggle for Black females is to retain proper love of self and significant others without becoming or being seen as "heartless bitches" for the choices they make.

Under the reconstructed African system, that of African American fictive kinship practices, the female was valued as a major element in newly imagined family units of survival. As explained by Miss Jane Pittman, during the enslavement era many "couples" didn't get married; it was more often the case that Ole Master put people together and encouraged them to jump over the broom handle for his own purposes of economic exploitation. In response to that practice, Miss Jane refused to jump over the broom handle when Joe Pittman asked her to marry him. Miss Jane, in her *Autobiography of Miss Jane Pittman* written by Ernest Gaines, says that she and Joe Pittman just agreed that they would live together and support each other. In Miss Jane's situation, she was barren and single (except for a young man, Ned, that she loved and raised as a son). Joe Pittman was a widower with two daughters. Jane and Joe's mutual affection for each other as Black people and their understanding of fictive kinship and mutual reciprocity brought them together. This didn't mean that they didn't love each other. It just meant that they agreed to support each other. Because they were now free and not bound to respect slavery customs, they refused to dignify the slavery conventions with their true affection for each other. Thus, using White supremacist and middle-class standards and theories to understand the constitution of the Black family and marriage obscures their function as units of spiritual, cultural, economic, and emotional survival.

Another social construction influencing the literacies of African American females is the value of autonomy or independence, not to be confused with individualism. Historically, the Black woman has been socialized to be the backbone of African American culture. During enslavement loved ones could be sold away and even oneself placed into new and dangerous situations at the discretion of the enslavers in the blink of an eye. Thus, the Black woman had to devise ways to live with herself, inside of her own mind. Paradoxically, from a White supremacist patriarchal perspective, she didn't feel it, and even if she did, she could handle it. On the other hand, "Maid" to serve as Mammy in slavery, she was socialized to be the backbone of the dominant culture, as well. As such, the autonomous and independent Black woman is often distorted as Superwoman, someone who can be there to comfort everyone else, with no time or need to be comforted. Contemporarily, the value of autonomy and independence is deeply instilled among low-income pre-adult Black females (Hubbard, 1997). Several factors account for this socialization. One factor is the strong possibility of being the single income earner as Black females who desire a Black male mate are more likely to end up without one. (Contributing to this situation is the status of Black men—endangered species.) The critical point here is that autonomy and independence need not sentence females to a death sentence of life imprisonment to the stereotypical images. Joan Morgan's (2000: 104) thoughts are helpful:

> When you're raised to believe that the ability to kick adversity's ass is a birthright—a by-product of gender and melanin—you tend to tackle life's afflictions tenaciously. This is a useful quality, no doubt. However, this [stereotype] also tricks many of us into believing we can carry the weight of the world.

While I understand Morgan's use of the term "melanin" to signify White supremacist distortions of African females' autonomy and independence, I think "social cultural conditioning" is more accurate as it takes into account precolonial influences as well as the semantic inversion of White supremacist images on the part of African Americans.

Another social construction influencing African American female literacies is early knowledge of the self as racially and sexually marked objects, to a degree greater than many European American girls or boys. In the chapter "The Trials of Girlhood," in Harriet Jacobs' *Incidents in the Life of a Slave Girl*, Jacobs describes the "slave girl's" uneasy transition from child to woman. She writes (Jacobs, 1861: 362–3):

> She will become prematurely knowing in evil things. Soon she will learn to tremble when she hears her master's footfall. She will be compelled to realize that she is no longer a child. If God has bestowed beauty upon her, it will prove her greatest curse.

Jacobs' statements suggest that because of the Black female social position, essential to her own survival is her early knowledge of evil things, the high likelihood of her being "discovered." Whiteness studies reveal that European Americans generally are not raised to connect their race to their privileges or their class status (MacIntosh, 1992). African Americans have had to do so as their lives depended on understanding their race as being connected to their lack of privileges.

Black female sexuality is constructed as a target for immorality. Jacobs identifies that most important time in every young female's life when she becomes aware of herself as the object of some man's sexual-economy program. Though this is the case for all females, African American females have to develop different strategies to guard themselves because they are generally in less insulated environments (from the hood to the United States government). Unlike females from the dominant culture, it is likely that the Black female may be sexually or racially harassed continually and not be backed by society.

An example of the sexual vulnerability of the Black woman is exemplified in the United States Supreme Court's non-support of Professor and Attorney, Anita Hill against "Justice" Clarence Thomas, who apparently internalized distorted images of the Black woman. Stories like the one of the professional African American woman being racially profiled and beaten by an officer because she drove a nice car through an affluent neighborhood exemplify the imaging of the Black woman as worthless. Episodes like the one of the young woman sleeping with a gun between her legs in her car in Los Angeles and being subsequently shot to death by LA's finest also demonstrate the way that Black female life is unprotected, disrespected, and yet devalued in American culture.

African American females' literacy practices

Multiple consciousness plays a significant role in the development of African American female language and literacy practices. The Black woman's consciousness of her condition/ing, her position/ing in American society, the condition/ing of her audiences must be factored into her language and literacy practices. Literacy practices encompass "the events and patterns of activity around literacy [linked to] something broader of a cultural and social kind" (Street, 2000: 21). In applying Street's definition of literacy practices to African American females' literacy practices then, that something broader to which events and patterns of activity are linked is African American discourse—a way of being in the world. The literacy practices identified here include: storytelling, performative silence, strategic use of polite and assertive language, style shifting/codeswitching, indirection, steppin'/rhyming, and preaching.

Storytelling remains one of the most powerful language and literacy practices that Black women use to convey their special knowledge. This is evident in many African American women's creative works, Paule Marshall's, "The Making of a Writer: From Poets in the Kitchen," for example. Alice Walker's

"In Search of Our Mother's Gardens" locates the centrality of storytelling: "[T]hrough the years of listening to my mother's stories of her life, I have absorbed not only the stories themselves, but something of the manner in which she spoke, something of the urgency that involves the knowledge that her stories—like her life—must be recorded" (1806). I can testify on this. My mother's stories about her childhood, the choices and circumstances of her life, saved me from the street life and forced me to become a woman that my daughters could be proud of. My mother was born in a rural area, known as Logwood in Jamaica, (British) West Indies during the 1920s. She grew up an avid reader. One of her favorite stories was Helen Keller's, but she also loved to recite the poetry of Omar Khayyam. She was an excellent student, and though her family was dirt poor, she had a stable childhood until her father was killed, hit by a truck, when she was in sixth grade. Since my grandmother was pregnant with the family's seventh child at the time of her husband's death, her only choice in her mind was to take my mother (the oldest child) out of school and put her to work so that the family could eat and stay together as much as possible.

My mother's sixth grade teacher begged my grandmother to let Evelyn (my mama) live with her and continue her education. The teacher had already taken over the responsibility for raising her niece, a classmate of my mother's, whose family felt that was their best shot at a better life. The teacher promised my grandmother that mama would get a fine education. She said that my mother could be raised along with mama's classmate, a very fairskinned, "threatened for White," girl. This choice, the teacher argued, would be better for our family in the long run. Only 13 years old, mama wanted to stay in school, but my grandmother's word was bond: "yu nah give way pickinny, yu give way dog and cat." My grandmother believed that with all her heart and soul. Thus began my mother's entry into the Black woman's world of that time: washing White folks' clothes, washing bottles in a soda factory, doing every kind of "honest" work she could for little or nothing. Even after moving to Kingston as an adult, she sent a portion of her money back to Logwood. Meanwhile, her classmate went on to finish school. She chose to marry a White man who moved her to England to begin life as a White woman.

My mother worked from that time, the age of 13, until she met my father about 23 years later. When she married my father, a Black man, and came with him to America, my father thought it his duty to husband her by restricting her to "woman's" work. At first, she liked the idea. She could just have children, my brother and me, and be a "homemaker," have the life that she deserved, something that she always dreamed of. But my mother soon grew tired of asking my father for money for things that she wanted for herself, or for us; she got a job doing days work as soon as my brother and I were old enough, against my father's wishes. She eventually got a job in the field of education, mopping and cleaning my junior high school. She mopped for the Board of Education for 24 more years. She used to say, "Hard wuk neva kill nobody." Mama and daddy argued many a night because of her working and spending her money the way she saw fit. She used to tell my father, "You marry me, I didn't marry you, you just pay these bills and take care of your kids."

My brother and I grew up on East 68th Street, in Cleveland, Ohio, in the hood. I fell in with my surroundings. I was smart in school, like my mother. Though I was often lured away from it. Mama made friends with all my junior high school teachers and kept an eye out on my whereabouts. I thought I was much smarter than her or anyone who worked a jay oh bee. I thought they were all suckers who ended up in the ghetto or with low prestige teaching jobs. Falling prey to slick brothers who had no idea of the value of their lives or mine, I got into the streetlife, had babies out of wedlock, and almost left them for my mother to raise. But eventually, my mother's stories welled up inside of me. "Yu nah give way pickinny, yu give way dog and cat." My mother's words, her mother's words, her mopping made me reflect on my situation, and I began to struggle against my environment, to keep and care for my own children, to face the choices I had made and the ones I'd been dealt. My mother always wanted an education and so I wound up getting it for her. I always tell her, "My PhD is yours mama." I proved mama's teacher wrong.

Similarly, Sojourner Truth's rhetorical use of storytelling exemplifies its centrality in the African American female language and literacy tradition—the same tradition that my mother's storytelling fills. In Truth's crusades and anti-slavery speeches, she invoked her mother's words to display the power of mother wit, a transformative element in the Black woman's production of knowledge:

> I remember my parents: my father died, and I think I can see my mother now as she stood many a night in the old apple orchard, under the open heaven, when the moon and stars were brightly shining. My poor mother would weep and say, in Dutch, "Oh! mein Got, mein Got," which means in English my God. "My poor children will be sold into Slavery." I did not know what that meant then, but I have learned since. My mother cried bitterly, and I took the corner of her old apron, and wiped her eyes and asked what she cried for. She said "my poor child we are going to be sold, and we shant see one another again; when you are far away; remember that I shall see the same moon and stars that you look at, and, when we die we shall both go to heaven among them." [57]
>
> ("New York Anti-Slavery Society", 1853)

Truth's recollection and retelling of her mother's words demonstrate their formation of her consciousness, a consciousness that developed over time to shape Truth's spirit and ability to triumph over life's circumstances. Additionally, Truth's words act to celebrate the Black females' metronymic[3] experience. Through this process Truth inherits the language of struggle which she is now able to share with her audience to persuade them of the need for their heightened awareness of the human condition. Truth is standing on her mother's words, her mother's wit, her mother's shoulders. Internalizing those words put her in the position to become a freedom fighter. African American females repeatedly use their stories as vehicles for the transmission of their special knowledge and truth. While I won't discuss them here, proverbs serve the same function. As defined by Smitherman, "proverbs constitute an essential dimension of communication in Africa and the African Diaspora that reinforces cultural authenticity while simultaneously facilitating literacy, critical thinking, and technological development" (Smitherman, 2000: 232).

African American females negotiate their racial and sexual status situation by using both verbal and nonverbal communication strategies. One such nonverbal literacy strategy is silence, which can be employed as a performative act in truth seeking. Harriet Jacobs' *Incidents in the Life of a Slave Girl* contains several examples of this. Jacobs' grandmother (Aunt Marthy) was supposed to be set free upon her mistress' death. But when the executor of her will, Dr Flint, the mistress' brother-in-law, took over, he decided to sell Aunt Marthy. Though Dr Flint was a slaveholder, pervert, and tyrant, he hid his latter two qualities from the general public and was respected in the White community as a man of integrity and honor. Knowing this and knowing how to work from her position as an enslaved woman, Aunt Marthy acts to expose Flint's "honor" (Jacobs, 1861: 347; emphasis added):

> On the appointed day, the customary advertisement was posted up, proclaiming that there would be a "public sale of negroes, horses &c." Dr Flint called to tell my grandmother that he was unwilling to wound her feelings by putting her up at auction, and that he would prefer to dispose of her at private sale. My grandmother saw through this hypocrisy; she understood very well that he was ashamed of the job . . . When the day of the sale came, she took her place among the chattels, and at the first call she sprang upon the auction block. *Many voices called out*, "Shame! Shame! Who is going to sell you, aunt Marthy? Don't stand there! That is no place for you." *Without saying a word*, she quietly awaited her fate. No one bid for her.

Aunt Marthy's silent action spoke loudly. She was bought by her former mistress' sister, an elderly White woman, who set her free. This passage underscores the strategic use of silence as a speech act. First, Aunt Marthy casts herself as a chattel. "She took her place among the chattels." Jacobs' description underscores Aunt Marthy's agency in exposing Flint's hypocrisy and inhumanity. Second, Aunt Marthy "sprang upon the auction block." She didn't shrug or shrink, nor did she have to be led or dragged. All of this signifies Aunt Marthy's agency, proving herself to be human, in fact more human than the animal that was about to sell her along with animals. Finally, Aunt Marthy's silence provokes the voice of the community.

The strategic use of silence is also a communication strategy used by African American women to resist perpetuation of distorted images of Black female sexuality and womanhood. Some acts and thoughts have no need to be discursively detailed since "everybody's business ain't nobody's business." Harriet Jacobs' understated title is instructive on this point. It is *Incidents in the life of a slave girl*, rather than "Every abuse a slave girl ever suffered at the hands of White men during enslavement."

African American females assert themselves in ways that are somewhat different from those of European American females due to their socialization as laborers outside the home (Houston, 1985). Denise Troutman's (1995) analysis of conversations between Anita Hill and the senators in the hearings shows that Hill skillfully interrupted them and used a strong forceful tone, managing to be polite and assertive simultaneously and appropriately. Troutman (1995: 214) writes:

> One mark of attaining womanhood is knowing when to be polite and when to assert oneself. This aspect of African American women's code of feminine politeness is passed on verbally or learned through nonverbal behavior.

A heightened consciousness of the rhetorical situation influences the literacy strategies that the Black female rhetor chooses to employ.

To be successful in environments where White middle-class values dominate, Black females must learn the language and literacy practice of style shifting/codeswitching. Of course people from all ethnic and racial groups codeswitch. Several factors contribute to the heightened importance of this practice in African American language and literacy traditions. One of the factors is doubleconsciousness as defined by William Edward Burghart Dubois. For Dubois, doubleconsciousness represented the psychic ambivalence experienced by Black people in their negotiation of conflicting European/Anglo and African/American identities. In some cases the values involved in negotiation are derived from White supremacist assumptions about Black people. This is not to say that Black people codeswitch when talking to Whites because all Whites are racist, but rather because many of the stereotypes of the past (yet lingering) equated Black speech styles and behaviors to cognitive (dis)ability and culturelessness.

Thus, AAVE speakers may use more standardized American English behaviors when speaking to Whites. Black folks' style shifting demonstrates that they are well aware of stereotypes. Further, doubleconsciousness reflects a juxtaposition of differential knowledge. In other words, there is a White supremacist concept of African American ideas and behaviors versus African American epistemologies. Codeswitching is also a valuable resource since each language represents a way of knowing and expressing the world. Style/code switching allows Black people to move between worldviews. Codeswitching has been defined as "a shift between different language systems; with reference to dialects, it refers to the change between overall dialect systems, such as that between a standard and vernacular dialect" (Wolfram, 1991: 300). In this definition of code/style shifting one may overlook the fact that code/style shift to AAVE discourse can be accomplished with the use of standard English grammar and/or writing conventions. Code/style shifting can also be done to move toward a more holistically Black style. Speakers/writers vary their rhetoric or discourse depending on audience and motive. John Baugh's (1983) construct of situational styles of usage for AAVE speakers suggests four contexts that govern language usage from familiar to least familiar: Black core culture, Intra community contact, Intercommunity exchange, and Outsider contact. In general, more conscious attention is paid to speech as the speaking context becomes less familiar, in the direction of standardized forms. However, as Alim's (2001) work on Hip Hop nation language (HHNL) indicates speakers may also consciously manipulate their language in the direction of vernacular forms, in order to represent certain ideologies and solidarity with their audience. In a society where dominant discourse is perceived to be White and rewards and privileges are connected to dominant discourse, African Americans may consciously perform Whiteness or Blackness (by varying their speech patterns) to meet their needs. The function of these performances could be to create ethos, pathos, authenticity, distance, familiarity, irony, or for purposes of critique, to name a few.

Zora Neale Hurston's ethnographic text *Mules and Men* offers an interesting example of code/style shifting as a rhetorical strategy. It demonstrates the principle of audience governance of language use. In this text, Hurston is presenting African American folklore, documenting various aspects of African American oral traditions and epistemologies, which celebrate African Americans' struggle for self-definition. One excerpt in particular exemplifies Hurston's struggle to expand the concept of scientific discourse and methodology to include a Black perspective on the world. She writes:

> Folklore is not as easy to collect as it sounds . . . [African Americans] are most reluctant at times to reveal *that which the soul lives by* . . . You see we are a polite people and we do not say to our questioner, "Get out of here!" *We smile and tell him or her something that satisfies the white person* because, knowing so little about us, he doesn't know what he is missing.
>
> The theory behind our tactics: "The white man is always trying to know into somebody else's business. All right, I'll set something outside the door of my mind for him to play with and handle. He can read my writing but he sho' can't read my mind. I'll put this play toy in his hand, and he will seize it and go away. Then I'll say my say and sing my song."
>
> (Hurston, 1935: 1,033; emphasis added)

Here, Hurston demonstrates the Black style shift to "satisfy the white person."

This type of style shift shows the double worldview of the speaker. The Black speaker *performs* non-verbal (smiles) as well as verbal speech acts "to satisfy the white person." These literacy practices developed from cool (related to shuckin', jivin' [forms of masking]) are adapted to resist racism. This excerpt serves Hurston doubly. It serves to critique her audience (consisting of fellow cultural anthropologists).[4] Insensitive anthropologists "want to know into somebody else's business" and cannot get beyond the surface structure of the culture to appreciate it fully. On the other hand, Hurston valued the culture and the people and used her insider status to obtain sensitive reflections of the soul(s) of the culture. Black folk, of whom Hurston herself was one, shift to mask their soul(s). Hurston's critique is rather indirect yet she shows her audience more than she scolds them, that there is method and theory to Black behaviors. The constraints upon Hurston were ethnically and structurally determined. She works her way through this dilemma by focusing her presentation on the theorization of Black thought and the reason that Black folk smile and give White folks something to satisfy them, as Hurston herself does. How might Hurston have presented the idea of Black thought patterns in a different rhetorical situation? Perhaps if the rhetorical situation were different, African American folklore would be a lot different.

Further, Hurston's excerpt also demonstrates the function of indirection as a rhetorical strategy that aids the Black rhetor/ess in maintaining that which the soul lives by while at the same time satisfying one's audience. Hurston's example points to indirection and signifying as powerful self-affirming rhetorical strategies in the tradition of African American female language use.

Codeswitching is so useful for Black interlocutors because it allows them in writing or speech to direct their audiences to a wealth of shared knowledge, to take the conversation to another level more expeditiously. Linda Williamson Nelson in her study of "Code-switching in the Oral Life Narratives of African American Women: Challenges to Linguistic Hegemony" found that women in her study used African American Vernacular with her because they sensed a shared background. Nelson found this out through listening to tape recorded discussions that she had with her consultants and then going back and translating their AAVE discourse into standardized English. Afterwards she asked her consultants the difference in the meanings and they explained that the AAVE usage referenced a range of meanings, which were lost in the standardized English translations and needed to be elaborated upon at length to get close to the meaning of the original speech.

Steppin' and rhyming are other Black Vernacular expressive behaviors exploited by young and adolescent females and traditionally absent from official literacy education sites. Steppin' involves spelling of words or the saying of rhymes to dance routines which feature hard body movements. These movements and rhymes are interpreted by some to be rude and associated with African American vernacular culture and were perceived by school officials and some middle-class African Americans as markers of resistance (Gilmore, 1983).

Rhyming is sometimes done in jump rope routines or other hand clap and dance performances by young and adolescent females. For example, I can recall from my youth the rhyme "A Sailor Went to Sea Sea Sea." We had steps that went with each verse and that helped to accentuate aspects of the rhyme. One verse is:

A sailor went to sea sea sea
To see what he could see see see
But all that he could see see see
Was the bottom of the big blue sea sea sea.

These rhymes can teach homonymy, rhyme structure and along with movement teach physical, intellectual, and vocal coordination. Further, some childhood rhymes contain race conscious social knowledge such as the often recited "If you White, you right; if you yellow you mellow, if you brown stick around; If you Black git back."

Researchers such as Foster (1992) and Ladson-Billings (1994) find that the Black preaching style is an effective medium of instruction for many African American students. Foster (1992: 306) notes that:

Black artful teachers incorporated many of the stylistic features found in the Black preaching style, in the verbal art of Black adolescents and Black males, and in the stories and playsongs of Black children—variation in pace, rhythmic language, repetition, alliteration, creative language play into reading lessons. Students taught using this style scored significantly higher on standardized reading tests than children taught using another style.

She notes that ethnographic studies of Marva Collins' classroom teaching style show that Collins herself uses Black communicative behaviors when she teaches reading and writing to such students. Collins has been highly successful in getting students as young as third grade of Westside Preparatory School in Chicago to quote Shakespeare and Emerson (though the struggle is not about quoting Shakespeare but about the development of critical consciousness for social change) and to demonstrate literacy proficiency on standardized tests, using Black delivery and interactional styles.

African American female strengths and educational issues

Some of the major socializing values surrounding African American females' literacies—life protector, nurturer, and independence—have been used against them in their in and out of school literacy experiences. I find the mantra of law enforcement, "To Protect and Serve," to be a useful metaphor to illustrate these issues. The general mission of the police is to protect American citizens and make sure that law and order are maintained. However, "To Protect and Serve" represents a unique set of ideas and experiences for African Americans, especially females.

As mentioned earlier, Black females have been socialized to protect and serve. This survival strategy comprises helping those inside and outside of the Black community to feel less threatened. Black females use this strategy at school and at work. As early as first and second grade this feminine African American literacy becomes recognizable. Classroom research has shown that African American females are socialized to function as "messengers," "caretakers," and "enforcers." It was found that African American girls in integrated classrooms had a wider net of social interactions: they befriended children from all backgrounds more than European American girls and boys. In contrast to the European American female classmates who only befriended students liked by the teacher, African American girls risked reprimand when they played the role of caretaker or messenger (Grant, 1984).

Further, many Black students do not like to go to teachers for help as they think it will be perceived as deficiency on their part (Collins-Eaglin and Karabenick, 1993). In their role as enforcer, socialization rather than academics is emphasized as Black female students are encouraged to help the teacher to maintain order in the classroom. For all intents and purposes, Black girls are reinscribed as Mammy in the classroom. It is hypothesized that this type of social literacy experience plays an important role in orienting Black females to service jobs in later life, rather than to more professionalized positions (Ladner cited in Grant, 1984). This shows us that careful attention must be given to African American female strengths, so that teachers do not encourage their use in ways that help females to participate in their own oppression.

Even when African American females pursue careers in fields where they are not expected such as sciences and engineering, they often meet resistance. Research on African American students on predominantly European American campuses has shown that when African American females show up in majors such as engineering, they receive less support, are asked to change their majors, and are expected to fail by White male professors (Arnold and Murphy, 1994). When dealing with gender inequity in the context of racism, African American females who persist have somehow avoided the fate of the "normal" Black female of lower test scores, higher dropout rates, and higher unemployment rates as compared to European American females (Ford, 1996: 121–2). Environments that emphasize social roles rather than academic excellence, as well as environments that alienate and dehumanize Black female students, perpetuate society's failure of the African American female (Boykin, 1984).

Black communicative styles and Black culture have been reported to operate adversely as barriers to literacy access. One example of this can be seen in Perry Gilmore's research on literacy access. The behavior that she calls "Stylized sulking" usually occurs in a student-teacher confrontation when a Black female student resists a teacher in a dominant/subordinate relationship by using silence and body language. Black female students, usually fourth grade through sixth grade, are labeled as having "bad attitudes" and are, subsequently, tracked into lower ability courses.

Similarly, differential interactional styles of AAVE speakers may interfere with acquisition of higher order literacy when teachers dismiss the thinking that students express and are not trained to work with these styles (Foster, 1992). Students may have alternative knowledges or approaches expressed in non-mainstream ways that remain untapped.

The Black female perspective is rendered entertaining at best and marginal, invaluable, or irrational at worst. I've had several undergraduate educational experiences and several graduate ones, where because I articulated my opinion through story-telling, influenced by my Black and female socio-cultural orientation, my thoughts were not acknowledged or even seriously engaged. Even now as I have been struggling to articulate an alternative African American-centered theory and praxis, one of my colleagues who has given me feedback on aspects of my thinking in successive drafts said to me: "You're not using the right language. You have to enter the conversation in the current way that other scholars are discussing it or you won't get heard." I understand playing the game, but I don't want to erase my voice from my work. I have three daughters and I want to help teachers rethink and recreate ways to incorporate Black language and culture into the literacy education of Black people. As you can see my thinking has been greatly influenced by many language and literacy theorists, but I don't want my main message hidden in a narrowly conceived academic discourse. I want to broaden our conceptualization of academic knowledge and discourse. Along the same lines, Lisa Delpit (1988) discussed her graduate students who had recounted the many times that their dialogues had been silenced because the first-hand experiences that they wanted to share with their professors and colleagues were not authorized by Vygotsky or some other big-named theorists.

At the high school level, a similar situation is experienced by African American female students. Fordham (1993) reports on an ethnographic study conducted at a predominantly African American New York city school which focuses on the complex intersection of "gender passing," gender diversity, culture, racism, and African American female student achievement. She found that the common features among high achieving African American females are that "they work hard, they are silent; when they vocalize, they speak 'in a different voice'" (1993: 83). Further, they sometimes adopt a male voice, image, or persona in speech, writing, and activities. These strategies are employed in young females' attempts to cast off low expectations of them by authority figures. Further, these strategies are employed to deflect high visibility that would make the young ladies vulnerable to ridicule, and/or labeled as "those loud Black girls" who speak AAVE and refuse to conform to standards of good behavior without really breaking school rules.

Similarly, Michelle Fine reports on a year-long ethnographic study of silencing in a low-income predominantly African American and Hispanic high school. She defines silencing as "words that could have been said, talk that should have been nurtured, and information that needed to be announced" (1995: 220). Silencing is prevalent for low and high achieving male and female African Americans throughout all levels of the academy. Although it is not exclusively the experience of African American students, it is a factor in the school achievement of African American females. Fine's portrait of "Patrice" (1995: 218) is telling:

> Field Note: February 16
> Patrice is a young African American female, in 11th grade. She says nothing all day in school. She sits perfectly mute. No need to coerce her into silence. She often wears her coat in class. Sometimes she lays her head on her desk. She never disrupts. Never disobeys. Never speaks. And is never identified as a problem. Is she the student who couldn't develop two voices and so silenced both? Is she so filled with anger, she fears to speak? Or so filled with depression she knows not what to say?

Fine's portrait illuminates the type of controlling literacy education that has left such students mentally out of school and all but engaged, or simply just going through school to get their diplomas and degrees.

Coming from the heart

Rather than being a barrier to literacy achievement, Black female language practices, knowledges, and understandings can be and have been used advantageously to help Black females in their literacy experiences in schools. Michele Foster's (1992) work on effective African American teachers offers alternatives to heartlessness. Foster's work is on literacy educators who use an effective style, or what one researcher coined the "Black artful style." As mentioned previously, she cites educators such as Marva Collins who exploit Black styles and ways with words to boost student comprehension and achievement by using "familiar language patterns, including repetition, call and response, analogies, aphorisms, and moral messages that resemble the secular and religious speech events in the African American community" (Foster, 1992: 306). Foster (1992: 307) notes that teachers who used this style were able to create a "bridge between text and experience." I think this style is also useful at higher levels of education. Black teachers who can code switch can help students to decode texts and contexts, offering them models of learners who go both ways—across the borders. The strategies of Black female educators can teach us a lot about the educational and literacy experiences of Black fe/males, as they demonstrate such alternative pedagogies to bring out the voices and best performance of all students (hooks,

1994). bell hooks notes that one aspect of her teaching that she developed was to implement Black vernacular into her writing and teaching. In the classroom she encourages students to articulate their ideas in their native tongue and translate it so that the higher education experience does not alienate them from the languages and cultures of their nurture. This practice affirms the intellectuality of Black and other languages and their speakers. On the other hand, hooks encourages White students, some of whom resent this practice (because they do not comprehend the meaning), to see it as an opportunity to learn to hear without "mastery" and to hear non-English and different types of English (hooks, 1994: 172).

Similarly, women of color can use their backgrounds and experiences to help younger females of color. Hudley (1992) found that the attitudes of such students toward literacy improved immensely in such a setting. Hudley notes students connected with successful role models who shared similar backgrounds. Use of role models in combination with culturally relevant literature offers a way to illuminate the perspectives and experiences of women of color, how they have overcome obstacles and fulfilled dreams which simultaneously inspires young women and builds on their language and literacy foundations.

Carol Lee's (1993) work demonstrated how teachers can use the African American discourse genre of signifying systematically to help students understand such features as innuendo, metaphorical use of language, and irony (etc.) in literature. Lee demonstrated that a teacher may scaffold students from implicit knowledge to explicit knowledge of strategies—to infer meaning from figurative language in texts. Similarly, Mahiri's (1998) work showed that rap can be used in much the same way. Rap lyrics employ innuendo, metaphorical language, word creation through grammatical innovations. Students can be taught language analysis skills using material that is culturally interesting to help connect them to the classroom from a position of authority. Further, many middle, high school and college students write their own raps and employ these linguistic processes in their own productions (Yasin, 1999).

Steppin' represents a vernacular practice that can be used as a scaffold to instruction in other literacy practices. Because steppin' uses rhythm and rhyme, it could be used to teach many concepts. Steppin' involves call-response, which as Smitherman (1977/1986) has outlined, seeks to bring speakers into a unified consciousness. Gilmore (1983) noted that teachers had never paid attention to what the steppers were saying or doing. They were more interested in the sexual connotations of some of the body movements used to embody some of the letters—for example "krooked ledda" or "s." Like Gilmore, teachers should be curious: ask about the rhymes, and spellings and explore underlying patterns.

Looking at the literacies of African American females from the point of view of agency, there are many aspects of Black female language practices, knowledges, and understandings that can be used advantageously. Additionally, the home environment instills the value of independence, and along with this is the push for a good education. The Black folk saying "Black women raise their daughters and love their sons" may be reflective of this pattern. One problematic aspect of this phenomenon is that in the classroom Black girls have been assigned caretaker–enforcer–messenger roles to the detriment of themselves. African American females must be encouraged to value themselves and their own good thoughts first. It is not the job of the Black student to make others feel comfortable or to provide the proper atmosphere. Another area of concern is the need to see, hear, and read African American females in any and every successful, productive, and positive career or role that they can imagine themselves in.

The literacies, language, and literacy practices of African American females should be acknowledged and exploited to their advantage "to protect and serve" the African American female. Including vernacular practices in formal literacy education provides us with opportunities to build from that foundation. As the Black female is her child's first teacher, mother tongue literacy must be factored in as a crucial element of theory and practice.

4

African American-centered rhetoric, composition, and literacy: theory and research

Tantamount to the effectiveness of any second-dialect pedagogy designed for Black English Vernacular Speakers (and especially adult BEV speakers) is a considerable amount of "debrainwashing" (for both student and teacher) regarding cultural differences, particularly as these apply to social differences in the use of language. The stigma which American society attaches to identifiably Black patterns of behavior (of which Black language behavior is but one) must be openly and honestly confronted by both student and teacher, before the desired attitudinal changes can be effected which are necessary for productive classroom interaction. More specifically, the student (and his teacher) must be helped toward an appreciation of his native dialect, Black English, as a unique and valid linguistic system; he must be enabled to throw off unfounded and injurious notions about his dialect as "non-language" or, at best, "incorrect" or pathological English, indicative of inferior intelligence. This debrainwashing away from such negative psychologically debilitating attitudes toward his native dialect must occur before productive use can be made of that dialect in the instructional process.

(Reed, 1973: 290)

Brief theoretical overview

Theoretically, my approach can be called Afrocentric, or more specifically, African American-centered. In the context of this work, African American-centered means that I cull ideas, knowledge, data, strategies, and experiences from the epistemologies found in analyses of African American rhetorical, cultural, and literacy traditions (some of which I presented in Chapter 2). I use these as a basis for teaching rhetoric and composition. As an African American-centered teacher-researcher, my task is to connect students to these discourses, rhetorics, and literacies developed by African Americans, to describe historic and transformational literacies from the viewpoints of Black experiences, to interpret data from these subject positions. Fox's (1992) position theory influenced my thinking on incorporating the social, historical, institutional, cultural, and gender considerations in writing instruction. Further, scholars such as Giroux (1991) who've constantly underscored the politics of literacy and difference have helped to shape my understanding of literacy as politically and socially constructed (also found in the work of critical literacy theorists— Freire, 1990; Macedo, 1994; Gee, 1996; Shor, 1996, and others). The theme that connects their arguments to mine is the importance of understanding how societies define and exploit literacy for political, social, economic, and cultural needs. Of course for African Americans the mere act of reading and writing has historically and literally been a political act. In this African American-centered approach the political and critical cultural legacy of writing and reading "men and nations" (Sojourner Truth) is emphasized to African American students as they are heirs to these traditions. Also critical in shaping my thoughts on pedagogy have been the works of Gloria Ladson-Billings (1995) and Mary Hoover (1982). Their works underscore the need for culturally relevant and multicultural literacy practices in the teaching of African American (and all) students. Furthermore, African American discourse and rhetoric scholars such as Gates (1988), Baker (1984), and Smitherman (1977/1986) have steered my thinking in the direction of the theory of African American Signification. It is in the written and oral tradition that authors of African descent repeat and revise themes of the Black experience to create an intertextual chain referring to shared experience/cultural identity. Within these Black oral-literate and post-literate traditions, rhetors revise forms, modes, and strategies—twisting the chain, while doing they own thang, in a word "playin' with the patterns" (Gilyard, 1996: 126).

The freedom through literacy theme in Black experiences is a major example of Signifying in African American literacy traditions. I see it as the heart of African American culture, because this trope can be used to describe the African American experience of "makin' a way outta no way," the quest for freedoms and literacies, from enslavement to the present day. As such, this theme is central to African American-centered approaches to composition and rhetoric. And lastly, the line of thought arguing that the vernacular should be used to teach the standard steered me in the direction of using the syntactic level as a contrastive measure. This line of thinking goes back to dialect readers for African Americans (Baratz and Shuy, 1969; Simpkins, Simpkins, and Holt, 1977; Rickford and Rickford, 1995). Scholars such as Baxter and Reed et al. (1972) expanded this idea to include writing. Drawing on this line of research, both the syntactic and discursive levels are exploited to heighten student facility with the all-encompassing nature of language, rhetorical stance and worldview negotiation in writing (and critical consciousness development).

African American-centered composition theory is based on these assumptions:

- Form and content are inextricably bound
- Black Discourse is an Academic Discourse in constant flux, in negotiation with other discourses, including the dominant discourse
- Contrastive analysis of AAVE syntax and discourse against standardized syntax and discourse will result in students' improved critical language facilities
- Increased historical and cultural self consciousness and critical awareness can be realized in writing and discourse showing Black discourse features.

In the remainder of this chapter I want to share data with you that I have gathered through teaching an African American rhetoric and composition course. I designed the course because I wanted to know if African American students' literacy achievement would be improved if they were positioned within African American language and literacy traditions. I wondered: what would happen if Black students were taught to value and exploit African American Vernacular English discourse and syntax as a systematic rule-governed language? As a way of knowing and being in the world with others? This chapter explores these questions by looking at various analyses of writing produced by students who participated in the course. To conceptualize African American language and culture as technology is to see Black experiences rhetorically. The point of exploiting African American literacies is to develop systematic approaches to connecting students to public and academic discourses without disconnecting them from their cultural and linguistic heritage in educational settings. As mentioned earlier, AAVE discourse is defined here as ways of living and communicative practices that have been largely developed by people of African American descent, as survival and self-advancement strategies. One of the defining characteristics of African American identity is the reality of living one's life against a dominant, often oppressive, text. In an oppressive society, it behooves African Americans to constantly reaffirm themselves. In African American literacy traditions, African Americans re-appropriate language and manipulate conditions to define their own realities for themselves. Hence, students are being asked to use Black rhetorical and discourse practices as means of developing their critical consciousness, their (Bl)academic literacies.

Research

The data presented here comes from my ongoing work in Big Ten university basic writing classrooms where the majority if not all of the students were African American and in which I taught written composition and critical literacy consciousness using AAVE language and literacy traditions as the composition curriculum. Students were solicited through advertisements throughout the campuses of a basic writing course, which featured Afrocentric topics. When students inquired about signing up for the course, I explained course objectives, gave students syllabi and obtained permission to use their writing (anonymously) in any report of research done on the course. The 52 student-subjects received writing instruction, over a one-quarter, ten-week time frame using African American-centered materials and instructional stimuli. (See note for a more complete account of the methodology).[1] This study can be classified as quasi-experimental since it employs pre- and post-testing. However, rather than comparing student-subjects to a control group, as is the case in true experimental design, students are compared within their group. We can call this study then a reflexive comparative study, employing both qualitative and quantitative dimensions. Beyond the reflexive comparative aspect of the study, we can also identify this study as quasi experimental because we cannot control (as an ideal or true experiment can) for external factors on students: whether they will come to class every day, be attentive at all times, finish every assignment, be simultaneously enrolled in other courses which stimulate critical thinking or writing etc. Even still, I preferred this design because I am both testing and developing theory. As far as I know, none of the students in this study had experienced an African American-centered composition curriculum. So, we can study the effect of this curriculum on the writing development of student participants. In this study, I am also exploring and developing African American methodology, which aspects of the curriculum and theory seem most applicable to developing writing and critical consciousness.

Issues in the study

Many African American students enter the universities through basic writing classrooms. Shaughnessy's famous definition of the basic writer gives us three problematic reasons why such is the case.

> [1] They have never written much, in school or out . . . [2] they have come from families and neighborhoods where people speak other languages or variant, non-prestigious forms of English and . . . while they have doubtless been sensitive to the differences between their ways of speaking and their teachers', [3] they have never been able to sort out or develop attitudes toward the differences that did not put them in conflict, one way or another, with the key academic tasks of learning to read and write and talk in standard English.
>
> (Shaughnessy, 1987: 179)

Well, it may be true that some of us come from the hood; but in my experience, I've found that many students placed in basic writing are also so-called middle-class Black folks (some of which are included in the population under discussion here). Nevertheless, the reasons Shaughnessy gave are all interrelated, and the tie that binds them is a combination of cultural difference and educational cultural bias. Heath's (1983) study found that literacy practices of the school coincided with practices of middle-class White and Black students, while the

98

literacy practices of poor Whites and Blacks did not. Heath's study strives to de-emphasize race and focus on language behaviors that are influenced by cultural socialization. Though that is a valuable and very revealing analysis, my focus in this study is on the intersectionality of racism and its influence on culture and language behaviors. Racism is a major factor in the development of critical literacies that undergird African American people's responses to the environment, and it is these literacies that are suppressed in the school setting, though these literacies may be vital to a Black person's physical, psychic, social, and emotional well-being. Historically, African American students have suffered from self-fulfilling prophecies which hold that some Black students are cognitively deficient or that they just can't write. Middle-class Black students, regardless of their ability to master standardized English and produce academic essays, have some concerns in common with those who have been labeled as basic writers—the struggle against stereotypes. My feeling is that centering students in African American language and literacy traditions will help develop their critical literacies regardless of socio-economic status.

Shaughnessy went on to point out another characteristic of so-called basic writers, the restricted and tangled nature of their prose. I believe that a factor which contributes to tangled discourse and restricted prose is stereotype threat. In this case, the "Blacks are illiterate" stereotype is the threat. Steele and Aronson's (1995: 808) work on "Stereotype Threat and the Intellectual Test Performance of African Americans" confirmed my personal and anecdotal knowledge with empirical data. In discussing their findings, they explain that a stereotype of that magnitude can "be disruptive enough . . . to impair intellectual performance" of members of the designated cultural or social group. Some African American students may write very little and suppress their language use because they've been taught (as we all have) that AAVE usage is a sign of so-called "intellectual inferiority" and they don't want any trace of it to be detected in their prose. This is not to say that all Black students speak or write AAVE, but their Blackness alone subjects them to the threat of the stereotype. And the threat is enough to suppress written fluency. So, when we say that Black people live their lives against racist texts, this is but one example.

Another issue pertinent to the literacy education of marginalized African American students is that of linguistic divergence. In the 1980s, Labov's research showed that AAVE is developing in a different direction than White vernaculars, that AAVE is going its own way (Labov, 1985); Labov reasoned that AAVE's divergence is proof that segregation and poverty continue to isolate a significant proportion of the African American population. Analyzing her data in view of the divergence controversy, Smitherman (1992) found that use of Black syntax features in students' writing declined from 1969 to 1988; and that students were not being penalized by instructors for AAVE syntactical usage. Smitherman's (1994) study found that Black discourse in students' writing reflected higher quality writing and intellectual depth. Black discourse in this sense refers to ways with words that are spoken more frequently among African Americans, though non-African Americans may use them. Black discourse was operationalized as smaller units of expression including: rhythmic dramatic evocative language, references to color–race–ethnicity, use of proverbs, aphorisms, biblical verses, sermonic tone, direct address-conversational tone, cultural references, ethnolinguistic idioms, verbal inventiveness, cultural values/community consciousness, field dependency, narrative sequencing, tonal semantics, signifying, structural call-response and testifying. (Examples of each are given in the more detailed methodology in note 1 to this chapter.) Smitherman surmised that work in leading professional language arts organizations such as CCCC has helped educators to understand AAVE as different and not deficient. But as indicated by the recent CCCC's Language Knowledge and Awareness Survey study (Smitherman *et al.*), many language arts educators have not had the sociolinguistic training that would allow them to build on AAVE communicative patterns.

To summarize, I conceptualized this African American-centered rhetoric and composition study to address the following issues: language suppression induced by stereotype threat, AAVE discourse in academic writing/settings. In what follows, I attempt to answer these questions:

1   Is AAVE syntax usage in African American students' writing an impediment?
2   Does Black discourse usage work to excel or arrest the development of academic writing?
3   Can student writing showing obvious Black discourse features be considered (Bl)academic?

The main question is: Is written fluency enhanced by African American methodology?

Prompt

On the first and last day of class, I asked students to compose an essay in response to a prompt that revolved around African American language and literacy traditions, as discussed in Gates (1986: 403):

> When authors of African descent began to publish imaginative literature in English in the eighteenth Century, for example, they confronted a collective and racist text of themselves which Europeans had invented. This helps us to understand why so very much Anglo-African writing—whether Phillis Wheatley's elegies, or Olaudah Equiano's autobiography, or Ignatius Sancho's epistles—directly addressed European fictions of the African in an attempt to voice or speak the African into existence in Western letters.

100

Using this passage as the backdrop, students wrote 50-minute in-class essays on the question: What does it mean to be Black and write or to be Black and literate? Both the question and the passage were employed because they explore an aspect of the AAVE political-literate tradition, writing/speaking the self into subjectivity. This aspect of African American literacy traditions provided a major underlying assumption of the curriculum. As preparation for writing their responses to the passage, I asked students to discuss the passage with colleagues for five or ten minutes, engage in any pre-writing strategies with which they were comfortable for five or ten minutes (clustering, outlining, free writing etc.), compose a draft for fifteen or twenty minutes, and use the remaining time to revise and edit what they had produced. I asked them to use their best prose including Black discourse styles, if they felt more comfortable doing so. Our data analyses will begin with AAVE syntax. (NB: all data and analyses are aggregated over four semesters.)

Findings

AAVE syntax usage[2]

Our analysis of AAVE syntax usage will begin with the "ed morpheme" on the pre-test essay. There were only seven cases out of 52 (13.5 per cent) using the AAVE "ed morpheme," as can be gleaned from Table 4.1.

The AAVE variants under scrutiny are represented in the following sentences:

(a) He look 0 for it yesterday.
(b) He had look 0 for it yesterday.
(c) The boy name 0 John did it.
(d) It is frown 0 upon.

Table 4.1 Showing AAVE "ed morpheme" usage on the pre-test essay (N = 7)

Ed morpheme	Subject						
	3	*18*	*32*	*33*	*35*	*39*	*40*
MV + 0	0	1/1	0	3/4	1/1	1/3	1/2
He look		100%		0.75	100%	0.33	0.50
Have/had + MV + 0	0	0	0	0	0	0	0
He had look							
V + 0	1/1	0	0	2/2	0	0	0
A boy name	100%			100%			
Be + MV + 0	0	0	1/4	0	3/5	0	0
He frown at her			0.25		0.60		

Table 4.2 Showing AAVE "s morpheme" usage on the pre-test essay (N = 14)

S morpheme	Subject						
	7	13	17	24	30	32	35
N + 0	0	0	1/1	1/1	0	6/7	3/4
Five girl			100%	100%		0.86	0.75
N + 0 poss	1/1	1/1	0	1/2	0	0	1/1
My man car	100%	100%		0.50			100%
V + 0	2/4	0	1/1	2/8	0	0	1/3
He look	.50		100%	0.25			0.33
N pl + s	0	0	1/1	0	1/4	0	0
mens			100%		0.25		

It should be mentioned that, for the pre-test essay, there were no occurrences of the AAVE variant represented by example (c). It is equally important to keep in mind that for cases showing 100 per cent AAVE variant usage, the opportunity to employ an AAVE variant only need arise one time for 100 per cent usage to occur. It is for that reason that I use the fraction so that the reader can see the ratio of actual occurrences to the probability of occurrences. In the seven cases, the AAVE "ed morpheme" was used at the rate of 40 per cent, determined by the crosstabs test to be statistically insignificant. To put it another way, the over-whelming majority of the students writing on the pre-test essay used the standardized variants for the "ed morpheme."

Table 4.2 shows cases employing AAVE variants in the following four tar-geted linguistic environments for the "s morpheme": noun + 0 (Five girl); noun + 0 possessive (My man car); verb + 0 (He look); plural noun + s (mens).

Fourteen cases (14) representing 26.9 per cent of the total sample employed the salient AAVE pattern "s morpheme" with a frequency of 0.32 per cent, which was statistically insignificant as determined by a crosstabs analysis.

The copula category is one of the features of AAVE, which has been most frequently identified, though more often than not, in speech than writing. The copula contexts examined in this study are: 0 + main verb (He doing it); 0 + noun (He my brother); 0 + adjective (He tall); 0 + preposition (Now we inside); 0 + adverb (He here now); plural subject + is (They is in that car); plural sub-ject + was (The legs was long). Ten (10) of the 52 cases (or 19.2 per cent) exhibited these categories. The percentage of AAVE copula for the pre-test essay was 0.22 per cent, quite low and statistically insignificant.

Although "habitual be" or "aspectual be" is widely cited as a highly distinc-tive syntactical feature of AAVE (Labov, 1972; Smitherman, 1977/1986; Baugh, 1999; Rickford and Rickford, 2000, and others), its usage is almost nil among this group of students. I presume that the stigmatization of this feature is a major reason that it is avoided, especially at this stage in the educational

Table 4.2 (continued)

S morpheme	Subject						
	36	37	40	46	47	48	50
N + 0 Five girl	2/3 0.66	2/3 0.66	2/3 0.66	0	0	2/7 0.28	1/17 0.06
N + 0 poss My man car	0	0	0	0	0	0 1	0
V + 0 He look	0	0	1/10 0.10	1/3 0.33	0	1/5 0.20	0
N pl + s mens	0	0	0	0	0	0	0

experience. By the time many AAVE-speaking students have matriculated into the university, it has been "corrected" out of their writing, if not their speech, in the academic setting. There was only one instance of "habitual be" in the written works of these students on the pre-test essay. There was only one case employing the AAVE category "perfective-done/have" (0 have/has/had + main verb), as in: "He gone home already."

The next category I examined was the category "irregular verb." Examples of irregular verb categories investigated in this study are represented below.

(a) He give it to me yesterday, she say.
(b) She had knew it.

There were only three cases exhibiting use of this category, with an almost nil percentage of use. There were only two cases on the pre-test essay exhibiting the "it expletive" category, as in "It's a lot of people." Again, the percentage of usage was insignificant.

The same situation of insignificance pertained to the remaining AAVE syntax categories: "undifferentiated third-person plural pronoun" "pronominal apposition," "stressed been," and "unstressed/past been."

The final test that I did with AAVE syntax on pre-test essay data was to look for correlations between AAVE syntax, discourse usage, and essay scores. The results are highly significant. A Pearson correlation analysis confirmed an association between essay length and AAVE syntax usage. Basically, the longer the essay, the lesser the amount of AAVE syntax usage, R-value −0.549, P < 0.008, significance at the 0.05 level. [P indicates significance.] Similarly, the statistical analysis found an association between pre-test discourse features usage and AAVE syntax usage. To put it plainly, the more Black discourse features, the lesser the amount of AAVE syntax usage, R-value −0.515, P < 0.014, significant at the 0.05 level. The higher the R-value or the correlational value, the greater the effect. These two tests indicate fairly strong correlations. Even more importantly, they match findings in other studies. For example, Smitherman's (1994) study found that greater usage of AAVE syntax occurs in non-Black styled discourse. I believe that what may account for this situation is that conscious usage of Black discourse features may have the effect of making students more careful in their writing, not less. Thus, students may exhibit more control over syntax as a result. These ideas lead me back to Shaughnessy's (1987) observations about the tangled prose of the culturally different writer. Students are striving so hard to avoid the negative stigmatization of their language usage that they don't write from within their comfort zones, which may help to fragment and tangle their written expression.

To summarize, there were a total of 22 cases showing AAVE syntax activity in any one or a combination of the categories under investigation at 0.33 per cent. The crosstabs analysis revealed this percentage to be insignificant. Now that we've looked at AAVE syntactical (non) activity on the pre-test essay, I will now summarize overall syntax use on the post-essay and then compare pre- to post-syntax usage.

"Ed morpheme" usage decreased from a mean of 0.40 per cent on the pre-test essay to 0.30 per cent on the post-essay. Ironically, on the pre-test essay seven cases exhibited usage of this variant, while on the post-test essay that number rose by four—showing 11 cases. This means that although more students used the variable they used less of it on average.

The overall "s morpheme" percentage of usage decreased from a mean of 0.32 per cent on the pre-test essay to 0.19 per cent on the post-test essay. Again, although there were 14 cases showing usage on the pre-test essay, there were 23 on the post-test essay.

For the "copula," the overall percentage of usage on the pre-test essay was 10 cases at 0.22 per cent, decreasing on the post-test essay to 0.16 per cent and nine cases.

The next category, "perfective-done/have," showed up on the pre-test essay in one case at a percentage of 0.50 per cent, while on the post-essay two cases showed this usage at the percentage of 0.41 per cent.

On the post-test essay, seven cases showed "irregular verb" usage at 0.88 per cent, while on the pre-test essay there were three cases at 100 per cent.

As with the pre-test essay, the usage of AAVE syntax in the remaining categories was almost nil: "undifferentiated third-person plural pronoun," "pronominal apposition," "stressed been," and "unstressed/past been." As for gender variance, there was no significant difference in usage between males and females in overall AAVE usage.

To summarize overall AAVE syntax activity pre- to post-test essay, then, there were 22 cases exhibiting AAVE syntactical variants on the pre-test essay at 0.33 per cent versus 30 cases on the post-test essay at 0.28 per cent. Though the pre- to post-test essay decrease in AAVE syntax is not statistically significant, this is due to the altogether low frequency and distribution of AAVE syntax in the students' writing. This finding matches other studies of African American students' writing (Chaplin, 1987; Taylor, 1991; Smitherman, 1992; Chapman-Thomas, 1994).

Recall that one of my major research questions was: (1) Is AAVE syntax usage in African American students' writing an impediment? My answer to that question is: no. New teachers need to be aware of this information so that they do not penalize students who may show even small amounts of AAVE syntax in their writing. A new teacher need not see this as an impediment to students' acquiring standardized English syntax. Teachers need to know what the AAVE patterns are and whether or not a student is using them to their rhetorical benefit.

Several studies have found that Black discourse styled writing has helped to boost the written achievement of African American students (Ball, 1992; Redd, 1993; Smitherman, 1994). For this reason, I believe we will find analyses involving discourse most interesting. Table 4.3 shows the results of a bivariate correlations analysis of mean scores for Black discourse (pre-dis) and essay ratings (pre-rating), and pre-word counts (pre-word) for the pre-test essay.

Overall, I found a positive and significant relationship between use of Black discourse, amount of words written, and essay scores. In this particular data, the higher the pre-test Black discourse score (mean 5.05), the higher the pre-word count (mean 240.82), (R-value = 0.734, P < 0.000); the higher the pre-test score (mean 1.96); and the higher the pre-test word count (240.82), (R-value = 0.513, P < 0.000). This does not mean that *every* writer with a high Black discourse score in his or her writing wrote more or scored higher; it just means that this was the (quite) strong tendency. The post data shown in Figure 4.1, for the same variables (discourse score, word count, and essay score), bears this point out.

The mean post-test essay score (post-rate) was 2.56, the mean essay length (post-word) was 439.6, while the mean post-discourse score (post-dis) was 6.70.

Table 4.3 Quantitative discourse analysis showing correlations between Black discourse, raters' scores, and word counts on pre-test essay

		Pre-dis	Pre-rate	Pre-word
Pre-dis	Pearson correlation	1.000	0.319*	0.734**
	Sig. (2-tailed)		0.021	0.000
	N	52	52	52
Pre-rate	Pearson correlation	0.319*	1.000	0.513**
	Sig. (2-tailed)	0.021		0.000
	N	52	52	52
Pre-word	Pearson correlation	0.734**	0.513**	1.000
	Sig. (2-tailed)	0.000	0.000	
N		52	52	52

* Correlation is significant at the 0.05 level (2-tailed).
** Correlation is significant at the 0.01 level (2-tailed).

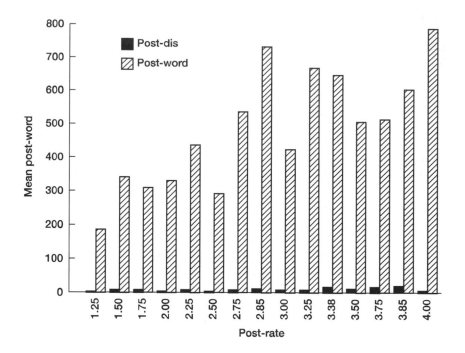

Figure 4.1 Correlation of post-word, post-discourse, and post-rate

Let's look at the data from pre- to post-curriculum to discern the amount of change in students' essay length, use of Black discourse, and essay scores using African American methodology (see Table 4.4). The study's prediction was that students would be able to write longer essays, use Black discourse patterns, and score higher on their essays than they did before taking the course. All of these elements combine to operationalize African American methodology. Of course, everyone should presume that any worthwhile writing course should increase students' essay length and writing achievement. But conventional wisdom has it that AAVE discourse is not conducive to academic writing. Thus, the null hypothesis is that there will be no significant gain in students' writing from pre- to post-curriculum using African American methodology. I used the t-test of paired samples to find out whether there was a significant change in the observed variables pre- to post-curriculum. As I already had evidence that there was a positive association between discourse scores, essay length and essay score, I wondered what would be the pre- and post-result of each dependent sample: the pre- and post-discourse, pre- and post-word, and pre- and post-essay rating. I chose the t-test because it is a precise test for matching before and after results. I found a significant change in sample results from pre- to post-curriculum.

Table 4.5 reports the Pearson correlation coefficient for word, discourse, and

Table 4.4 Showing mean change from pre-to post-curriculum for word count, Black discourse, and raters' scores

	Mean	N
Pair 1: *pre-word*	241.5	51
Pair 1: *post-word*	440	51
Pair 2: *pre-dis*	5.11	51
Pair 2: *post-dis*	6.7	51
Pair 3: *pre-rate*	1.9	51
Pair 3: *post-rate*	2.5	51

Table 4.5 Paired samples correlations showing significant mean change from pre- to post-curriculum for word count, Black discourse, and raters' scores

	N	Correlation	Sig.
Pair 1: *pre-word* and *post-word*	51	0.541	0.000
Pair 2: *pre-dis* and *post-dis*	51	0.541	0.000
Pair 3: *pre-rate* and *post-rate*	51	0.541	0.000

rating before and after the course. The R-values of 0.541, 0.589, and 0.304 suggest the existence of a positive association with fairly strong effect for this sample size between these variables before and after the course; the P-values (or significance values) of 0.000, 0.000, and 0.030 indicate that the observed association is highly statistically significant at the 0.05 level. Therefore, the hypothesis that there will be no significant gain in students' writing from pre- to post-curriculum using African American methodology is rejected. Thus, the answer to research question (2): Does Black discourse usage work to excel or arrest the development of academic writing? The answer: African American methodology was generally valuable for the students.

Because one dimension of the exploration of the language and literacy practices of African Americans has a gender focus, I wondered if there was any significant difference in the performance of males and females in the course. For this reason, I ran the t-test for independent samples because it is the test most often used to compare two groups. I ran a descriptive statistics test first to compare the mean scores of both groups on the variables pre-discourse, post-discourse, pre-rating, post-rating, and pre-word, post-word. Levene's test for equality of variance was not significant so both groups were assumed to be equal. The t-test for the equality of means showed only one aspect of this analysis to be significant. Inspection of the two groups' means indicated that the average post-discourse score for females was significantly lower (5.16) than for males (8.9). Thus, for post-discourse scores, the results were t (49) = −2.22, and P = 0.031 [where the number in parentheses represents the degrees of freedom or valid number of cases]. The difference between the means was −3.74. The

95 per cent confidence interval of difference was between −7.12 and −0.3545. This means that if we repeated this study 100 times, 95 of the times the true population difference would fall within this confidence interval. This raises an interesting issue. In early research on AAVE, Black males were generally thought to use more AAVE than Black females. However, that line of thought is problematic because earlier research was overwhelmingly conducted with Black male subjects on their use of AAVE syntax, not discourse. Black females' discourse practices were hardly studied. Recent research on Black women's language usage challenges the earlier assumption (Stanback, 1983; M. Morgan, 1989; Smitherman, 2000; Troutman, 2001).

Though none of the other variables were significant with regard to gender, it is interesting to note the difference in the means for all variables as demonstrated in Table 4.6.

It is interesting to note that, generally, the males used more Black discourse features than the females in both pre- and post-test essays; however, the females' essay ratings were nevertheless higher than the males' on both measures. It is also interesting to note that the males wrote more on both the pre-test and post-test essays. It is equally important to keep in mind though that there was not enough difference between the groups for any of this to make a significant statistical difference, except in the post-discourse category. In any case, I think it was important to show that Black males in this study showed improvement. In Hip Hop words, they *represented!*

Now that I have given an overall view of pre- to post-data on discourse usage, I'd like to focus here on discourse and rhetorical analyses of an out of class essay (post-middle essay), non-impromptu, where students had time to work outside of class on the essays for at least two weeks. I asked the students to

Table 4.6 Showing differences in means between females and males on pre- and post-variables (F = females, M = males)

	Gender	N	Mean
Pre-dis	F	30	4.83
	M	22	5.36
Post-dis	F	30	5.16
	M	21	8.90
Pre-rate	F	30	2.10
	M	22	1.76
Post-rate	F	30	2.64
	M	21	2.44
Pre-word	F	30	237
	M	22	246
Post-word	F	30	427
	M	21	457

compose an essay in response to a prompt that revolved around the African American rhetorical tradition, as discussed in Bormann (1971).

Prompt

> Perhaps the greatest distinction between current black rhetorics and the rhetoric of abolition is that the main audience for the latter had to be the white community, because in the 1830s and the 1840s the great bulk of the blacks were slaves and could not be reached by the words of the speakers and writers. Today a rhetorician planning a persuasive campaign for reform of race relations can decide to adopt a strategy of unity with the entire society, white and nonwhite, as did Martin Luther King and his followers and as did some leaders of the biracial Congress of Racial Equality (CORE), or they may choose to adopt a strategy of divisiveness and appeal primarily to the black audience.
>
> (Bormann, 1971: 238)

For reasons already mentioned, my prediction was that essays exploiting more Black discourse would score higher than those which did not. To test this hypothesis, I did a Pearson correlation analysis focusing on writing assessment score, Black discourse score, and word score/essay length. As with the pre- to post-essay, these results proved significant.

The strongest correlation is that between the Black discourse score and essay length (0.000 at $P < 0.01$, R-value 0.796). The second strongest correlation was essay rating and essay length (0.000 at $P < 0.01$, R-value 0.576). The third strongest correlation is between essay rating and Black discourse score (0.031 at $P < 0.05$, R-value 0.316). It is important to note that the R-value (0.316) shows a moderate effect for the strength of this relationship. It is not as strong as the relationship between Black discourse score and essay length. This points to the fact that, generally, Black styled essays correlated with higher scores.

The most frequently used Black discourse features were "Cultural Values—Community Consciousness" and "field dependency." The nature of the prompts, their basis in the Black experience, may have influenced the students' heightened involvement with the topic. Since person-centeredness is a central aspect of AAVE culture, literacy experiences might be developed with that in mind. It is not surprising then that expressions of concern for all African Americans (Cultural Values—Community Consciousness) and field dependency (lack of distance from topic) were the most prominent discourse features. Incorporating AAVE culture and thought and its representation (Black discourse features) into academic work may help us to develop a sensibility about which features work well for specific kinds of writing tasks, as well as features that do not work. Among the many Black discourse features, it is interesting to note the employment of field dependency. I would argue that field dependency is the hallmark of the Black style, a signature feature. It is as salient a discourse feature as "Zero copula" is for AAVE syntax. Field dependency epitomizes the person-centered assumptions of AAVE culture. It helps a writer to engage more deeply with the subject. Generally, field dependency is in opposition to traditionally conceived "objectivity" and "neutrality" that characterizes academic discourse. Some scholars see "Presence in the Essay" as highly problematic, bordering on anti-academic (see for example, Harvey, 1994).

Increasingly, scholars are denouncing these traditional and static conceptions of academic discourse (Bizzell, 2000). No one has struggled to flip the script on academic discourse better than Smitherman (1977), in the fields of English studies and socio-linguistics. In fact, her entire academic career has been dedicated to signifying on the official dis-course on African American language and literacy. In literature, Toni Morrison provides another of the many examples. Allowing students to write from areas of cultural strength could help to level the cultural bias of traditionally influenced literacy experiences.

Qualitative evidence

To get a sense of the students' experiences of the curriculum it may be helpful to look at student reflections on ways in which the learning about AAVE and Black literacy traditions was beneficial to them:

> It helped me develop a better understanding of our language and possibly why other people may not get it. I was exposed to some excellent literature.
>
> Student #20, Fall 96

> The course helped me understand more about the AAVE culture and language.
>
> Student #15, Fall 96

> This course has helped me to recognize the difference between standard English and Black English and to be able to write according to my audience.
>
> Student #21, Fall 96

> This course has helped me to identify my weakness in writing. I also feel more comfortable about my writing style and the Black discourse I use because now I have control over it.
>
> Student #3, Fall 96

> I have become more aware about the language of my people. I learned that to talk Black is not to talk improper; it is just a different way of talking. I learned to take more pride in my people and my ancestors.
>
> Student #14, Fall 96

It has opened my eyes to the struggles of African Americans. I learned to write in the language of Wider Communication and Black English at the same time. It has been very useful, and will continue to be as I pursue my English degree.

Student #6, Fall 96

I have learned to coincide my voice with the voice of the work I am critiquing to come up with a proper analysis of the subject.

Student #12, Fall 96

I honestly feel that I learn and comprehended so much information because I was learning about my people. In addition I was learning with my peers. I am happy that Sister Elaine was the instructor of this course. She knew the course material very well therefore it was easier for the class to learn. She was able to teach from her heart and soul. You don't find many instructors like that. This class has not only given me the opportunity to learn more about my culture, I have also had more confidence toward all my classes because of my new found identity.

Student #1, Fall 96

I feel that I now have some knowledge of self and can break down the African American English. I feel my writing that I do now is better than before because I can feel and relate to the writing and feel good when I get done. Unlike these other classes were they only want the European English.

Student #6, Fall 97

I do feel differently about African American English because I even thought that it was not in existent. Now I understand that Black English does exist and everyone I think needs to know and learn that it is in existent.

Student #1, Fall 97

My views on Black topics has change. It was easy for me to write in here because AAVE is a part of me and the way I think.

Student #2, Fall 97

Before I took this class, I thought it was a joke. Now I have a high respect for AAVE. The writing I did before was similar to the AAVE style except I didn't elaborate on thoughts.

Student #3, Fall 97

I am now more convinced that African American English exists. As before my ignorance led me to believe there was no such thing. The writing that I did before was always adjusted to what the intructors wanted to hear. Now I can write in my own voice and use patterns of discourse that are related to my culture.

Student #5, Fall 97

I feel more connected to african american english because I have a better understanding. I don't think I will change the way I write because this is probably the only class where I will be allowed to use AAVE. It wouldn't be accepted in other classes.

Student #8, Fall 97

Before I was enlightened with the true meaning of Ebonics, I was one of the ignorant ones who thought Ebonics was bad and that "Black English" was Broken English. I am more able to produce metaphors and supporting evidence in a lengthy format that adheres to the college writing expectations. AAVE enhanced my ability to think and signify to my brothers and sisters.

Student #13, Fall 97

This small sample from the course exit questionnaires demonstrates that this course was important to the students. Several themes emerge. Some students mentioned that they didn't believe African American English was a reality. They mentioned that prior to taking the course, they knew it to be "Broken English," or "a joke." This points to the way that oppression and racism influence the ways that people know. These students showed that what they knew was discredited knowledge. To put it another way, if something that is distinctly African American does exist, it is worthless. Educators must work against this type of oppression.

Another obvious theme in students' statements is a new understanding of the differences between the language of wider communication and AAVE. Students' commentary pointed to surface level syntax as well as more global concerns. It's one thing to say that language varieties other than the official standard are worthy and equal from a purely linguistic standpoint. It's another to exploit these for cognitive advantage in academic settings. Students' commentary pointed to their gain in analytical competence, as well as feeling more connected to their writing and feeling good. These are certainly not the typical remarks Black people in historically Eurocentric influenced academic settings are used to hearing.

These disclosures remind us of the problem of using grading itself as a measure of student achievement. Attitude affective motivation is very significant in leading to demonstrable achievement in written literacy as well.

I've heard so many conversations wherein teaching culturally diverse students writing was equated with changing clothes and superficial codeswitching:

112

"When one goes to church, a suit of clothes is appropriate." I think the situation is much deeper—so much more than meets the eye. As Canagarajah (1990: vii) succinctly stated:

> Literacy for minority students . . . involves more than knowing the "standard" codes, necessary literate skills or the ability to switch language patterns as explained by current sociolinguistic and composition studies; literacy is an ideological act of negotiating between competing discourses and identities.

I think that by integrating the speech styles, rhetorical, and literacy traditions of African Americans into academic writing, we invite students to have a fair fight with discourses. Disconnecting them from their cultural histories and the heterogeneity of their language and literacy practices is restricting their classroom literacy experiences from the word go. Competition between discourses is healthy if the "true" proper attitudes are developed. That proper attitude is rooted in respect for one's own culture and language. Forced suppression of one over the other is not healthy.

In this chapter, I have presented quantitative and qualitative evidence to answer the main research question: Is written fluency enhanced by African American methodology? In the next chapter, I take a closer look at students' writing and the assignments that generated that writing in relation to research question (3): Can student writing showing obvious Black discourse features be considered (Bl)academic?

5

Composition in a fifth key: rhetorics and discourses in an African American-centered writing classroom

Booka-booka-booka-booka-booka-booka
Ha hah
You know the deal
This is me yo
Beats by Su-Primo for all of my people, negroes and latinos
and even the gringos
Yo, check it one for Charlie Hustle, two for Steady Rock
Three for the fourth comin live, future shock
It's five dimensions, six senses
Seven firmaments of heaven to hell, 8 Million Stories to tell
Nine planets faithfully keep in orbit
with the probable tenth, the universe expands length
The body of my text possess extra strength
Power-liftin powerless up, out of this, towerin inferno
My ink so hot it burn through the journal
I'm blacker than midnight on Broadway and Myrtle
Hip-Hop past all your tall social hurdles
like the nationwide projects, prison-industry complex
Broken glass wall better keep your alarm set
Streets too loud to ever hear freedom ring
Say evacuate your sleep, it's dangerous to dream
but you chain cats get the CHA-POW, who dead now
Killin fields need blood to graze the cash cow
It's a number game, but shit don't add up somehow
Like I got, sixteen to thirty-two bars to rock it
but only 15% of profits, ever see my pockets like
sixty-nine billion in the last twenty years
spent on national defense but folks still live in fear like
nearly half of America's largest cities is one-quarter black
That's why they gave Ricky Ross all the crack
Sixteen ounces to a pound, twenty more to a ki
A five minute sentence hearing and you no longer free
40% of Americans own a cell phone

so they can hear, everything that you say when you ain't home
I guess, Michael Jackson was right, "You Are Not Alone"
Rock your hardhat black cause you in the Terrordome
full of hard niggaz, large niggaz, dice tumblers
Young teens and prison greens facin life numbers
Crack mothers, crack babies and AIDS patients
Young bloods can't spell but they can rock you in PlayStation
This new math is whippin motherfuckers ass
You wanna know how to rhyme you better learn how to add
It's mathematics.
From Hip Hop artist Mos Def—"Mathematics" (1999)

In the verse that opens this chapter, Mos Def is addressing "negroes, latinos and even the gringos." His overarching theme is the ideologies, values, and practices of capitalism and its far-reaching effects on society. Some bodies gotta suffer and they are disproportionately people of color. Another connection that Mos Def makes and draws his audience's attention to is the effect that some technologies have on the literacy education of Black youth: "Young bloods can't spell but they can rock you in PlayStation/This new math is whippin motherfuckers ass/You wanna know how to rhyme you better learn how to add/It's mathematics." Briefly, Mos Def critiques one of the fallouts of education for the marketplace, the decontextualized and autonomous literacy education that stunts political holistic critical social self-consciousness development and by extension societal development. If we can make technological games like Playstation that young folks can't put down, how come our educational technologies can't keep up? It just don't add up! It's mathematics. The results of such education equip young people to proceed purposelessly through society becoming highly competent playas/players or consumers being pimped by the system to their own degradation. "You wanna know how to [write] you better learn how to add/ It's mathematics." In other words, what good is the flawless sentence, the rhetorically stylish argument, if that still leaves you powerless? To put it in terms of the Word: What does it profit a man or a woman to gain the whole world and lose his/her soul? Or his/her own center of self-consciousness? (Influenced by Mark 8: 36.)

The purpose of this chapter is to offer educators and students a new song to sing. I want to provide notes that will lead us toward new refrains of free at last and bridges that swing both ways. Toward that end, I will describe a course I taught wherein I made African American rhetorical and discursive practices the center of the curriculum. By describing the course and the pedagogical approaches in it, and sharing examples of the kinds of writing students produced, I want to move to a discussion of specific practices that can follow from this pedagogy and can serve to encourage the development of African American voices (and those of all our students) rather than continue their subjugation.

115

Theory/practice

I developed an African American-centered approach to rhetoric, composition, and literacy as an holistic approach to improve the writing and critical literacy of African American students. African American rhetoric, composition, and literacy is grounded in six theoretical traditions: (1) The theory of Afrocentricity (Asante 1991); (2) Giroux's (1991) theory of literacy and difference; (3) Fox's (1992) theory of "position"; (4) vernacular theory exemplified by Gates' (1988) theory of "Signifyin(g)," Baker's (1984) vernacular theory, and Smitherman's (1977) theory of Black language and Black modes of discourse; (5) culturally relevant literacy as presented by Ladson-Billings (1995) and Hoover (1982); and (6) Baxter and Reed's (1973) bi-dialectal/contrastive and historical approach to teaching academic writing.

African American-centeredness influenced by Afrocentricity is an inclusive approach to phenomena which encourages knowledge and centeredness of self. I use the term African American-centered rather than Afrocentric to underscore the focus on African American experiences that influence language use and knowledge production. Pedagogy based on this view of reality seeks to fuse the self and the subject of study, in this case literacy education, acknowledging self and subject as inseparable. Education for African American students is predicated on the assumption that one is at once subject and agent of her experience. From this perspective, an African American student's literacy education should involve her experience and be experienced by her.

Literacy acquisition is not a set of skills to be mastered. It is a looking inward into one's own thought and cultural/language patterns and history, while looking outward into the world's, seeking to intervene in one's own context. The student of African American descent should not be dislocated so that she has to reinvent herself in order to negotiate new information. Rather, the student develops from her own cultural position, so that new information can be effectively mastered. Asante (1991: 29) writes:

> The fact that an African American or Hispanic person—in order to master the white cultural information—has had to experience the death of his or her own culture does not register with most teachers. The true "centric" curriculum seeks for the African, Asian, and Hispanic [student] the same kind of experience that is provided for the white [student].

Of course Asante is not talking about creating within students of color the feeling of superiority over other cultures when he says that the same kind of experience should be provided. He is talking about the fact that students have a right to be reinforced in their historical experiences. Maybe Black students have heard African American spirituals but don't know the significance of the folklore embedded within them. Maybe students have read Langston Hughes or Phillis Wheatley but don't know the significance of the literature from a political, historical, and cultural perspective. Maybe students have read Zora Neale Hurston's *Their Eyes Were Watching God*, but don't understand why Hurston included AAVE or maybe students have not ever been given a reason to feel pride in the language used. Valuable epistemological traditions can be gleaned from African American cultural productions. Centering this perspective in African American literacy education may be productive.

Giroux's suggestion, that best practices in literacy instruction acknowledge literacy's political context, and our students' need to locate themselves in the contested site of literacy as it is practiced in these United States, complements the African American-centered approach. Giroux (1991: xv) puts it this way:

> Our students do not deserve an education constrained by the smothering dictates of a monolithic and totalizing view of culture, literacy, and citizenship; they deserve an education that acknowledges its role in the preparation of critical political subjects and that prepares them to be agents capable of locating themselves in history while simultaneously being able to shape it.

The African American-centered approach to writing instruction makes the pursuit of literacy more than a positivistic academic exercise. Students' own culture and literacy experiences are recognized as valuable tools which inform ways in which they explore and help shape society. Giroux's theory of explicating the political nature of literacy instruction is highly compatible to the situation of the African American student. From its beginnings, Black literacy has been political. The enslaved Africans knew that their ways of knowing and being in the world meant nothing in the "New World" and that the only way they could survive was to try to assimilate. They had to learn to manipulate the language and use it to free themselves. When an enslaved African learned to write, she did so knowing that Black lives were at stake (most immediately one's "own" life). Literacy was a way of uplifting and freeing the enslaved. Thus, the first Black American texts (enslavement narratives) were political acts. Students need to know that they are heirs to this tradition of struggle. The contemporary fight is for freedom of the mind, freedom to conceive and achieve in a new and better world. Agreeing with Giroux, I believe students deserve an education that locates them within their history and encourages them to define their futures.

Fox's (1991) concept of "position" is an important theoretical influence in the African American-centered approach to teaching writing. Position is a geographic metaphor that locates African American writers in relationship to race and history, race and institutions, and race and gender (Fox, 1991: 292):

> "Position" as a central concept in the exploration of African American student writers requires a pedagogy that would investigate the ways in which history, culture, institutions, social relations . . . intersect and influence writing.

117

Educators start from the viewpoint that students are positioned, that they come from somewhere with something worthwhile, valuable, and fundamental to the educational process. Students are not blank slates waiting to be written upon. Rather, they are members of gender-ethnic-social groups with histories and all sorts of political and religious affiliations. Their literacy education should invite them to find where they are coming from and where they can go by developing their talents. The African American-centered approach strives to achieve this by connecting African American students to Black language and literacy traditions and stimulating their critical awareness.

Gates' (1988) theory of "Signifyin(g)" illuminates the importance of acknowledging racial/cultural identity in literacy education. Gates calls the Black language and literacy traditions the "language of Signifyin(g)." For Gates, Signifyin(g) is the Black language tradition! Signifyin(g) is the all-encompassing term for the ways in which African Americans use language to critique the dominant culture's view of reality. Black experiences as represented in African American literature, especially autobiography, offer fascinating studies of Signifyin(g). Authors repeat and revise themes of the Black experience creating an intertextual chain which refers to that shared experience/cultural identity. In *The Signifyin(g) Monkey*, Gates traces the oral and literate political tradition of the African American experience, highlighting African Americans' preoccupation with the Black tradition of resistance to objectification by talking and reading and writing their way into subjectivity. In other words, African Americans continually redefine their own reality. In Gates' words (1988: 51):

> Signifyin(g) is black double-voicedness; because it entails formal [literal restructuring of forms] revision and an intertextual relation, and . . . it is the ideal metaphor for [B]lack literary criticism for the formal manner in which texts seem concerned to address their antecedents.

In this way then, the preoccupations and cultural elements that are concerned with teaching writing to Black students include themes of the Black experience as represented in African American literature, identifying the "freedom as literacy" trope as most crucial. "Freedom through literacy" emerges as one of the earliest traceable themes of the African American experience. This theme is repeated, though with the authors' own sense of difference, in many African American texts, for example, texts such as those written by J. A. Gronniosaw, Olaudah Equiano, Frederick Douglass, Nathan McCall, Kate Drumgoold, Maya Angelou, and Sister Souljah. Therefore, these works are useful in African American-centered literacy curricula.

Following Houston Baker, in this work, vernacularity is conceptualized as the guiding impetus for the epistemological development of African American literacies and rhetorics. Baker (1984: 39) writes of his project:

> The [creative Black] subject's very inclusion in an *Afro-American* tradi-

tional discourse is, in fact, contingent on an encounter with such privileged economic signs of Afro-American discourse. The "already-said," so to speak, contains unavoidable preconditions for the practice of Afro-American narrative.

Baker's metaphor for vernacularity is the blues matrix, which is a "cultural invention . . . that generates (or obliges one to invent) its (her) own referents" (Baker, 1984: 9). Baker's "blues matrix" is akin to Smitherman's "Forms of things unknown" (adapted from Richard Wright). Like Baker, Smitherman (1977/1986: 103) identifies an overall formulaic structure for Black language use, wherein "individuals are challenged to do what they can within the traditional mold." From this point of view, Black creativity is a response to absence and desire, which can often be traced (in part) to an "economics of slavery." Taken together then, resistance to oppression, response to absence and desire, and economics are some important elements of teaching rhetoric, composition, and literacy to African American students. The vernacular approach guides us to an ideological analysis of the cultural productions of African American speakers and writers, in their quest for equal access to society's resources. This is what is meant by culturally relevant literacy instruction.

From an African American perspective, culturally relevant education involves the integration of content from African American cultures, perspectives, and ideas, including European American cultures, perspectives, and ideas, teacher facility with a wide array of culturally appropriate practices and attitudes, and the engagement of different ways of knowing and learning. Culturally appropriate literacy approaches should acknowledge, exploit, and expand the epistemological and cultural traditions, which students bring with them to the classroom. I use the terms "culturally appropriate" and "culturally relevant" synonymously. I borrow these terms from Mary Hoover (1982) and Gloria Ladson-Billings (1995). To date, however, empirical studies in culturally relevant literacy development such as those focused on the impact of AAVE-centered curricular strategies on African American students and their writing are quite scarce. Researchers interested in researching and teaching African Americans' acquisition of literacy and critical literacy development, bidialectal and bilingual literacy are often met with resistance. Yet, culturally appropriate approaches to education and literacy remain a promising response to cultural conflict. Interesting comparisons can be made among the unequal education situations between African Americans and other castelike groups around the world. An example is the Maori of New Zealand (Cazden, 1992; Airini, 1998; Hemara, 2000).[1]

Pedagogically, work on Black students and composition (as discussed in Chapter 1) points to the fact that students should explore African American cultural knowledge and "ways with words" in order to develop their abilities as writers with improved critical literacy. Pedagogy should include Afrocentric topics, contrastive rhetoric and discourse analysis, and a genuine incorporation of African American Vernacular English as a discourse, not simply a set of grammatical features to be eradicated from speech and writing.

Nuts and bolts of the course

As a curriculum, then, this African American-centered rhetoric and composition course begins by exploring African American language and literacy traditions, starting with the literature of the enslaved or newly freed African. Such literature is rich with problems and ideas that are still of concern to contemporary African Americans as it includes major themes of Black experiences and offers excellent stimuli for critical thinking, reading, and writing material. I like to begin with James A. Gronniosaw's *A Narrative of the Most Remarkable Particulars in the Life of James Albert Ukawsaw Gronniosaw, an African Prince, Written by Himself*, and Olaudah Equiano's *The Interesting Narrative of the Life of Olaudah Equiano, or Gustavus Vassa, the African, Written by Himself*. I also use Frederick Douglass' *Narrative of the Life of Frederick Douglass*, Kate Drumgoold's *Slave Girl's Story*, and Harriet Jacobs' *Incidents in the Life of a Slave Girl*. Students are encouraged to focus on the meaning and uses of literacy, and ways of knowing and surviving in these texts, for they exemplify the importance of critical reading, thinking, acting, and writing in Black experiences. In particular, they introduce students to the important African American literacy trope, Signification, through examples of early searches for freedom and self-determination.[2]

Gronniosaw's quest to be able to read his world, the obstacles he encountered as a man of color, literally, his struggle to learn to read the Bible, stands as a powerful example of the power of the human will to achieve. This Talking Book Trope (literacy as freedom), or a variation of it, can be seen in many African American autobiographical texts. The AAVE literary version of it originated in 1770, when Gronniosaw, the first author of African descent of a full-length autobiography brought a fresh voice into the New World. When he wrote of the book that would not speak to him, he gave visual representation, symbolically and in print, to the invisibility of the Black experience. In Gronniosaw's version of this trope, he had a fascination with his master's ability to read and identify with the Bible or a prayer book. In stolen moments Gronniosaw puts his ear to the book hoping to communicate with it as his master had. Ashamed of his ignorance and aware that he is seen as subhuman, Gronniosaw connects his inability to read to his Africanness, his cultural difference, his invisibility. His life goal is to become literate and to transform his status from object to human. The transcendent self is literate or at least articulate and thus worthy to be free (Gates, 1988: 167). This struggle to master the master's tongue, to negotiate between competing discourses, to constantly reaffirm the self, and gain knowledge, is the focus of the African American-centered classroom.

To be successful, therefore, it is essential to begin the course by getting the students to connect their own experiences as African Americans to narratives of the enslavement era Africans. Themes of Black experiences in the texts become a focus of instruction. Other themes subsumed under literacy/literacies are assimilation, identity politics, multiple consciousness, self-doubt, racism, oppression, sexuality, class, religion, relationships, Black cultural expression, and the struggle for self-determination. Then, once students have a handle on themes, I introduce contemporary texts as a way of demonstrating the intertextuality of past and present Black lives and their representation. For contemporary texts, I use excerpts from Carter G. Woodson's *Miseducation of the Negro*. I use Woodson's *Miseducation* as a bridge text that helps students connect their individual experiences to these histories of literacy and the conditions of their educations. Woodson identifies many issues that work against the political, social, spiritual, and democratic education of Black people that still apply today. I use *Makes Me Wanna Holler* by Nathan McCall, and *The Autobiography of Malcolm X* by Alex Haley and Malcolm X because they illuminate many of the themes of Black experiences from a male viewpoint, while *No Disrespect* by Sister Souljah offers insight to the dilemmas from a Black female's perspective. Claudia Mitchell-Kernan's "Language Behavior in a Black Urban Community" and Geneva Smitherman's *Talkin and Testifyin* are highly accessible texts that introduce students to the linguistic and cultural practices of African Americans. Students also analyze song lyrics, and have to read articles printed in magazines and newspapers with Black and mixed audiences. I also supplement these with other handouts and articles on AAVE syntax and discourse.

A major focus of the course is on AAVE. While we do some contrastive analysis of syntactical forms, I am also extremely interested in the rhetorical/discourse level. We focus on Black language strategies. I strive to make the students meta-conscious about language usage. For example, we learn semantic inversion or flippin' the script. A passage from Equiano in which he describes the customs of his Nigerian culture before his enslavement displays this and other important strategies, which students can be taught to discern and execute in writing. Equiano writes:

> [O]ur children were named from some event, some circumstance, or fancied foreboding at the time of their birth. I was named Olaudah, which, in our language, signifies "vicissitude or fortunate," also, "one favoured, and having a loud voice and well spoken." I remember we never polluted the name of the object of our adoration; on the contrary, it was always mentioned with the greatest reverence; and we are totally unacquainted with swearing, and all those terms of abuse and reproach which find their way so readily and copiously into the language of more civilized people.
>
> (Equiano, 1789: 20)

Most students get turned on to the story by this passage. First of all Equiano's style epitomizes Anglo African writing. Not only does Equiano exhibit great lexical range as exemplified in his employment of words such as "reverence," "unacquainted," "copiously," but the content of his writing shows his highly sophisticated understanding of Europeans and their social, economic, and governmental systems. Closer examination reveals Signifying in the sense of semantic inversion or critique. Equiano implies that Black people are considered to be uncivilized, when they revere words as sacred, unlike the more "civilized" Europeans who swear and abuse words and by extension people. A passage such as this serves the African American-centered classroom quadruply as it passes on pre-enslavement cultural knowledge, demonstrates critical awareness, teaches close reading, and exemplifies an AAVE language device, Signifying.

Reading the enslavement narratives was both an interesting and difficult experience for the students. Most students found *Douglass* to be the most accessible text. Some complained that *Slave Girl* seemed too accommodating to Whites. And on the level of readability, they found it hard to follow because of the text's adherence to oral strategies. I saw the students' frustration with the text as an opportunity to critically analyze the context of Drumgoold's text. I asked the class who they thought was Drumgoold's target audience, pointing out that the number of literate Blacks was disproportionately low during that time as compared to Whites. One student said "her text was written for Blacks and Whites because she wanted to uplift Blacks, by showing Whites that she could think and write."

Another student pointed out that Drumgoold's obsession with talking about her love for her "White mother" (an uncommonly kind mistress who had all but adopted Drumgoold) was generated by her knowledge of the text's function. As a Black female, Drumgoold hoped to generate empathy for the cause of freedom and literacy. Her text stressed her experience of human equality with Whites and human ability to achieve even in the face of adversity. Drumgoold's text offered a prime example of audience awareness and the rhetoric of unity. Drumgoold knew that her text was going to be used as a tool for abolition. She wrote extensively about her "White mother" and how much the White mother loved and cared for her. We discussed the fact that there were many Whites who had helped Blacks achieve literal literacy and freedom. Drumgoold's mistress was rich and powerful and could afford to educate her Black "daughter" without risking her own life or that of her daughter. Drumgoold devoted a considerable amount of her text to thanking God for her "mother" and her literacy. Her text stressed a concern for the literacy training of all Blacks. After discussion of audience, purpose, and the conditions under which Kate Drumgoold's text *(Slave Girl)* was produced, we decided that her text was nevertheless a critique of the system, and therefore worthy of all of their attention.

After the first semester of teaching this class, I began emphasizing the ideas of public discourse versus private discourse. I began to push students to think about the difference in arguments African Americans make in unofficial versus official spaces. What Black semantics are invoked in a Black space that will not be successful in a public space? What do Black audiences require of a Black rhetor even when that rhetor is publicly speaking or writing? Why?

122

We studied the Black modes of discourse as described by Smitherman (1977). Students had to learn to identify and create their own examples. We studied the history behind the language. Most students developed an appreciation for the language and a different view of African American Vernacular English culture. The Black language and discourse section of the curriculum was contextualized by Smitherman's "Forms of Things Unknown" and Mitchell-Kernan's "Language Use in a Black Urban Community." We read portions of the Mitchell-Kernan article and Smitherman's "Forms" in class so that I could make sure students knew how to identify the forms and what made them distinctly Black. One of the assignments for this section of the curriculum consisted of students' bringing in an article that addressed a topic of utmost concern to the AAVE community. They were to write a piece refuting or agreeing with the article's ideas and to make the discussion their own. Students could choose their audience and the style of their prose according to their audience analysis. They were provided with a list of Black discourse features (i.e. "direct address," "ethnolinguistic idioms" etc.) from Smitherman (1994). It was stressed that the Black discourse had to sound authentic. That is, students had to concentrate on discourse not grammar. AAVE grammar was to be employed sparsely because even in Hip Hop magazines every sentence does not have AAVE grammar! One of the papers had to be sent out for publication, depending on its compatibility with a publishing outlet's audience.

This assignment was work intensive for students because they had to peruse local or national Black and mainstream magazines and papers to scope out possible publishing outlets. This entailed getting a feel for the type of writing favored by the prospective outlets. Further, students had to research submission information on their own. They worked in groups sharing information and writing cover letters to editors for their articles. The assignment was very time consuming for me, too, as I had to do a lot of conferencing with students on their texts to oversee writing quality. Three students had pieces accepted for publication, all in Black outlets. Figure 5.1 shows an excerpt from one of the student's essays that was published in a local Black newspaper.

I varied this assignment after the first time teaching the course. In subsequent classes the assignment became to create a web page for a Black community organization. As in the earlier version of the assignment, students had to do all of the research on their own. They had to find a community organization and interview someone at the organization to find out what services they rendered, the mission of the organization, their needs. If that need could be helped in any way by a web page, the students had to make the web page happen and solicit the guidance of a member of the sponsoring organization. One of the directives also included making sure that the page met the aesthetic and communicative criteria of the organization. Some of my students already knew how to do HTML and this aided me greatly in the classroom. It gave certain students opportunities for leadership and to demonstrate their "skillz." This way all of the students got something published for an audience beyond our classroom.

AAFS offers support groups

Rufus Brown

Insight Intern/Contributing Writer

African American Family Services (AAFS) offers many support groups and treatment programs for adolescents and adults. Each program is well structured and accessible to African Americans and other different Ethnic groups.

AAFS is nationality acknowledged and is thought of as highly reputable in many school districts. The organization teaches seminars which cater to interests of a diverse population.

"If you keep doing what you've been doing, you'll keep getting what you've been getting," said Rufus Brown, the chemical dependency counselor at AAFS. His mission to keep young adolescents off the streets and away from a negative environment is clearly justified in his self-instructed eight to 10 week Adolescent Outpatient Treatment Program (AOTP).

Since AOTP's start-up date in the early 1990s, it has greatly inspired a diverse age group of Africans Americans. The program is specifically designed to challenge young males and females and to encourage them to reconsider their decision-making skills which affect their well being and essentially, that of the entire community.

The curriculum for the AOTP includes: substance abuse prevention; discussion of emotions; African American history; family involvement; criminal justice awareness; sexuality education and career development.

Each week is geared towards teaching a particular subject. Also, the program features speakers from the community and videotapes exploring numerous social issues that impact the adolescents' environments. Brown's approach provides young adults with the ability to maintain chemical free lives and to repair damaged relationships among family members and friends.

Different organizations, schools and public officials refer clients participating in the AOTP. Prior

Figure 5.1 Student article published in American local Black newspaper

Some of them did the local urban league, or a community center. Others created pages for churches or organizations within their churches. The main thing about this assignment besides the writing and research activities was that students became familiar with grass roots, self-help, African American agencies as part of the literacies of African Americans.

As part of the course, we also listened to lots of Black music, studied themes of Black experiences in the music, the rhetoric of the sounds and the lyrics. To the extent that we could, we talked about the importance of aesthetics as ways of knowing. We listened to selections from the CD that is part of the *Norton Anthology of African American Literature*. We also listened to much Hip Hop discussing beats, styles, and how they spoke to us. Students had to learn to identify syntax and discourse strategies operating in the songs.

I taught discourse analysis, by having students bring in rap lyrics and discuss the functional and rhetorical usefulness of AAVE syntax and discourse strategies. Students had to write papers showing their ability to identify examples of AAVE syntax and how they added to the ethos, logos, or pathos of the rhetor or the message. Further, they had to identify at least three discourse or rhetorical strategies and find an overall theme in the lyrics and discuss how this was enhanced by the use of the Black language features.

We also watched several excerpts from movies to put a visual aspect to the course. For example, we watched the excerpt from *Roots* wherein Fiddler (Americanized/Colonized African) is charged with turning Kunte Kinte (the newly captured African) into a "proper field hand, who does exactly as his master tells him to do and speaks the King's English"—as Master Reynolds put it to Fiddler. We watched a few more important scenes from that movie—the (in)famous scene where Kunta is beaten into submission and made to call himself "Toby." We also watched the scene in which Kunta's daughter Kizzy is caught reading by Master Reynolds' brother, and the uses to which she puts her literacy. These scenes help to underscore the violence of language and literacy (Stuckey, 1991), how they can be used or suppressed to dominate people and control their thinking. Additionally, we analyzed these videos to explore the centrality of language to human identity, how African American people used language and literacy to protect and advance themselves.

The rhetorical focus of the course also included instruction on composing processes. Students were encouraged to use pre-writing strategies (clustering, freewriting, brainstorming, outlining, researching). Further, the class also participated in writing workshops, wherein students could offer each other advice on how to strengthen their arguments and persuasive strategies.

I would like to turn here to examples of student writing in response to the assignments. In order to try to share a range of the writers and their writing, I will begin with examining the pre- and post-tests of one of my most struggling souls and proceed to other student essays and excerpts, showing a range of writing abilities.[3]

African American-centered writing

The first piece of writing you will see here was produced by one of my students who had not had a lot of writing education prior to my class. He was a heavy AAVE speaker and in some instances his writing reflects his idiolect. On the other hand, in some ways, his writing hardly reflects his face to face communicative competence. Below is his impromptu in class pre-test essay response.

To be a member of the African American Vernacular English

To be able to fluently speak the American language it_ (**zero s**) a hassle in some cases. Words you never ***herd*** (**sp**) of seem to be twisted a little bit. It seems that although ***a words may be right in when saying them*** (**IL**) but**,** (**comma**) it comes out different ***then*** (**ww**) when its (**desyl**) pose_ (**zero ed**) to be pronounce_ (**zero ed**). Like the word "the" in (**0 da**) bible is said **the** (**sp**) (**0 comma**) different in old script. There is a lot of culture tie_ (**zero ed**) into the American language (**0 p**) (**0 cap**) for example (**0 comma**) German, Spanish, French, England etc. (**0 cap**) those thing_ (**zero s**) make American [language] today what it is. A lot of times I thinks (**hypercorrection or aspectual s**) its (**0 appost**) hard for African American_ (**zero s**) to

say the right words but, (comma) ease (**sp**) for them to say the wrong. That_
(**zero s**) why you may hear words floating out people mouths that is [IRV]
not in the dictionary but, (**comma**) at that time and place is the proper word
to used. (**hypercorrection**)

The African American Vernacular English writing is the only thing known
to an American. I can't really say if it is hard are (**ww**) not because I have
not took it upon myself to be educate_ (**zero ed**) on the subject how the
African write_ (**zero s**).

Student #4, Fall 97: pre-writing sample

Surface level analysis

- 184 words in 50 minutes
- 3 SP – spelling
- 1 IL – interlanguage pattern (not standardized English or AAVE)
- 2 WW – instances of wrong word
- 1 0 da – omission of definite article
- 7 mechanics/convention errors (1 period omitted, 1 sentence initial letter not capped, 3 misplaced commas and 2 commas omitted)
- Total errors in usage and mechanics = 14

Use of AAVE syntax in student's text

This writer has five (5) AAVE "zero s." In two instances the "zero s" represents
copula deletion (as in "it a hassle" where standard American English would use
"it's a hassle"). Two of the "zero s" represent difference in demonstrating plu-
rality (as in "those thing" where standard American English would use "those
things"). The other "zero s" is demonstrated by third person differentiated differently (as in ". . . the African write" where standard American English would
use "the African writes." This writer also employs four (4) instances of "zero ed"
and demonstrates two (2) hypercorrection patterns. There is one (1) instance of
desyllabification ("pose" for supposed). I think this is due to a phonological rule
operating where the /s/ sound from the preceding word, "it's" is elided with
"suppose" and the writer represents this just the way it is pronounced. Altogether, the student employs twelve (12) instances of AAVE syntax.

Content/discourse evaluation

I will here discuss form and content together as I think they are inseparable. I
really like this writer. I can see a lot of potential here. Although it's a mixed
metaphor, I notice creativity in the sentence that contains the comment "you
may hear words floating out people mouths." The writer has not had a lot of
experience with using his language competencies for the purposes of analyzing

literature. The student's discussion is off the topic. He is not addressing the prompt. The content of this essay actually complements the surface features. His voice is really turned in against itself. "A lot of time I thinks its hard for African American to say the right word but ease for them to say wrong." He knows that certain words used by African Americans are not sanctioned by the official culture and thus not in the dictionary, but that they are appropriate in certain contexts. I've heard that line so much in the academy. The question is really one of control and consciousness—who is saying what to whom and under what conditions. One thing is for sure, his education has taught him that his language is wrong, and he clearly states that he's not taken it upon himself to be "educate on the subject." What kind of system lets students go all the way through school not knowing anything positive or systematic about their language?

The next example is the in-class impromptu post-test essay of the same student.

The African

When the Authors of the African descents (**hypercorrection**) began to publish imaginative literature in English in the eighteenth century the writing was meat (**typo**) for White people_ eyes to see. The African American_ discover_ all the lies that had been force_ upon them. Then they took action to translating the literature of AAVE. That_ why there are writers such as Phillis Wheatley. The European writings of the African American is (IRV) false. Europeans have never understood the African ways of learning and living. Blacks (**hypercorrection**) people have their own way of learning (**0 p**) (**0 cap**) it goes with our culture. Ebonics is something that came from the old slavery days. Black_ are able to read and write on the European level.

To be a member of the African American Vernacular English culture our descended from Africa had their native speaking (IL). Be able translated or convert to different language entirely would take too much to do so (IL). Knowing how to read and write in the AAVE is difficult if you are limited to education from the school systems. Our language is different in many ways, all because of the past history which we have accepted. In MSED (*The Miseducation of the Negro*) they talked about the need for more teaching on the AAVE. Blacks in general don't really know about they (AAVE per pro) culture enough to make progress in advancing to the level of such writers like Carter G. Woodson who understand the needs of the Afro-American to make advancement in learning to cope with the European style of writing. White people_ perception of Black people_ writing is limited unless it is translated to their form of reading. The chance for African American_ to voice themselves clearly is a chance to be acknowledge_ as people, something we_ been denied.

Student #4, Fall 97: post-test essay

Surface level analysis

- 240 words written in 50 minutes
- 1 typo
- 2 IL – interlectal errors (not mainstream and not AAVE)
- 1 0 cap-1 – sentence initial letter not capped
- 1 0 p-1 – period omission
- 5 surface level errors in 240 words
- Surface level errors reduced over one-half. Word gain of 56 words (from 184 to 240).

Use of AAVE syntax in student's text

The writer has (6) six occurrences of the "zero s" pattern—two of them in the possessive dimension, two occur where standard American English would have a contracted copula, and two where standard American English uses "s morpheme" for plural. The "zero ed" shows up (3) three times. The writer uses (1) one AAVE/IRV form. He also employs (1) one personal pronoun undifferentiated. There is one (1) usage of "unstressed been." There are (2) two hypercorrect patterns for "s." On the post-test essay, the student has 14 AAVE syntax occurrences.

Content/discourse evaluation

Again, we will evaluate form and content. In the post-test essay piece, the student is addressing the ideas in the prompt. The content of the student's essay actually complements the surface features. The writer is striving to deal directly with the topic at hand. Also, we see progress toward the development of a confident voice. Instead of the student succumbing to the power of the dominant discourse which says that "its hard for African American to say the right words but, ease for them to say the wrong," the student writes, "The chance for African American to voice themselves clearly is a chance to be acknowledge as people, something we been denied." This shows the beginnings of the student connection to the power of African American literacy traditions, what it means to be Black and literate. It is obvious that this writer does not have total rhetorical mastery over his usage of AAVE syntax or discourse yet. With both "ed" and "s" pattern usage, we can see that the student uses neither AAVE pattern 100 per cent categorically, but that the writer varies between the AAVE pattern and the standardized pattern for both linguistic environments. Even though there is increased AAVE syntax usage on the post-test, the writer demonstrates intellectual engagement with the prompt and the question. The writing is clearly more fluent, and I don't think it impedes the points the writer is trying to get across. However, it should be understood that increased control over these features is the goal so that the writer can use them skillfully for rhetorical effect.

Interlanguage seems to be a factor in at least two of the student's sentence constructions. Interlanguage is a form of language that appears in writing or speech, a production of idiosyncratic rules or patterns not a part of a speaker's heritage language. Likewise, it is not a part of the code that a student is striving to acquire (Scott, 1993). Interlanguage posits that some mistakes are made as the language learner (re)adjusts native speaker rules in an effort to acquire the target code. Both of the interlanguage patterns seem to me to occur as the writer strives to integrate the main theme of the essay into the second paragraph, but isn't quite sure of how to structure the topic sentence. Here is the complex string of discourse in the second paragraph: "To be a member of the African American Vernacular English culture our descended from Africa had their native speaking." It appears that what the writer wants to write is something like: "To be a member of the AAVE culture, our descendants from Africa had their native speech." In wanting to be sure to stay on topic, the writer tries to integrate the excerpt language, which I think is a good move. The second sentence only needs two minor editorial changes to be understood clearly. The writer writes: "Be able translated or convert to different language entircly would take too much to do so." Two interesting moves are demonstrated here. The writer has been working to get the "ed morpheme" under control. Notice the words "translated" and "convert." The writer doesn't need the morpheme on either word as it seems that what the writer is striving for is something along the lines of: "To be able to translate or convert to different language entirely." Another interesting point is that this student and I had worked on sentence variety. He runs into a problem in the effort to avoid creating two adjacent sentences with the same structure. In any case, what I want to demonstrate here is self-construction. This is a writer under construction. (NB: I think it is important to keep in mind that both the pre- and post-tests were written in a 50-minute time frame.)

I would like to present here the pre- and post-test essays of another writer. The pre-test essay score was judged as mid range by the raters.

I understand the passage below to mean that early African American writers used their literacy skill to express who they really are. Celebrating and paying tribute to their culture and people in their new land. (**frag**) Giving a more accurate face to African American culture. (**frag**) This also ties into the question, What does it mean to be a member of the AAVE (African American Vernacular English) culture and literate? (no indent) In my opinion it means to be able to communicate your thought to the world from an African American perspective. Being a literate member of AAVE is very important to the individual but also to the entire culture (comma) literate and illiterate included (comma) because that particular individual is able to disprove myths and stereotypes of their people and therefore uplifting you and your people. But form (**typo**) another point of view being a literate member of AAVE also mean_ (**zero s**) being in a position where you could possibly misrepresent and create or strengthen stereotypes that already exist. This is what I believe happens when you have a bunch of mis-educated literate AAVE people that think they are educated because they have their BA, masters, or PhD.

Student #3, Winter 98: pre-test essay

Surface level analysis

- 191 words in 50 minutes
- 1 typo
- 4 mechanical errors
- 2 sentence fragments
- 7 surface errors in 191 words

Use of AAVE syntax in student's text

The writer has one instance of "zero s."

Content/discourse evaluation

I think this is a very thoughtful piece of writing. The student is clearly addressing the topic and has a clear idea of the rhetorical problem at hand. The writer has some idea of the complexity of literacy for Black people. The writer demonstrates this through problematizing the idea as represented in the following: "But form [i.e. from] another point of view being a literate member of AAVE also mean being in a position where you could possibly misrepresent and create or strengthen stereotypes that already exist . . . when you have a bunch of mis-educated literate AAVE people." The phrase, "But from another point of view . . ." shows argumentative or critical skill. What I really find interesting is that she understands the concept of educated fool, those who have been educated away from their culture, someone who's lost his mother wit.

Below is the post-test essay for the same student.

The struggle continues

In this essay I will be discussing the question what does it mean to be a part of the African American Vernacular English group? I will also be interpreting Gates passage in relation to the question.

Gates passage talks about how authors of African descent challenged the fiction that European Americans wrote and said about African Americans by excersizing (**sp**) their ability to use western letters or in other words, to read and write. This is the same kind of literacy that we have been discussing in this class. Not simply being able to read or write but writing knowledgeable and self affirming literature that voices what it means to be an African American. (**frag**) Wheatley, Equiano, and Ssancho (**typo**) wrote literature that represented all Africans at that time that weren't able to express themselves for a number of reasons. The first and most common reason was because it was against the law for an African American or at that time "nigger" to learn to read and write.

I believe that the European Americans knew how powerful the tool of literacy was and would be threatened if African Americans ever acquired that skill because then they would be able to tell the truth from their own perspective therefore empowering themselves.

What it means to be a part of the African American Vernacular English group is to be able to understand the struggles of my people and having the right to give an Afrocentric view of things. This is very special to me because I know that I have one of the most powerful weapons of literacy to fight against all of the damaging lies and stereotypes that exsist (**sp**) in the text_ (**zero s**) and in society. Just as my ancestors Phillis Wheatley, Olaudah Equiano, and Ignatius Sancho, I too can "speak the African American into existence in Western letters" (Gates passage).

For example in the American school system students are not taught about African traditions, contributions, and culture. The only difference between the eighteenth century and the present is that back then the damage was done by what the European text_ (**zero s**) said about the African. Now because of "civil rights" and laws like it the European text isn't suppose_ (**zero ed**) to say negative things about African American or the African culture. Instead they say nothing at all. I believe this to be just as harmful.

Pretending as if the African American doesn't exsist (**sp**) is an insult to all of the many people that died building and defending this country. Me being a member of the AAVE gives me the chance to say that, Yes the African American has built this country and defended the same America that has written us out of history and written itself as the innocent, land of the free and the brave. Being a member of the AAVE gives me the instrument to speak the truth in a society where the truth must be told so that the next generation of African American_ (**zero s**) will have self-esteem and love themselves and where they come from, Africa.

Student #3, Winter 98: post-test essay

Surface level analysis

- 507 words in 50 minutes
- 1 typo
- 3 spelling errors
- 1 sentence fragment
- 5 surface errors in 507 words, a gain of 316 words from the pre-test.

Use of AAVE syntax in student's text

The AAVE "ed morpheme" pattern is used once as well as two instances of "s morpheme." Overall, low AAVE syntax usage.

Content/ discourse evaluation

Though the student is using a personal voice, I wouldn't call the writing style informal. I think it is rather formal, thoughtful, strong, and authoritative. The writer is clearly addressing the issues of the prompt. Thesis statement, topic sentences, and paragraphing are employed. And the writer draws on examples to supplement opinions. The writer claims the AAVE literacy tradition for purposes of empowerment in the statement: "Just as my ancestors Phillis Wheatley, Olaudah Equiano, and Ignatius Sancho, I too can 'speak the African American into existence in Western letters'" (Gates passage).

I think it is important to underscore the fact that the student is finding meaning in the writing she is doing. The student's imagination and political consciousness have been stimulated through learning about the complexity of literacy in African American experiences. The student is definitely connecting her individual experience to past histories of literacy and conditions of Black education. This is most noticeable in the sentences: "Now because of 'civil rights' and law like it the European text isn't suppose to say negative things about African American or the African culture. Instead they say nothing at all." She may be overstating the case a bit, but the critique is nonetheless well taken. She has been Kindergarten through twelfth grade and knows very well what she didn't learn in school. She is not just writing a paper for class. She is writing for her life.

Thus far, I have shared low range and mid range essays. I would like to offer here examples of the pre- and post-test essay from a student in the high scoring range.

I think that being a member of the AAVE really in itself means that Africans are ready to be recognized, not just by White people, but by other Africans as well. Those individuals with the insight and the desire to progress and take the necessary steps to be productive in their society are ready to use their own voices, to let others know what they are thinking and to let them know what is important to them, to let them know what they want to learn about in their schools, and to let those who are listening know what limitations they will recognize and which ones they will not accept.

I think that being a member means being active and involved, being aware of the expectations that have been set, the ceilings that have been laid and evaluating whether or not these have been done beneficially for myself as an African American, and for those other voices which long and deserve to be heard by those who do and don't have preconceived notions.

It is important for us to challenge the negative stereotypes and the negative notions of our ability that do exist now and have existed for hundreds of years. I think being a member of the AAVE means that we acknowledge our ability to be a star and shine brightly, we acknowledge our humanness, our beauty, our uniqueness and we also demand the right to not be penalized for this. Being a member of the AAVE to me, (**comma splice**) means me recognizing my personal talents, my personal light that is ready to shine, and being able to do this and express myself intelligently and equally through the knowledge that I have gained from my elders, and peers, from those who are also a part of my culture and those who I feel have taken the first strides for me, and those who I intend to follow after.

Student #2, Winter 97: pre-test essay

Surface level analysis

- 317 words in 50 minutes
- 1 comma splice

Use of AAVE syntax in student's text

The writer doesn't use any AAVE syntax patterns.

Discourse/content evaluation

The writer is responding to the prompt accepting the ideas in the Gates passage and interpreting them from a personal perspective. The writer's voice is confident and strong to begin with. The arguments and style of the post-test essay are even stronger.

To be a member of the AAVE culture and be literate, you must be aware of the social construction of race within this country, that was set up to aid the oppressor in oppressing the ethnic groups contained within the term "race." A member of the AAVE culture must be knowledgeable in the truth of our enslavement, knowledgeable in the truth of who we are as a people, where we come from, and knowledgeable of the ancestors who went before us and still guide us within our African spirits. To be a member of the AAVE culture, African Americans must realize the depth of the word literacy and its true meaning. In the following essay, I will expand on the above characteristics that I feel encompass members of the AAVE culture, and I will explain why I feel that possessing the knowledge offered by the above characteristics is necessary in order to really be literate and free.

The meaning of literacy goes beyond the basic understanding of the word. Literacy still includes being able to read, write, and critically think for oneself, but it also means being literate about one's history and the origins of one's ancestors. African Americans today must go beyond the basic "education" that is presented to us within the classrooms. We must aspire to know the truth about who we are as people. We must aspire to know the truth about where we come from, and we must aspire to know the truth about the society in which we are now living. In order for a member of the AAVE culture to share this knowledge that comes with being literate, we must be capable of intelligently speaking our opinions, our concerns, and our demands. We must possess the strength that comes with being confident about ourselves as an African American. We cannot afford to fall and stumble over our own ignorance and incapabilities. To be literate means to be scholarly and educated, and for us, as African Americans, it means we must devote the time and energy necessary for us to interact within this oppressing culture and bring forth some changes that are long past due.

Being literate means also being aware of the social conditions that affect our lives daily. We must become aware of the social construction of race in this country. We must acknowledge that we are all one race, human, but be aware that the government constructed these different racial categories to aid it in the oppression of those individuals who were not intended to be a part of American society. Even deeper still, we must accept that we were not seen as human not so long ago. We cannot deny the truth, we cannot hide the truth, and we can no longer be afraid to reveal the truth to those who are still unaware. It is critical that we do share this truth with every individual in our communities, so then we can each be dealt with and taken seriously as literate individuals. Our people have been mis-educated, right along with the White folks of this nation, about the intentions of life, liberty, and the pursuit of happiness that ring out as our national creed. African Americans have been lied to, lied on, and lied about through the propaganda that our media and television feed off of. Our schools are mis-educating our children by teaching them that their history begins with slavery, and not with Egyptian empires where we resided as kings and queens. Being a literate member of the AAVE culture means being aware of this mis-education, and having the knowledge and determination necessary to combat it and save our ancestors from any further degradation.

Student #2, Winter 97: post-test essay

Need I give you the whole shebang? This writer went on to produce an 807-word essay.

Use of AAVE syntax in student's text

As in the pre-test example, this writer uses no AAVE syntax features, but many of the discourse features of AAVE.

Content/ discourse/ evaluation

It is evident that the writer is addressing the issues of the prompt. The voice is confident. The writer is able to bring to bear knowledge gained through the course and apply it to the essay response.

Examples and discussion of Black discourse features in student texts

I would like to turn here to other writing examples. Instead of analyzing a single text or concentrating on a single student, we will look here at several samples from students' texts in order to get a feel for the Black discourse-styled texts discussing and discerning the Black language patterns employed. (See Chapter 4 notes for taxonomy used to describe Black discourse patterns.)

> By feeding into the stereotypes that America has created the African American race will never advance being ignorant, militant, and extremely violent because all that is just adding fuel to the fire. Instead we need to take that same energy and convert it into something positive and productive for the upliftment of our race. By creating wise, well researched criticism America will [have] no choice but to listen especially if the information that is being presented is reaching through to mis-educated Americans, (not only the African Americans) and is ***turning them on to the light.*** Causing positive ruckus is far more beneficial than negative ruckus and you can't go to prison for speaking the truth. That's a right we are protected under by the Constitution. ***By enlightening the darkened*** we will be threatening the "secure" establishments America has created to prolong oppression.
>
> Student #1, Winter 97

There are several Black discourse patterns that can be discerned above. One pattern above is rhythmic, dramatic evocative/imagistic language use. Notice the play above on "light." The "mis-educated Americans" are those Blacks and non-Blacks and Whites who have bought into racial stereotypes. The rhetor has turned this stereotype upside down and inside out, revealing another Black language pattern, signifying. The "darkened" or the "mis-educated" will be "en*light*ened." The quality of light has been traditionally associated with "knowledge," "goodness," and, hence White folks. Darkness has traditionally been associated with a "state of ignorance," or "evil," and consequently, Black folks. But here, the Blacks possess or will possess the qualities of knowledge and light. This is an instance of signifying, also known as semantic inversion.

> Unity consists of several movements that need to take place within the African American community. I believe first and foremost we, as a people, must deal with the disease of Black on Black crime. We must cry out to our young brothers out there who are destroying themselves, and everyone around them, by murdering one another. I remember very recently hear a quote on the radio stating that the number one killer of young, Black men today is young, Black men. When we begin to really take militant steps in an effort to stop the murder rate in our communities, then we will begin dealing with this deep seeded self-destruction and self-hate that has planted its poisons into the hearts and souls of our young adults.
>
> Student #2, Winter 97

There are several Black discourse patterns that can be identified from the above essay excerpt. This essay evinces "direct address/conversational tone," in that it assumes an immediacy with the audience. Notice the sense of audience that the writer displays. Her rhetoric is directed toward Black people. For this reason, the writer uses the pronoun "we," and the ethnolinguistic idiom "brothers," which is a lexical item for Black man. Also interesting is the rhetor/writer's incorporation of a narrative interspersion as a testimony to Black on Black crime. The most interesting Black discourse pattern here though is the use of rhythmic dramatic, evocative/imagistic language. "[T]hen we will begin dealing with this deep seeded self-destruction and self-hate that has planted its poisons into the hearts and souls of our young adults" is loaded. "Deep seeded" is itself an instance of "verbal inventiveness." The LWC standard term that this item brings to mind is "deep seated." However, the writer here creates "deep seeded" as it is more in line with the writer's meaning expressed through the metaphor of poison garden. This garden has been grown through the seeds of "self hate" and "self destruction" that have been planted in the Black communities.

> Trust and honor make up the soul of African Americans. Is that trust and honor still with us? Where did it go? During a time when we were lost in a strange land some four centuries ago the only face to bring comfort was that of another African lost in the same wilderness far from home, far from our roots. Within those last four hundred years we have struggled to gain our freedom and our African hearts. The price we paid for this American freedom was our ability to trust and the fire to come together as one. Our satisfaction with freedom in America overshadowed our dream to be Africans again. Four hundred years of losing our languages, morals, and originality has reduced us to rearrange our ways to seek the same gods that

caused Europeans to bring us to this country, such as money, cars, and a million dollar home. I say, head for the underground railroad one more time African, because you are not free if you can't love your brother.

Student #3, Winter 97

The above writer/rhetor is clearly adopting the rhetorical strategy of directing his/her rhetoric to a Black audience and is styling her/his discourse to reflect this. The discourse evidences no non-standard Black Vernacular but is yet styled in AAVE discourse. Notice the conversational tone/direct address, the use of the questions, and the admonition, "I say, head for the underground railroad one more time African, because you are not free if you can't love your brother." This sentence contains evocative-imagistic, ideographic symbologic language use in its employment of the "underground railroad" symbol. Here the underground railroad symbolizes a freedom from thinking of oneself in terms of European ideals. Further, the essay uses a common Black discourse pattern, used in some of the other essays as well, cultural values/community consciousness, which are expressions of concern for Black community.

To me this [the rhetoric of divisiveness-focus on a Black audience] sounds like a wonderful rhetorical strategy. Unfortunately, this strategy will only take us so far. I believe Blacks in this nation will not come together because there is too much jealousy and greed between our people. Our people struggle with the concept of working together and having unity. The economic situation has most of the money in the hands of White people. The only way to solve problems we have between various cultural backgrounds is to work with other Whites.

Divisive rhetoric is like a bunch of Black people knocking on the door of the White House. On the other side of the door, are a bunch of White people. The scenario becomes that you will never get in no matter how much you knock unless the White person on the other side of the door opens it. My point is that divisive rhetoric will get Blacks to the door, but not inside the door.

Student #6, Winter 97

The above and the next essay excerpts are included to show the diversity of ideologies within the Black speech/writing community. The above writer/rhetor is arguing for and employing the rhetoric of unity which in Bormann's terms is directing his/her rhetoric to a racially mixed (White, Black, multicultural) audience and is styling her/his discourse to reflect this. An interesting observation can be made here. This essay is very problematic, for the most part because of its inherent contradictory premises. The writer argued against Black unity (divisiveness rhetoric), but at the same time used an analogy with Black people

137

united. "Divisive rhetoric is like a bunch of Black people knocking on the door of the White House." In any case the essay employs a conversational tone and a familiarity with its audience.

> The diverseness rhetoric would not work for this plan of action, because the decisions needed to be made would have to be made with all Americans' in mind. I'm not saying that diverseness would not work in easing race relations, But it is not the means I would choose to fix whats been brokien for so long. Race, Race is a term a ignorant word, it has nothing to do with people it was [a] term used for seperating people, and I think this is what caused all of this trouble in the first place. Let me explain, if you use race to catagorize someone, there must be a dominant race of people. A White person made up race so who do you think thinks they're the dominant race, that's right you guessed it. Unity is the key, once White America is turned into everybody America, this place will finally be what everybody makes it out to be, a great country.
>
> Student #7, Winter 97

This writer/rhetor is arguing for the rhetoric of unity, directing his/her rhetoric to a racially mixed (White, Black, multicultural) audience. The writer seeks to deracialize the problem while at the same time showing that the problem is White domination of America. Again, here the writer employs a conversational tone as a rhetorical strategy to create a credibility and a relationship with his/her reader, hoping to persuade readers to his/her point of view.

Clearly the above excerpts from students' papers demonstrate various levels of written and critical literacy development. The rhythmic language, the imagery, the analogies appear to have the effect of heightening the level of involvement with the ideas. Field dependency is a strength that is often unexploited as an African American epistemological resource. Not all of the student writers have realized their potential, but they are certainly on their way. If we truly want to develop Black students rather than transform them into people who act, sound, and write White, we must allow Black students to develop their Black voices as an academic convention. Black and academic voices live harmoniously inside many of our great thinkers and writers, well perhaps not harmoniously. But the point is that this struggle is productive. Would you really want to read Toni Morrison or Geneva Smitherman if they didn't know how to capture the Black experience? June Jordan (1985) states,

> One main benefit following from the person-centered values of [AAVE] is that of clarity. If your idea, your sentence assumes the presence of at least two living and active people, you will make it understandable because the motivation behind every sentence is the wish to say something real to somebody real.

I believe that Black experience—music, culture, and rhetoric in all of its forms and content—provides visible, and internally persuasive, usable material for students who are learning to appropriate the university and its inquiry. Black ways of knowing, Black language, idioms, proverbs, proofs, and principles provide a way to do critical inquiry that is both intellectual and inspirational, that engages history as well as the heart. In another sense, this vernacular approach in the composition and rhetoric classroom operationalizes a politics of "keepin' it real." I opened this chapter with Mos Def, first of all because he is a gifted rapper and he is socially conscious. Secondly, if we are really going to be serious about creating new songs we do well to use the sweet wild melodies of the African American to recall W. E. B. Dubois' words. African American Vernacular English gives us more than enough notes to work with to help cultivate new voices.

In the next chapter I deal with the complexities of African American-centered classrooms. All that glitters . . .

6

Dukin' it out with "the powers that be": centering African American-centered studies and students in the traditional curriculum

> To be educated in the next century will necessarily mean encoun-
> tering the humanity of other people in both domestic and
> international cultures. This will involve much more than taking
> one or two "periphery studies" courses. It will require being
> knowledgeable of other cultures, struggles, achievements, aspira-
> tions, and ways of thinking. A truly multicultural education is not
> European Americans studying Europe or African Americans
> studying Africa and so on. The ideal is to study one's own cul-
> ture, literature, and history as well as at least two others—one
> domestic and one international. It is possible to have a university
> in which no single historic group dominates the core experience.
> Under these circumstances, the university may become a much
> more dynamic and potentially unifying institution.
>
> (Bowser 1995: xxii)

This chapter is a subjective reflection on the implementation of African American methodology into the traditional curriculum. This overview is offered to
provide insight into the problems and pleasures of overcoming "the powers that
be." I offer a little herstory behind the course so that anyone who may want to
design such a course will have an idea of the kinds of problems that may be
encountered. Nobody told me it was going to be easy. Teaching the African
American-centered rhetoric and writing course is clearly the most enjoyable
experience I've had in the university. It was also the most real to me. It allowed
me to be that teacher that I wanted and needed so desperately as a college
freshwoman, someone who could point me toward the knowledge that I felt was
relevant to my life. But now here I was and it was me against the world. The
course was marginal on two accounts. First, it was experimental. Second, theoretically and pedagogically the body of knowledge centralized in the course is
discredited knowledge. Finally, as a Black woman, I face issues of authority and
credibility because of my race and gender.

Institutional experiment

The course was experimental because though anyone could sign up for it, we wanted the courses to be overwhelmingly African American. The first time I taught the course I was a graduate student, and I had to write a proposal outlining my objectives, goals, and rationale, which had to be approved by the department head. The first flag went up upon the submission of the first draft of the proposal when I mentioned that I would focus on centering African American students in rhetoric and composition, using Afrocentric topics and instructional stimuli. The first thing that the head found problematic was that I needed to stress that ALL students could take the course. And of course, ALL students could take the course, but I wanted to attract Black students—the focus of my research. This idea is problematic for many reasons from an institutional perspective. Most universities are historically White institutions and have been made to open their doors to all citizens via Civil Rights and Affirmative Action. Theoretically, any financially and educationally qualified student can attend, but we know that many factors contribute to the fact that most students of color have not had an equal opportunity to matriculate. Even when we make it to the university, we are at higher risk of not graduating than traditional students.

If we want to change the university, we have to create access for all students with the desire to achieve. This will necessitate a change in our methodologies and philosophical understandings of what education is and its purposes. The change in demographics in our classrooms should affect the ways we teach. When we have 23 European American students and one Black one, a teacher must be careful not to make the one Black student's voice the universal position on the Black perspective. By sheer reason of numbers, classroom dynamics will be dominated by the views of the European American students. The same thing applies to the university as a whole. Without more people of color, there is no need for the university to change. What I am getting at here is that filling up university spaces with Black bodies will automatically shift the learning dynamics. And that is something I wanted to do. I wanted to clear a space where we could invert traditional dynamics. What would that feel like? I believe that land grant universities have a duty to offer such spaces.

Luckily, my major professor had juice. She advised me to stress the fact that ALL students could take the course. I did that. She worked her magic on the department head, and the course was approved. My challenge was to advertise the course in an attractive manner and get it filled up with a majority of Black bodies. It was always surprising to me how many people not of color signed up for the course or wanted to take it. This illuminates the fact that many mainstream students are hungry for different perspectives as well. I didn't have the problem of institutional resistance at my next school, after I had written my dissertation. In my new position, I was at a school that was hungry for multicultural perspectives. My new department head had juice and an understanding of the importance of my project, and he let me do my thing. I was able to teach the course for the entire two years that I worked there with no problems. The ironic part about that was that it was an institution that was itself under attack because it was an Open Admissions college within a university. Periodically, the state would try to shut down the college, complaining about the amount of money it took to keep the college open. So, the college was always under pressure to track its students' graduation rates. In general, all such institutions that offer spaces to students who have been underprepared for college work are under attack. The traditional thinking is that they should be at community colleges, rather than "the ghetto" of universities. Again, our society is stratified to the core.

At my current institution, I've not taught the course again with a predominantly African American class. In fact, every time that I've taught the course since has been with *all* European American students and an occasional Asian American. Since I am no longer collecting data, "the experiment is over" and I don't have a rationale for continuing the course with a predominantly African American student body. That would be seen as "reinstituting apartheid." If that don't beat all. When I teach at my current institution, the Freshman Honors Composition course—comprising a survey of African American rhetoric—to majority White students, I expect resistance for the first few weeks of class (sometimes I get it all semester from some of them). They sign up for the course not knowing that they're gonna get me and African American rhetoric as the subject. For those who stay and resist all semester, it's not a real course. How can it be real to them when universities are struggling with ways to meet their so-called diversity requirements? Such diversity should be centralized but this would take a total restructuring of knowledge. It can't be fixed by requiring students to take a certain amount of classes from different cultural perspectives. Most of the White students who stay find the course very valuable and although they resist, they develop critical resistance in their quest to think beyond stereotypes and traditionally one-sided curricula. Many of them have become open to different kinds of inquiry and thinking after taking the course.

The same is true of the African American students who take the course. Of course they are not coming from the same places in terms of privilege as the White students, but in the sense of biased education, they are. Most have not escaped the experience of mis-education. Mis-education here is employed in the sense in which Woodson (1933) so thoroughly explained it—a form of training designed for the uplift of the dominant society, which inadvertently works to the demise of the oppressed people in the society.

What counts and what's real?

The second source of forces working against an African American-centered course centered in the traditional university relate to what counts as reality or credible knowledge. Although African American-centered theory and practice should be viewed as a push for multicultural education, it is often seen as a push to eradicate the best that Eurocentric education has to offer, not as an expansion of the world's knowledge base. White supremacy is so deeply embedded in our society that any challenges to it are interpreted as challenges to a so-called democracy. bell hooks (1994) discusses the ways in which we were indoctrinated into the precepts of White supremacy through the idea of "civilization," and how "heroes" like Columbus with their "discoveries" provided the cultural capital on which White supremacist capitalist society is based. Any knowledge that doesn't fit within that paradigm is discredited. Thus, the course is marginalized and discredited. That fact leads to the third set of forces working against an African American-centered course in a traditionally White institution, that is the teacher of such a course is also suspect, especially if she is a Black female. With these issues as the backdrop, I would like to discuss the ways that the African American students responded to the curriculum.

Me against the world

As Cornel West (1993: 31) argues, part of the mission of the Black cultural worker is to "demystify power relations that incorporate class, patriarchal, and homophobic biases; and construct more multivalent and multidimensional responses that articulate the complexity and diversity of [B]lack practices in the modern and postmodern world." A part of the work in the course then was to try to identify why cultural practices such as African American language were identified by us as lower-class, uneducated, language of poverty, etc. etc. etc. Other important questions were: Why do many so-called middle-class African Americans distance themselves from some African American cultural practices? Why do we deny that racism exists? What is middle-class African American culture? Why is everybody in the world from Miami to Morocco trying to be ghetto fabulous and down (up) with Hip Hop culture? What does it mean to be Black and literate? These and other questions like them were the center of class discussions and written assignments. This search for Blackness should not be seen as a rejection of Whiteness. It is not. In fact, such exploration in the literacy classroom helps us to understand the depth of race and just how influential Whiteness is in African American experiences. Yes, I know that race is a social and cultural construction—how do constructions of race affect people? That was my point—to help students become critical about these experiences, to see them from vernacular perspectives. For the majority of their educational experiences, students are encouraged to analyze life through standardized and official perspectives. This flipping of the script is not done in an effort to bash Whitey, but to affirm and celebrate our humanity, our resourcefulness, and to encourage us to develop strategies for making ourselves and the world better.

The first time I taught the course was Spring 1996. Every semester the course was a little bit different, depending on the students, their vibe with one another and me. The curriculum always begins to take on a life of its own. I could not anticipate the restlessness that it would create in the classroom atmosphere. The first class did not give me a glimpse as it served basic introductory purposes (i.e. completion of questionnaires, introductions, overview of course and syllabus). But usually from the second week onward, it's like students don't know what to do with their new-found liberation. They become at once liberated and bewildered. The students become liberated because this classroom provides a space where they can wrestle with experiences and ideas that they could not in other official spaces. As AAVE culture is presented to the students, they are sometimes so excited that they begin talking in pockets among themselves. For example, a student would be responding to a probe only to be cut off and drowned out by an eruption of dissonant and unharmonic voices. This is a good thing. It's like church in a way. I'm always excited by their excitement. On the other hand, students are sometimes bewildered because indeed it is very difficult for them to explore their Blackness. The idea that Black anything is nothing is so deeply embedded into our consciousnesses that sometimes our behaviors reflect this sad truth. I don't think any Black person is above this. It is a constant struggle to throw off these deeply embedded internalized racist beliefs that sometimes cross the minds of even the best of us. To put it plainly, the closer one's complexion to White, the more access to better treatment and material goods one could expect. This White supremacist system of the color caste in nineteenth-century America is well known and alive today.

A biracial rhetorical stance

One student in particular, Student #9, Fall 96, wrote a very superficial paper about how she couldn't relate to the experiences of the Africans because she was biracial. After all of the background knowledge and context provided to counteract mis-education, I saw this as clear resistance to the curriculum. I directed her to re-read *Douglass* which discussed the creation of classism and the development of the mulatto class in the enslaved African communities and his own suspected biraciality. Further, we went back to the discussion of Black/White relations in *Gronniosaw*. We also discussed the fact that most everyone in the world is at least biracial. I wanted the student to explore her clinging to "biraciality." What are the benefits of distancing oneself from a wholly African American identity? Is there such a thing? What are the benefits of being more White? These types of questions help us to explore more deeply what it means to be Black. Is it a color? A culture? A set of practices? A political orientation? All of these? What are the practices that families participate in that identify them as African American? As biracial? In order to get historical perspectives, we looked back at excerpts from Douglass, Gronniosaw, and Harriet Jacobs. We got into discussions on passing. Why do lightskinned people pass for White? After subsequent discussions on the matter and rereading of the texts, the student managed to write a paper directly addressing the topic. I didn't force her to relinquish her claim to biracial identity. I invited her to explore it in the context of what it means to distinctly identify oneself as biracial from histor-

144

ical, political, cultural, and contemporary perspectives. This type of experience could not be captured in a traditional classroom, where the majority of students are White. We all learned things that would more often be marginalia or omitted in a traditional classroom. As pointed out by Williams (1991: 10–11)

> acknowledging, challenging, playing with these as rhetorical gestures is
> . . . necessary for any conception of justice. Such acknowledgement complicates the supposed purity of gender, race, voice, boundary; it allows us to acknowledge the utility of such categorizations for certain purposes and the necessity of their breakdown on other occasions.

An objective rhetorical stance

Even more puzzling than that situation is that of Student #23, Fall 96, who wanted to become a journalism major. Her stance was that she did not see any of the structures of the past in the current experiences of Blacks. In other words, she said she had no knowledge or experiences of oppression or institutional racism. Upon learning of this, I read Peggy McIntosh's article, "White Privilege," to the class. This article stirs up a lot of conversation. The ironic part about it is that it takes a White person's testimony about the subject to give credibility to a sentiment that the student had been exposed to by several enslavement narratives and certainly in her own life. I attributed some of her resistance to her desire to be a journalist, which stresses objectivity and neutrality. It was as if this student believed that her own opinion and what she saw tainted her own truth. Putting herself into the equation negates it. She didn't want to invoke or acknowledge any Black discourses. It seems she was straining to make her prose reflect the sentiment "only the standardized facts please!"

Her academic posture was that of the "good student." As revealed in her responses to a language/writing questionnaire that all of the students answered, most of the characteristics that she associated with good writing are formal or superficial aspects of writing. There is no mention of writing to learn or understand, idea development, personal satisfaction, creativity, or interesting use of language. I attribute another part of the student's resistance simply to the fact that this African American-centered curriculum posed an opposition to everything the student had been trained to think and write. Needless to say, this student turned in several unacceptable drafts before she achieved one that revealed some semblance of her own thought as influenced by the context provided by the curriculum.

Some students complained that the students who wrote "racist stuff about White folks" were the ones who got the best grades on their papers. In fact, two students commented in an exit questionnaire that they thought their writing was not appreciated by me because I made them "revise, revise again, and re-revise" papers that did not conform to my ideology. As I tried to demonstrate in the example of the young lady and biracial identity, the papers don't have to conform to my ideology, students' papers have to demonstrate a historical understanding of the ideologies that they set forth. Students have to demonstrate to me that they know where they are coming from. I understand why people want to cling to biraciality or why they want to dismiss critical readings of society in the name of racial harmony. But we have to be real about what we are doing and why. We can't pretend that we don't live in a racist society and that we adopt certain (non)coping strategies because of this. Every semester I stress to the students that all of us have White friends and relatives that we love and that the class is not about bashing White folks, but learning to be critical of racist practices and naming oppressions as well as affirming African American ideas and practices that we've all been taught are ignorant.

A Black rhetorical stance that I almost (dis)missed

In my attempt to heighten student awareness of exactly what AAVE language and discourse practices were, I taught them how to do discourse analysis through having them analyze rap lyrics. A part of their assignment was to bring in a recording, scrutinize the lyrics and discuss the features that they were going to write about. The first time I taught the course, I was surprised that several students brought in raps that I felt were obscene. Although many would argue that that is acceptable, many of the same artists who have explicit lyrics have other "mainstream" songs, that do not exploit the plight of Black people under the guise of "that's the way it is" and capitalism. I believe elders of the AAVE community, myself included, (although I am young), should encourage students to look to the best of what AAVE culture has to offer. I saw their uninhibitedness to bring in this kind of "art" as resistance to the study of AAVE culture as a worthwhile intellectual enterprise.

The first time I taught the course, after about the third presentation of this kind, I intervened and preached a sermon on their failure to wake up and recognize their compliance in their own oppression. This sentiment was confirmed by one of my supervising professors observing the class on that night. I believe that African Americans comply in their own oppression when we become desensitized to our plight as the struggle to overcome "the powers that be." I believe we comply in our own oppression when our cultural artifacts become commercialized into a commodity from which corporate America benefits at our expense. I only listened to rap that celebrated Black culture and good old party rap.

Despite my early rejection of listening to anything other than the likes of Heavy D (I like him because he knows how to rap to a sista), KRS One, Queen Latifah, Public Enemy and such, I learned to explore the seeming underside of Hip Hop, profanity, bitches, hos, murderation lyrics, motherfuckuhs, and blatant materialism. I realized that Hip Hop and rap are political, about nation building and consciousness raising. Rappers are redefining and achieving even when they weren't supposed to. Even more than surviving, some artists are flourishing in hostile conditions. This recognition doesn't mean that we not critique what is going on with the political economy of Black music and its orchestration by corporate America. In subsequent classes, we expanded our discussions to include what I am calling Hip Hop literacies. Hip Hop literacies include ways of knowing and acting in response to social conditions. They are an extension of African American literacies. I talked to colleagues who were already offering courses on the culture about why we liked to shake our groove thangs to "devil music" as the old folks say. I added chapters from William Eric Perkins' *Droppin Science* particularly those by Robert Farris Thompson—"Hip-hop 101," and one by Robin D. G. Kelley, "Kickin' Reality, Kickin' Ballistics: Gangsta Rap and Post-industrial Los Angeles". We also read Tricia Rose's (1994) "Fear of A Black Planet" and "Bad Sistas: Black Women Rappers and Sexual Politics in Rap Music." Farris Thompson's chapter helped us to historicize Hip Hop as a manifestation and reinterpretation of Kongo, Afro-Brazilian and Afro-Cuban musical and cultural traditions including the griot function and aesthetics as a way of knowing and resisting. Kelley's piece helped us to explore the rhetoric of gangsta rap as a response to Reaganomics. Rose's pieces helped us to understand the politics of public space—who can say what to whom where and under what conditions, the ways in which Black bodies are policed. Rose's pieces also helped us to understand the importance of aesthetics in Hip Hop culture—how aesthetics is itself a resistance strategy. Most importantly for me as a Black woman and parent, Rose's work helped us to explore the sexual politics of Hip Hop and rap, how young Black female artists are inventing lives for themselves, exploiting patriarchal language and structures. All of this helped us to look beyond the surface of vernacular-styled lyrics, their delivery and style to the negotiation of discourses by Hip Hoppers as a means of survival. I am reminded by Smitherman (2001) that Hip Hop is no more vulgar than the Blues. "African American popular culture, music especially, has always been a resistance culture, operating way outside of the norms and conventions of [W]hite mainstream society." This is not to say that we all agreed with strong language use and images of violence in the music and videos, but our explorations of the topic and the discourses operating helped the students and me to think about the utility of Hip Hop expression. In short, I had to get over the fact that students were "keepin in real" with me. I had to begin to realize that young people are working with the scraps they've been given and that they've taken stuff thrown out on the trash heaps and made a way outta no way. Many of the students and I are still saddened about materialism and misogyny. Many students wrote against these themes, but were better able to historicize, contextualize, and politicize their analyses.

Can't please everybody

Now, I know somebody is thinking right about now, "Elaine uses her authority as an African Americanist." And I am happy to say I do. I am defending myself against the accusation that I oppressed the "biracial" student and the "raceless" student. Nothing could be further from the truth. I helped them to explore their topics more fully. Every writing teacher worth her salt has a duty to help students make credible arguments, in which students must connect their positions with the already said. In a science class, if the professor assigns a paper on Newtonian physics and a student writes about how the sun revolves around the planets, he'd flunk. As a professor teaching about culture, race, writing, and literacy why should I accept an off topic generalized piece that doesn't engage the readings and discussions in the name of relinquishing my authority? I'm an African American female, there is a resistance to my presence already in the classroom. Students wonder if I'm qualified; if my subject matter is intellectual; if they are themselves qualified to be in the university. They can call me Dr E because I'm young. We can talk about Hip Hop because I'm down. But the intellectual traditions that I bring into the classroom are serious as a heart attack, and that's where the buck stops for me. People like Geneva Smitherman and on down the line back to Kate Drumgoold and my great great great great great grand ma caused me to be here. They held up the blood stained banner and passed it to me.

I became frustrated many times during the course of implementing the curriculum. The source of my frustration was not due to students' failure to learn what I wanted them to learn, when I wanted them to learn it, but due to my recognition of the many societal factors that tugged at my students' lives. I sensed a lostness in some of the students' faces, not academic lostness, but purposelessness—no sense of direction. This points to the problem of retaining Black students in institutions of higher learning. I think Baldwin *et al.*'s (1987) finding that (Bl)academic settings or Black educational experiences increase African Self Consciousness may be a link to student achievement. Black students are struggling to define themselves in a high tech, materialistic, capitalistic society. More African American-centered literacy experiences would help these students create spaces for themselves in the university and in the larger society as agents of change. For these reasons, I think it is utterly important to connect these students to literature of the enslaved African and contemporary Blacks who are struggling to achieve freedom through literacy in spite of insurmountable odds.

In fact, I think that the problems encountered in implementing an African American-centered curriculum into the university curriculum attest to the need for African American-centered perspectives in Kindergarten through university level educational institutions, to counteract the monocultural influence of traditional orientation to the making of knowledge or "the powers that be."

This work examined whether using knowledge of the language and literacy traditions of African Americans in the acquisition of academic literacy is effective among college-aged students. The goals of the research were to improve the literacy achievement of African American students by incorporating the language and literacy traditions of African Americans into their literacy education, to provide research data on the literacy achievement of African American college students, and to add to the research basis informing multicultural/African American-centered approaches to academic literacy. I believe I have done that. Shaughnessy and others were right about the fact that there is cultural conflict. Like others, Shaughnessy saw this conflict as central, but her approach to the problem was to conflate the basic and culturally different writer and focus on error. In some senses, I have done the same thing, except I haven't focused on error, but rather I developed an approach to the teaching of writing that explored how culturally different writers have historically negotiated the American dilemma. Because it is problematic to implement and standardize knowledge of the Black language and literacy tradition into the curriculum (for various political reasons), AAVE students are disproportionately assigned to basic writing classrooms (i.e. Black student with dialect "problems" or the (semi) illiterate Black student). An African American student highly conversant in AAVE culture may also be a basic writer, which may have been the case with some of the students in my work. However, my tentative conclusions point to the fact that the path of least resistance (the road that Shaughnessy took) is not necessarily the one that is in the best interest of African American students. Paying attention to the attitudes and the language practices that students bring to the classroom may lead us down the path to equality. Let's walk down this road hand in hand.

I believe the struggle to change the conditions of the African in America is best expressed in African American rhetoric. Black discourse and rhetoric helped to evolve and revolutionize the meaning of equality in this country. We cannot afford to continue to subjugate this discourse in the classroom.

Notes

1 LITERACY, LANGUAGE, COMPOSITION, RHETORIC AND (NOT) THE AFRICAN AMERICAN STUDENT

1 [A]t grade 4, White students had higher average writing scale scores than Black, Hispanic, and American Indian students. At grades 8 and 12, the average writing scale scores for Asian/Pacific Islander (PI) and White students were similar and were higher than those for Black, Hispanic, and American Indian (Amer. Ind.) students. (available online: www.nces.ed.gov/nationsresportcard/www.nces.ed.gov/nationsres-portcard/pubs/main1998/1999462.asp)

	Below basic	At or above basic	At or above proficient	Advanced
	Fourth grade			
White	10	90	29	2
Black	31	69	8	0
Hispanic	28	72	10	0
Asian/PI	7	93	36	4
Amer. Ind.	24	76	11	1
	Eighth grade			
White	10	90	29	2
Black	28	72	8	0
Hispanic	31	69	11	0
Asian/PI	0	90	35	2
Amer. Ind.	27	73	9	0
	Twelfth grade			
White	16	84	26	1
Black	36	64	8	0
Hispanic	35	65	10	0
Asian/PI	22	78	24	1
Amer. Ind.	42	58	9	0

I'm with you. I'm tired of reading information like this that comes out of the report from the Executive Summary of the National Association of Educational Progress (NAEP) 1998 Writing Report Card for the Nation and States.

2 For a fuller discussion see Richardson (in press), "Race, Class(es), Gender and Age: The Making of Knowledge about Language Attitudes" in *Language Diversity in the New Millennium* [tentative title], Villanueva, V. (ed.) Studies in Writing and Rhetoric Series, Southern Illinois University Press.

3 The CCCC Language Knowledge and Awareness Survey reports on data collected from members of NCTE and CCCC on their attitudes toward language diversity and their feelings about their training to teach from a perspective of linguistic diversity. The research report is online at ncte.org. You may also read Richardson (in press), cited above, n. 2.

2 THE LITERACIES OF AFRICAN AMERICAN-CENTERED RHETORIC AND COMPOSITION

1 For an in-depth treatment see Wilson Jeremiah Moses' historical overview of the origins of Afrocentricity, mystical as well as reasonable conceptualizations of it in *Afrotopia* (1998).

2 I use the terms Black people, people of African descent/ancestry, African, Anglo African, African American, and American African interchangeably. When I use the term Negro it is to signify that time in America's development when the descendants of enslaved Africans referred to themselves as such (though they were first referred to as such in the fifteenth century by Portuguese). I realize that people of African descent were not considered citizens until 1868, so referring to them as American Africans or African Americans before this time is officially inaccurate; however, from a vernacular perspective, the blood, sweat, and tears that Africans contributed to the construction of this nation qualifies them as citizens from the jump, even if some of them wanted to go back to Africa or wanted free spaces designated for Blacks in this country. See Smitherman, 2000: 41–56, for fuller discussion of naming in the history of American Africans. Smitherman's article discusses "the history of racial labelling from the perspective of the changing material conditions of Blacks." Also, I refer to people of European descent as Anglo, Anglo European, White, or European American depending on their nationality or cultural location.

3 See Crawford, 2001, in which chapters by Nehusi, Blackshire-Belay, and Ernie Smith are very informative on the Africologist perspective. They argue that Ebonics are new African languages.

4 Although Dalby's explanation seems pretty straightforward, scholars haven't settled the matter of whether Ebonic languages are European languages that should be categorized as members of the Indo-European language family or if they are newly created African languages that should be categorized as Niger–Kordofanian derived languages. It appears that part of the problem of definition for scholars of language is ideological and paradigmatic. For example, in the case of US Ebonics, Blackshire-Belay (1996) points to the problem that scholars use traditional racist terminology and paradigms in discussing the speech of peoples of African descent. This tradition is inadequate as these paradigms were created to justify the social and political domination and oppression of peoples of African descent and so traditional terminology must be rejected. Schools of thought on the origins and development of US Ebonics can be divided into at least three categories: Dialectologist, Creolist, and Africologist. It is important to underscore the fact that these terms are very problematic as the term dialect has a pejorative connotation and creole is derived from Eurocentric

analysis of African phenomena. Dialectologists are those linguists who study African American Vernacular English identifying the similarities that it shares with features descended from Irish–English and Scotch–Irish varieties (Copeland-Lanier, 1974). Another school of thought about the historical development of AAVE is based on the creole hypothesis. These linguists produce evidence which indicates that AAVE developed as a result of the overlay of a largely English vocabulary on Africanized grammatical/syntactical structures. They argue that a "pidgin" (a simple language system which doesn't carry the nuances and intricacies of someone's native tongue, developed by two groups of speakers who come into contact and do not share a common language) was formed along the West African coast, expanded into a creole (a language which covers a wider range of experience than a "pidgin" because speakers are native to it and expand it to meet their needs and reflect their nuances and intricate ways of thinking), survived the middle passage, and became more and more "decreolized," as people of African ancestry have been brought closer and closer to the mainstream of American society. There are different schools of creolists and dialectologists; but overall, all agree that AAVE is a mixture of English, surviving African patterns, and contemporary innovations.

5 Herskovits (1941) is the seminal work on African retentions. See also Holloway (1988), Gates (1988) and Mufwene (1993). This text contains state of the art data on African retentions in Afro American cultures, languages, and dialects. Especially insightful is Mervyn Alleyne's discussion of continuity versus creativity in Afro American cultures. He finds that "Afro American music, storytelling, language, dance, and games can . . . be analyzed in terms of inventiveness within [African influenced] tradition" (Mufwene, 1993: 179).

6 Again Gates (1988) traces the trickster figure in African American literature to Esu Elegbara, of Yoruba Culture and Ifa Divination, which symbolizes indirection, critique, and multiplicity of meaning in language use. See Smitherman (1977) which discusses the cultural background, West African ways with words, and how these along with servitude and oppression helped to develop African American English syntax, discourse, and rhetorical practices.

7 Gundaker (1998) discusses African-oriented knowledges used along with Euro-American cultural conventions to resist domination.

8 For an excellent exploration of the topic of African American literacy and religion, see Cornelius (1991).

9 For a fuller explanation of warrants see Chapter 5 "The Logical Structure of Arguments" in Ramage and Bean (1998), p. 99.

10 For a fuller discussion of signifyin' see Smitherman, 2000: 26.

11 "For African-Americans, during the late 1600s individuals and organizations began to try to teach African Americans—mostly religious organizations. This brought about literacy laws in some states like South Carolina, in 1740. Literacy is in opposition to oppression and slavery. Because African American humanity still hung in the balance, they were not full citizens and barred from literate culture. From its inception, the United States was characterized by the universal belief in White supremacy" (Anderson, 1995).

12 Around the time of Walker's text, 1830, the Convention Movement began. Black businessmen, clerics, editors, and orators met to plan ways of uplifting their race. Their strategies of advancement ran the range of moral suasion, political action, self-help, racial solidarity, economic advancement, and emigration to Africa. Though many colonizationists at one time or another favored creating an independent state in Africa, members of the Convention largely opposed emigration to Africa on the basis that their forefathers and mothers had helped to build this country and they intended to enjoy its wealth and prosperity. In 1864, in Syracuse, New York, these

Black freedom fighters instituted a National Equal Rights League with abolition and political equality as their main goals (Meier, 1964: 4–5).

13   Gates (1988) describes the Talking Book Trope of African American literature as the Ur-trope. It can be traced back to James Albert Ukawsaw Gronniosaw's (1770) *A Narrative of the Most Remarkable Particulars in the Life of James Albert Ukawsaw Gronniosaw, An African Prince, as Related by Himself.* In it, Gronniosaw describes his master's reading of the Bible on board ship and how the book seems to speak to everyone except him. Gronniosaw equates the inability of the book to speak to him to his blackness. Black here signifies Gronniosaw's inability to read or speak in Dutch and his cultural and linguistic differences in relation to the European slavers. At a stolen moment Gronniosaw puts his ear to the book to see if it will speak to him as it had done to his master and crewmen, but of course, it doesn't. He spends the next 40-plus years of his life gaining European literacy and composes his own book filled with his voice (Gronniosaw, 1770: 135–8).

14   The editors caution that interviewers of the former enslaved persons were both Black and White and that it is likely that Black interviewers were able to get perspectives unavailable to White interviewers. Thus, it is possible that Mrs Alexander's account, since it was told to a Black interviewer, may reveal more of her unveiled thoughts.

15   According to Carawan and Carawan (1963), the song "We Are Soldiers" is an adaptation of a traditional song by members of the Student Non-violent Coordinating Committee. There do not appear to be any pre-existing in-depth studies of this song.

16   Although Nat Turner was unable to leave behind a thesis on his philosophy and opinions, we do know that he wanted to free all enslaved Black persons and that he took it upon himself, as God's anointed man, to lead an insurrection. It is also speculated that he read *David Walker's Appeal.*

17   Garvey was unable to meet with Booker T. Washington as Mr Washington passed away in 1915. Yet, Garvey set his sights on strengthening the UNIA across the African Diaspora, setting up shop in Harlem and offices in major metropolitan cities. His organization was one of the largest mass movements in African American history.

18   The Talented Tenth, simply put, was Dubois' idea that there should be a Black leadership educated to instruct and lead the masses of people of African descent. (Cf. Green, 1977.)

19   Kaestle (1991) states that Black literacy increased dramatically in the late nineteenth and early twentieth centuries, from 19 per cent reporting to be literate in the 1870 Census to 43 per cent 20 years later.

20   In this section on Jane Edna Hunter and the Phillis Wheatley Association, I rely heavily on Jones (1990).

21   Although Cleveland has neighborhoods in Cleveland Heights, Shaker Heights, and near West Side areas that are racially mixed, it is still very much a city of racially and ethnically segregated neighborhoods—with large numbers of Hispanics (and smaller numbers of poor Whites) on the near West Side, Blacks populating most of the East Side (with the exception of Little Italy on the Cleveland Heights border area), and many other Whites in the suburbs.

22   Pamphlet preserved by Western Reserve Historical Society, Cleveland, Ohio.

23   Cf. pamphlet of the Working Girls' Home preserved by the Western Reserve Historical Society, Cleveland, Ohio.

24   My emphasis. See "Find Law for Legal Professionals, Amendments to the Constitution of the United States of America," available online http://caselaw.lp.findlaw.com/data/constitution/amendments.html:, accessed on July 26, 2001.

25   "Chief Justice Earl Warren Opinion of the Court in Brown v. Board of Education,

NOTES

May 17, 1954" in Martin, W. E. (1998) *Brown v. Board of Education: A Brief History with Documents*, Boston, MA: Bedford/St Martin's, p. 174.

26 In the words of Kelley (1997) "soul in the 1960s and early 1970s was also about transformation. It was almost never conceived by African Americans as an innate, genetically derived feature of Black life, for it represented a shedding of the old 'Negro' ways and an embrace of 'Black' power and pride" (p. 26).

27 I must stress American version of Hip Hop since this music and culture has been adopted and adapted globally to reflect the lived experiences of its proponents.

28 See M. Morgan (2001) which outlines major cultural and ideological concerns of Hip Hop contextualizing language use and development. Hip Hop as a part of the African American Tradition exploits conflicting views of reality and co-constructs meaning with its core audience.

3 "TO PROTECT AND SERVE"

1 This definition is identified as now archaic in the *Webster's New World College Dictionary*, third edition, New York: Simon and Schuster.

2 I have consulted various sources in my search for an understanding of African American female literacy development: ERIC, dissertation abstracts, education abstracts, MLA bibliography, archival information, and government documents. In the databases, I used the search terms "(young/adolescent) Black girls" and/or "African American (women) females" and "literacy" and/or education. It would appear that we were a group recently immigrating to the United States, from the scant results that these search terms yielded. I also examined psychological, sociological, and creative literature from which I was able to glean more material. Another point of note is that not much of the extensive quantitative research in literacy studies has focused on African American females. Generally, when gender and literacy and education are explored, females of all cultural and ethnic backgrounds are lumped together. Ethnomethodological and ethnographic studies have proven helpful. Creative literature, as well as historical and contextual data have helped me to identify African American female literacies. In literacy studies, one must be mindful of the complex interaction of sociological variables which must be considered to get a clearer perception of the dynamics involved in acquisition of literacies.

3 Metronymic is defined in the *OED* as "derived from the name of the mother or other female ancestor" (p. 1,785).

4 Indirection is a major device used in the speech act of signifying. One of the functions of signifying as defined by Smitherman (1977/1986) is to critique an idea or to correct a behavior.

4 AFRICAN AMERICAN-CENTERED RHETORIC, COMPOSITION, AND LITERACY

1 **Instrumentation**

Six instruments were used to collect data: (1) a holistic assessment scale; (2) a demographic questionnaire; (3) a language/writing attitude questionnaire; (4) an AAVE syntax scale; (5) a Black discourse scale; and (6) field notes.

Students

The subjects of this study were 52 African American freshman students who were placed into basic writing. Thirty females and 22 males participated in the study. For

154

purposes of this research students did not necessarily have to use AAVE syntax in an introductory essay to be defined as students from the vernacular background. As I have already said in Chapter 1, AAVE is being conceptualized in this work as a total discourse including syntax, discourse, and rhetorical practices, thus, a student need not employ AAVE grammar in a so-called "diagnostic" essay to be classified as a member of AAVE culture. AAVE is conceptualized on a continuum from vernacular to standard forms, with vernacular forms and standard forms influencing each other and competing on the levels of grammar and discourse. Additionally, three or four students of other ethnic/racial groups took the course, but the majority of the students in my classes identified themselves as African American. The data comes from the African American students only.

Tests

The primary data reported here focuses on syntax, discourse, and rhetorical analyses of the essays written for the course. Students wrote a total of six essays for the course—a pre- and post-essay—which were impromptu—and four essays on which students had time to work outside of class for at least two weeks. These essays have been subjected to syntax, discourse/rhetorical analyses and compared with the presence or absence of selected syntax and discourse features found in other studies of culturally different student writing. AAVE syntax was assessed by creating a typology based on features identified by linguists as qualitatively or quantitatively particular to AAVE (Labov, 1972; Smitherman, 1977; 1994; Rickford, 1980; Wolfram, 1991). It is important to note that this scale of AAVE syntax represents a synchronic representation of features, not an exhaustive description. Black discourse was assessed by measuring the frequency and distribution of such features as they occurred in students' texts. Discourse features were coded based on a modified version of Smitherman's (1994) typology. A research assistant and I independently coded essays and then met to compare and synthesize our findings. One hundred and fifty-six essays were given a discourse rating from where we assessed the total number of discourse features used, scoring them 5–10 for highly Black discourse styled essay and numbers 4–0 for more European American discourse styled essays. Features of Black discourse that occurred in the data from this study are the following (original spelling from student writing kept intact):

1.   Rhythmic, dramatic, evocative language. Use of metaphors, significations, vivid imagery. Example: "Our history through the eyes of white America after it has been cut, massacured and censored is pushed down blacks throath."
2.   Proverbs, aphorisms, biblical verses. Employment of familiar maxims or biblical verses. Example: "there is a time and place for everything."
3.   Sermonic tone reminiscent of traditional Black Church rhetoric, especially in vocabulary, imagery, metaphor. Example: "The man should once again be the leader of the household as God intended and the female . . . the helpmate."
4.   Direct address, conversational tone. These two are not necessarily the same, but often co-occur. Speaking directly to audience—also, can be a kind of call/response. Example: "Would you rather be respected as Aunt Jemima and Sambo or Queen Nzinga? As yourself or someone else?"
5.   Cultural references. Reference to cultural items/icons which usually carry symbolic meaning in the AAVE communities. Example: "There are still those Uncle Toms . . . out to get you."
6.   Ethnolinguistic idioms. Use of language which bears particular meaning in Black community. Example: "Black English is a 'Black Thang' you wouldn't understand . . . That's on the real!".

7. Verbal inventiveness, unique nomenclature. Example: "[W]e will begin dealing with this deep seeded self-destruction and self-hate."

8. Cultural values—community consciousness. Expressions of concern for the development of African Americans; concern for welfare of entire community, not just individuals. Example: "Before Blacks can come together in racial harmony they need to strengthen their own people. Trying to unite . . . will only cause more problems if we have not taken care of our own business."

9. Field dependency. Involvement with and immersion in events and situations; personalizing phenomenon; lack of distance from topics and subjects. Example: "[w]e should first try to accomplish better race matters within ourselves. We can do this by patronizing and supporting our Black community."

10. Narrative sequencing. Dramatic retelling of a story implicitly linked to topic, to make a point. Reporting of events dramatically acted out and narrated. Relating the facts and personal socio-psychological perspective on them. Example: "I have learned . . . some things that never crossed my path in thirteen years of miseducation . . . This was very important for me because I . . . felt that [my] writing was wrong and far beyond improving."

11. Tonal semantics (repetition of sounds or structures to emphasize meaning). Example: "European views are the rules," "We are victimized . . ." [structure repeated four times in subsequent sentences].

12. Signifying—use of indirection to make points. May employ oppositional logic, overstatement, understatement—and/or reliance on reader's knowledge of implicit assumption that is taken to be common knowledge (shared world view). Example: "In light of having limited means of getting first hand information we then have had to rely on books and the media to provide us with an unbiased account of information . . . we know how honest the media is."

13. Call/response (structural)—writer returns repetitiously to the prompt as a structural device—checking for constant connection with the question or text at hand. A repeated invocation of the language from the prompt, manifesting as a refrain. Example: "to be a member of the AAVE Culture and literate," "Black and literate," "Blacks being literate" (repeated four times).

14. Testifying—telling the truth through story—bearing witness to the righteousness of a condition or situation. Example: "I use [the works of Angelou and Douglass] to liberate myself from my hardships to come."

Essays were analyzed for actual occurrences of these features and given an overall rating. The typology above is based on Smitherman (1994), except where indicated. All of the examples, however, were gleaned from students' essays.

The Statistical Program for the Social Sciences (SPSS) was used for all quantitative analyses and significance testing, using crosstabs, chi-square, Pearson correlations and t-test procedures appropriately. Quantitative analyses focus on degree of usage of AAVE syntax, Black discourse, essay scores, word counts, and correlations between AAVE syntax, Black discourse, and essay scores.

Procedures

The research population of African American college students received training that involved four components: (a) instruction in academic writing/rhetorical practices including rhetorical and discursive practices of African American Vernacular English (AAVE) culture; (b) examination of African American literacy tradition and culture through exploration of values, beliefs, and history as presented in African American texts and media; (c) writing processes (pre-writing, drafting, revising, editing, etc.); and participation in: (d) writing workshops. A fundamental aspect of the course was introducing students to Black discourse patterns from an analytical point of view. Most people, African Americans notwithstanding, have a vague idea of what is considered to be Black language. In order to familiarize students with Black discourse patterns, we studied excerpts from Smitherman's (1977) *Talkin and Testifyin*, especially the section on Black modes of discourse. We also studied examples from Smitherman's typology and other articles. We analyzed rap lyrics and studied various media and texts that exemplified Black discourse styles. We also looked at Black rhetorical devices in several enslavement narratives and other literature by African Americans such as Sister Souljah's *No Disrepect*. I developed several activities and assignments, which encouraged students to experiment with these Black discourse and rhetorical patterns. The course is discussed at greater length in Chapter 5

Holistic writing assessment, demographic, and language attitudes scales

The holistic writing assessment scale consists of eight categories, with "4.0" representing a well-developed and well-written essay that successfully attempted a thorough response to the prompt, moving to various scores "3.5," "3.0," etc., representing different levels of idea development and command of the written code, and "0.0," representing a poorly written response that did not address the task. AAVE was not specifically mentioned on the scoring rubrics. There are several reasons that Black discourse was not mentioned in the rubrics. The theory behind this strategy relates to the overall hypothesis of the research, that including Black language practices in academic writing instruction heightens argumentative and negotiative skills. Further, this type of discourse negotiation helps to expand the concept of academic discourse. The demographic/informative questionnaire functioned to provide socio-cultural information. The language/writing attitude questionnaire was used to uncover the subjects' perceptions of themselves as writers and to obtain subjects' language attitudes about writing, and the course experience and was administered pre- and post-curriculum.

Rater information

For each college student in the research population, a panel of experts assessed writing samples. Each essay received two ratings using the holistic writing assessment scale. The ratings were averaged. The raters were experienced composition professionals who regularly teach college-level writing to students of color and all college students. All of the raters were active professionals in the fields of composition and language and literacy studies, and they all were members of the National Council of Teachers of English (NCTE) or Conference on College Composition and Communication (CCCC). Twenty raters participated in this study, 12 women and eight men. Two of the women were of European American descent or Caucasian. Nine of the women were African American. One woman was of Asian descent. There were four European American male raters, three African American male raters and one Latino male rater. The average level of teaching experience for the raters was 18.2 years of college-level instruction. The least experienced rater taught writing for four years. The most experienced rater taught writing for 49 years.

2 The syntactic variables were coded following the standard procedure in language variation studies of ascertaining the frequency of potential AAVE patterns to actual observed patterns. This frequency is expressed as a ratio or a percentage. In the analysis for this study, the percentage figure was used. AAVE examples of the variables found in the data from this study are provided below.

Variable "ed morpheme" Main verb past (MV + 0)	*Example from essay* She **learn** that the remedial classes were filled with Blacks
Main verb perfect (have/had + MV + 0)	Being a member of the AAVE culture and literate makes me feel like I've **accomplish** something.
Verbal adjective (V + 0)	All throughout their educational careers African American youth are made to feel **belittle** because they don't speak standard English (proper English).
Passive (be + MV + 0)	Whites are **frighten** of the educated Black male.
"s morpheme" Noun plural (N + 0 pl)	**African** who are literate have been subjected to the views of Anglo-Saxon America.
Noun possessive (N + 0 poss)	It was mainly written from a white **person** point of view.
Third person singular (V + 0)	Being Black and literate **have** many meanings.
Hypercorrection Plural noun (N pl + s)	Those who choose to write against the common views of the Anglos show these and other **peoples** exactly how things are determined.
Copula Be + noun (0 + N)	I see that being Black and literate in America _ a threat to the white man.
Subject-verb agreement past (plural subject + was)	It was taken upon the Africans of that day and age to change some of the **myths** that **was** pounded into society's head.
Perfective done/have (0 have/has/had + MV)	As we _ seen in the past.
Irregular verbs	Our people **begin** to take more action after they became literate. The whites **had took** all of the fight out of Blacks.
Pronominal apposition	In Sister Souljah, she talks about this problem.

Analyses focused on overall usage and correlations with other variables—Black discourse, essay scores, and essay length.

5 COMPOSITION IN A FIFTH KEY

1 I realize that linguistically and culturally this comparison is weak, however, from the point of view that the Maori suspect European dominant education as a tool of colonial oppression and to the extent that they see Western based educational practices as non culturally sensitive, this comparison holds. Additionally, the Maoris are blamed for underachievement and indifference and their intelligence has been implicated as a reason for underachievement. Sound familiar?

2 There are two levels of "signifying." Gates distinguishes them as Signifyin(g) and signifyin(g). Capital "S" with the optional "g" is for structural intertextuality, interjecting a vernacular view of a received standard concept and/or revising a forebear's form and content to fit a current reality. When represented by the lower case "s" with the optional "g" this could be a playful or serious personal critique. In either case, the language used is indirect but direct enough so that if the shoe fits, the hearer/reader may be aware of the admonishment or behavior corrective. See Gates (1988) for literary examples, and Smitherman (1977) for oral examples.

3 NB: three of the classes represented in this study took place in computerized classrooms therefore some of the essays were word processed and some were handwritten. In some cases it is hard to distinguish typos from spelling errors. A research assistant and I discussed each case of typo or spelling error and came to agreement.

References

Abrahams, R. (1992) *Singing the Master: The Emergence of African-American Culture in the Plantation South.* New York: Pantheon Books.

Airini, C. (1998) Dreams of Woken Souls: The Relationship between Culture and Curriculum, ERIC document ED 427916.

Alim, H. S. (2001) We Are the Streets: Street Conscious Copula Variation. Paper presented at the American Dialect Society, January 4–7, Annual Meeting, Linguistic Society of America. Washington, DC.

Ampadu, L. (in press) Modeling Orality: African American Rhetorical Practices and the Teaching of Writing. In Richardson, E. and Jackson, R. L. (eds) *African American Rhetoric(s): English Studies Perspectives*, Carbondale, IL: Southern Illinois University Press.

Anderson, J. D. (1995) Literacy and education in the African-American Experience. In Gadsden, V. L. and Wagner, D. A. (eds) *Literacy Among African-American Youth: Issues in Learning, Teaching, and Schooling.* Creskill, NJ: Hampton Press, pp. 19–37.

Anoykye, D. (1994) Oral Connections to Literacy: The Narrative, *Journal of Basic Writing,* 13(2), pp. 46–60.

Arnold, K. and Murphy, P. B. (1994) Campus and Classroom: The Experiences of Minority Students in Predominantly White Universities. In Hood, S. and Frierson, H. T. (eds) *Beyond the Dream: Meaningful Program Evaluation and Assessment to Achieve Equal Opportunity at Predominantly White Universities.* Greenwich, CT: JAI Press, pp. 17–46.

Asante, M. (1974) A Metatheory for Black Communication. Paper presented at the Annual Meeting of the New York State Speech Association, Loch Sheldrake, April 1974, ERIC document ED 099945.

—— (1991) Afrocentricity and the African-American Student: A Challenge, *The Black Collegian* Mar/Apr, 21(4), pp. 132–4.

—— (1991/92) Afrocentric Curriculum, *Educational Leadership,* 49, pp. 28–39.

—— (1998) *The Afrocentric Idea: Revised and Expanded Edition.* Philadelphia: Temple University Press.

Baker, H. (1984) *Blues, Ideology, and Afro-American Literature: A Vernacular Theory.* Chicago and London: University of Chicago Press.

Baker, T. L. and Baker, J. P. (1996) *The WPA Oklahoma Slave Narratives.* Norman and London: University of Oklahoma Press.

Baldwin, J. (1987) Assessment of African Self-consciousness among Black Students from Two College Environments, *Journal of Black Psychology,* February 13(2), pp. 27–41.

—— and Hopkins, R. (1990) African-American and European-American Cultural Differences as Assessed by the Worldviews Paradigm: An Empirical Analysis, *The Western Journal of Black Studies*, 14(1), pp. 38–52.

Balester, V. M. (1993) *Cultural Divide: A Study of African-American College-level Writers*. Portsmouth, NH: Boynton/Cook.

Ball, A. (1992) Cultural Preference and the Expository Writing of African-American Adolescents, *Written Communication*, 9(4), pp. 501–32.

—— and Lardner, T. (1997) Dispositions toward Language: Teacher Constructs of Knowledge and the Ann Arbor Black English Case, *Journal of the Conference on College Composition and Communication*, 48(4), pp. 469–85.

Baratz, J. and Shuy, R. (eds) (1969) *Teaching Black Children to Read*. Washington: Center for Applied Linguistics.

Baugh, J. (1983) *Black Street Speech: Its History, Structure and Survival*. Austin: University of Texas Press.

—— (1999) *Out of the Mouths of Slaves: African-American Language and Educational Malpractice*. Austin: University of Texas Press.

Baxter, M. and Reed, C. (1973) *Teachers Manual for Teaching Standard English Writing to Speakers Showing Black English Influences in Their Writing*. Brooklyn, NY: Language Curriculum Research Group, Department of Educational Services, Brooklyn College.

Baydar, N., Brooks-Gunn, J. and Furstenberg, F. (1994) Early Warning Signs of Functional Illiteracy: Predictors in Childhood and Adolescence, occasional paper OP 94–01, ERIC document ED 372186. Reprinted from *Child Development* (1993) 64(3), pp. 815–29.

Berlin, I. (1998) *Many Thousands Gone: The First Two Centuries of Slavery in North America*. Cambridge, MA, and London, England, Belknap Press of Harvard University Press.

Berlin, J. (1987) *Rhetoric and Reality: Writing Instruction in American Colleges, 1900–1985*. Carbondale, IL: Southern Illinois University Press.

Berlin, J. (1990) Writing Instruction in School and College English, 1890–1985. In Murphy, J. J. (1990) (ed.) *A Short History of Writing Instruction from Ancient Greece to Twentieth-Century America*. Davis, CA: Hermagoras Press, pp. 183–220.

—— (1996) *Rhetorics, Poetics, and Cultures: Refiguring College English Studies*. Urbana, IL: National Council of Teachers of English.

Bizzell, P. (1982) Cognition, Convention, and Certainty: What We Need to Know about Writing, *Pre/Text*, Fall 3(3), pp. 213–43.

—— (2000) Basic Writing and the Issue of Correctness; or, What to Do with "Mixed" Forms of Academic Discourse, *Journal of Basic Writing*, 15(1), pp. 4–12.

Blackshire-Belay, C. A. (1996) The Location of Ebonics within the Framework of the Africological Paradigm, *Journal of Black Studies*, 27, pp. 5–23.

—— (2001) Linguistic Dimensions of Global Africa: Ebonics as International Languages of African Peoples. In Crawford, C. (ed.) *Ebonics and Language Education of African Ancestry Students*. New York and London: Sankofa World Publishers, pp. 164–90.

Bormann, E. G. (ed.) (1971) *Forerunners of Black Power: The Rhetoric of Abolition*. Englewood Cliffs, NJ: Prentice-Hall.

Bowser, B. P. (1995) *Toward the Multicultural University*. Westport, CT: Praeger.

Boykin, A. W. (1984) Reading Achievement and the Social-Cultural Frame of Reference of Afro-American Children, *Journal of Negro Education*, (53)4, pp. 464–73.

—— and Allen, Brenda (1992) African-American Children and the Educational Process: Alleviating Cultural Discontinuity through Prescriptive Pedagogy, *School Psychology Review*, 21(4), pp. 586–96.

Brooks, G. (1993) *Maud Martha*. Chicago, IL: Third World Press.

Camitta, M. (1993) Vernacular Writing: Varieties of Literacy among Philadelphia High School Students. In B. V. Street (ed.) *Cambridge Studies in Oral and Literate Culture: Cross-Cultural Approaches to Literacy*. Cambridge, UK: Cambridge University Press.

Campbell, K. (1993) The Rhetoric of Black English Vernacular: A Study of the Oral and Written Discourse Practices of African-American Male College Students, unpublished doctoral dissertation, Ohio State University, Columbus, Ohio.

Canagarajah, A. S. (1997) Safe Houses in the Contact Zone: Coping Strategies of African-American Students in the Academy, *Journal of the Conference on College Composition and Communication*, 48(2), pp. 173–96.

—— (1990) Negotiating Competing Discourses and Identities: A Sociolinguistic Analysis of Challenges in Academic Writing for Minority Students, unpublished doctoral dissertation, University of Texas at Austin.

Carawan, G. and Carawan, C. (eds) (1963) *We Shall Overcome: Songs of the Southern Freedom Movement*. New York: Oak Publications.

Cazden, C. (1992) *Whole Language Plus: Essays on Literacy in the United States and New Zealand*. New York and London: Teachers College Press.

Chaplin, M. (1987) An Analysis of Writing Features Found in the Essays of Students in the National Assessment of Educational Progress and the New Jersey High School Proficiency Test, unpublished manuscript, Rutgers University, Department of English, Camden.

Chapman-Thompson, I. (1994) Dissin' the Dialectic on Discourse Surface Differences, *Composition Chronicle*, 7(7), November 4–7.

Chude-Sokei, L. (1997) Dread Discourse and Jamaican Sound Systems. In Adjaye, J. K. and Andrews, A. R. (eds) *Language, Rhythm and Sound: Black Popular Cultures into the Twenty-First Century*. Pittsburgh, PA: University of Pittsburgh Press, pp. 185–202.

Coleman, C. (1997) Our Students Write with Accents—Oral Paradigms for ESD Students' *College Composition and Communication*, 48(4), December, pp. 486–500.

Collins-Eaglin, J. and Karabenick, S. A. (1993) Devaluing the Academic Success of African-American Students: On "Acting White" and "Selling Out." Paper presented at the Annual Meeting of the American Educational Research Association, Atlanta, GA, April 12–16, 1993, ERIC document ED 362 587.

Cooper, A. J. (1892) *A Voice from the South*. With an Introduction by Mary Helen Washington (1988). The Schomburg Library of Nineteenth-Century Black Women Writers. New York: Oxford University Press.

Cooper, C. (1995) *Noises in the Blood: Orality, Gender, and the "Vulgar" Body of Jamaican Popular Culture*. Durham, NC: Duke University Press.

Copeland-Lanier, D. (1974) Black Dialect: Selected Studies since 1865, unpublished doctoral dissertation, Commerce, TX: East Texas State University.

Cornelius, J. D. (1991) *"When I Can Read My Title Clear": Literacy, Slavery, and Religion in the Antebellum South*. Columbia, SC: University of South Carolina Press.

Crawford, C. (2001) (ed.) *Ebonics and Language Education of African Ancestry Students*. New York and London: Sankofa World Publishers.

Crowley, S. (1990) *The Methodical Memory: Invention in Current-Traditional Rhetoric*. Carbondale, IL: Southern Illinois University Press.

Cummings, M. (1977) Historical Setting for Booker T. Washington and the Rhetoric of Compromise, 1895, *Journal of Black Studies*, 8(1), pp. 75–82.

Dalby, David (1970) Black through White: Patterns of Communication (First Annual Hans Wolff Memorial Lecture). Bloomington, IN: African Studies Program.

Davis, A. (1998) *The Angela Y. Davis Reader*, Jones, J. (ed.). Malden, MA, and Oxford, UK: Blackwell Publishers.

Debose, C. (1992) Codeswitching: Black English and Standard English in the African-American Linguistic Repertoire, *Journal of Multilingual and Multicultural Development*, 13(1 and 2), pp. 157–67.

—— (2001) The Status of Variety X in the African-American Linguistic Repertoire. Paper given at the New Ways of Analyzing Variation in English (NWAVE) Conference, October, 2001.

Def, M. (1999) "Mathematics," *Black On Both Sides*. Rawkus Records, manufactured and distributed by Priority Records.

Delpit, Lisa (1986) Skills and Other Dilemmas of a Progressive Black Educator. *Harvard Educational Review*, 56, pp. 379–85.

—— (1988) The Silenced Dialogue: Power and Pedagogy in Educating Other People's Children, *Harvard Educational Review*, 58, pp. 280–98.

Douglas, W. (1976) Rhetoric for the Meritocracy: The Creation of Composition at Harvard. In Ohmann, R. M. (ed.) *English in America: A Radical View of the Profession*, New York: Oxford University Press, pp. 97–132.

Douglass, F. (1845) *Narrative of the Life of Frederick Douglass: Written By Himself*. In Gates, H. L. (ed.) (1987) *The Classic Slave Narratives*. New York: Penguin.

—— (1852) Fourth of July Oration. In Hill, R. L. (ed.) (1964) *The Rhetoric of Racial Revolt*. Denver, CO: Golden Bell Press.

Drimmer, M. (1987) Review of Black Politicians and Reconstruction in Georgia, *Journal of Negro History*, 69(2), pp. 90–4.

Drumgoold, K. (1898) *A Slave Girl's Story*. In *Six Women's Slave Narratives*, with an introduction by Wm. L. Andrews. New York: Oxford University Press.

DuBois, W. E. B. (1903/1997) Of Our Spiritual Strivings. In Blight, D. and Gooding, W. (eds) *The Souls of Black Folk*. Boston, MA: Bedford Books, pp. 37–44.

—— (1935/1962) *Black Reconstruction in America: An Essay toward a History of the Part which Black Folk Played in the Attempt to Reconstruct Democracy in America, 1860–1880*. New York: Russell and Russell.

—— (1973) *The Education of Black People: Ten Critiques*, Herbert Aptheker (ed.). Amherst: University of Massachusetts.

Engs, R. F. (1987) Historical Perspectives on the Problem of Black Literacy, *Educational Horizons*, 66(1), pp. 13–17.

Equiano, O. (1789) *The Interesting Narrative of the Life of Olaudah Equiano, or Gustavus Vassa, the African: Written by Himself*. In Gates, H. L. (ed.) (1987), *The Classic Slave Narratives*. New York: Penguin.

Evans, H. (1997) An Afrocentric Multicultural Writing Project. In Severino, C., Guerra, J., and Butler, J. (eds) *Writing in Multicultural Settings*. New York: MLA, pp. 273–86.

Farr, M. and Daniels, H. (1986) *Language Diversity and Writing Instruction*. New York and Urbana, IL: ERIC Clearinghouse on Urban Education Institute for Urban and Minority Education and NCTE.

Find Law for Legal Professionals, "Amendments to the Constitution of the United States of America," available online, http://caselaw.lp.findlaw.com/data/constitution/amendments.html; accessed on July 26, 2001.

Fine, M. (1995) Silencing and Literacy. In Gadsden, Vivian and Wagner, Daniel A. (eds)

163

Literacy among African-American Youth: Issues in Learning, Teaching, and Schooling. Creskill, NJ: Hampton Press, pp. 201–22.

Ford, D. Y. (1992) The American Achievement Ideology and Achievement Differentials among Preadolescent Gifted and Nongifted African-American Males and Females, *Journal of Negro Education*, 61(1), pp. 45–64.

—— (1996) Gender Issues in Underachievement and Educational Attainment. In *Reversing Underachievement among Gifted Black Students: Promising Practices and Programs.* New York: Teachers College Press.

Fordham, S. (1993) "Those Loud Black Girls": (Black) Women, Silence, and Gender "Passing" in the Academy. *Anthropology and Education Quarterly*, 24(1), pp. 3–32..

—— (1996) *Blacked Out: Dilemmas of Race, Identity, and Success at Capital High.* Chicago and London: University of Chicago Press.

—— (1999) Dissin' "the Standard": Ebonics as Guerilla Warfare at Capital High, *Anthropology and Education Quarterly*, 30(3), pp. 272–93.

—— and Ogbu, J. U. (1986) Black Students' School Success: Coping with "The Burden of 'Acting White,'" *Urban Review*, 18(3), pp. 176–206.

Foster, M. (1992) Sociolinguistics and the African-American Community: Implications for Literacy, *Theory into Practice*, 31(4), pp. 303–11.

Fox, T. (1990) Basic Writing as Cultural Conflict, *Journal of Education*, 172(1), pp. 65–83.

—— (1992) Repositioning the Profession: Teaching Writing to African-American Students, *Journal of Advanced Composition*, 12(2), pp. 291–301.

—— (1999) *Defending Access: A Critique of Standards in Higher Education.* Portsmouth, NH: Boynton/Cook Heinemann.

Franklin, J. H. (1957/1994) "Legal" Disfranchisement of the Negro. In Nieman, D. G. (ed.) (1994), *African-Americans and Southern Politics: From Redemption to Disfranchisement.* New York and London: Garland Publishing, pp. 119–26.

Freire, P. (1990) *Pedagogy of the Oppressed.* New York: Continuum.

—— (1994) Our Uncommon Culture. In Macedo, D. (1994) *Literacies of Power: What Americans are not Allowed to Know.* Boulder, CO: Westview Press, p. 102.

Freire, P. and Macedo, D. (1987) *Literacy: Reading the Word and the World.* Foreword by Ann E. Berthoff; Introduction by Henry A. Giroux, South Hadley, MA: Bergin and Garvey Publishers.

Gaines, E. (1971) *The Autobiography of Miss Jane Pittman.* New York: Bantam Books.

Garvey, M. (1986) *Message to the People: The Course of African Philosophy*, Martin, Tony (ed.), Foreword by Hon. Charles L. James. The New Marcus Garvey Library, No. 7. Dover, MA: The Majority Press.

—— (1987) Dialogues from the Black Man. In Hill, R. and Bair, B. (eds) *Marcus Garvey Life and Lessons: A Centennial Companion to the Marcus Garvey and Universal Negro Improvement Association Papers.* Los Angeles and London: University of California Press.

Gates, H. L., Jr (1986) Talkin' that Talk. In Gates, H. L. (ed.) *Race, Writing and Difference.* The University of Chicago Press.

—— (1988) *The Signifyin(g) Monkey: A Theory of African-American Literary Criticism.* Cambridge, MA: Harvard University Press.

Gee, J. P. (1996) *Social Linguistics and Literacies: Ideology in Discourses.* London, UK, and Bristol, PA: Taylor and Francis.

—— (1998) What Is Literacy? In Zamel, V. and Spack, R. (eds) *Negotiating Academic Literacies: Teaching and Learning across Languages and Cultures.* Mahwah, NJ: Lawrence Erlbaum Associates.

Gibbs, J. Taylor *et al.* (1988) *Young, Black, and Male in America: An Endangered Species*. Dover, MA: Auburn House Publishing.

Gilmore, P. (1983) Spelling "Mississippi": Recontextualizing a Literacy-related Speech Event, *Anthropology and Education Quarterly*, 14, pp. 235–55.

—— (1991) "Gimme Room": School Resistance, Attitude, and Access to Literacy. In Mitchell, C. and Weiler, K. (eds) *Rewriting Literacy: Culture and the Discourse of the Other*. New York: Bergin and Garvey.

Gilyard, K. (1996) *Let's Flip the Script: An African-American Discourse on Language, Literature, and Learning*. Detroit: Wayne State University Press.

—— (1999a) African-American Contributions to Composition Studies, *CCC*, 50(4) (June), pp. 645–61.

—— (1999b) Kinship and Theory, *American Literary History*, 11(1), pp. 188–95.

—— (2000) Literacy, Identity, Imagination, Flight, *CCC*, 52(2) (December), pp. 260–72.

Giroux, H. (1991) Introduction: Literacy, Difference, and the Politics of Border Crossing. In Mitchell, C. and Weiler, K. (eds) *Rewriting Literacy*. New York: Bergin and Garvey.

Gomez, J. (1993) Black Women Heroes: Here's the Reality, Where's the Fiction? In Castenell, L. A. Jr and Pinar, W. (eds) *Understanding Curriculum as Racial Text: Representations of Identity and Difference in Education*. Albany: State University of New York Press, pp. 148ff.

Grant, L. (1984) Black Females' "Place" in Desegregated Classrooms, *Sociology of Education*, 57(2), pp. 98–111.

Green, D. S. (1977) W. E. B. DuBois' Talented Tenth: A Strategy for Racial Advancement, *Journal of Negro Education* 46(3), pp. 358–66.

Gronniosaw, J. A. (1774) *A Narrative of the Most Remarkable Particulars in the Life of James Albert Ukawsaw Gronniosaw, An African Prince, Written by Himself*. Newport, RI, and Bath, England: reprinted and sold by S. Southwick, in Queen Street.

Gundaker, G. (1998) *Signs of Diaspora/Diaspora of Signs: Literacies, Creolization, and Vernacular Practice in African-America*. New York: Oxford University Press.

Haley, A. and X, Malcolm (1964) *The Autobiography of Malcolm X as Told to Alex Haley*. New York: Ballantine Books.

Hanley, M. S. (1995) Children of the Drum: Equity Pedagogy, Knowledge Construction, and African-American Student Learning through Drama. Paper presented at the Annual Meeting of the American Educational Research Association, New York.

Harding, V. G. (1987) Wrestling toward the Dawn: The Afro-American Movement and the Changing Constitution, *Journal of American History*, 74(3), pp. 718–39.

—— (1990) *Hope and History: Why We Must Share the Story of the Movement*. Maryknoll, NY: Orbis Books, third printing, July 1991.

Harrison, D. D. (1988) *Black Pearls: Blues Queens of the 1920s*. New Brunswick, NJ: Rutgers University Press.

Harvey, G. (1994) Presence in the Essay, *College English*, 56(6), pp. 642–54.

Heath, S. B. (1983) *Ways with Words: Language, Life and Work in Communities and Classrooms*. Cambridge, UK: Cambridge University Press.

Hemara, W. (2000) Maori Pedagogies: A View from the Literature, ERIC document ED 448892.

Herskovits, M. (1941) *Myth of the Negro Past*. New York: Harper and Brothers.

Hill, L. (1998) *The Miseducation of Lauryn Hill*. Ruffhouse/Columbia.

Hill, P. (ed.) (1998) *Call and Response: The Riverside Anthology of the African-American Literary Tradition*. Boston, MA: Houghton Mifflin.

Hill, R. L. (1964) *The Rhetoric of Racial Revolt*. Denver, CO: Golden Bell Press.

Hill Collins, P. (1991) *Black Feminist Thought: Knowledge, Consciousness, and the Politics of Empowerment*. New York and London: Routledge.

Holloway, J. (ed.) (1990) *Africanisms in American Culture*. Bloomington: Indiana University Press.

Holtzclaw, W. H. (1970) *The Black Man's Burden*. New York: Negro Universities Press.

hooks, b. (1994) *Teaching to Transgress: Education as the Practice of Freedom*. New York: Routledge.

Hoover, M. (1982) A Culturally Appropriate Approach to Teaching Basic (and Other) Critical Communication Skills to Black College Students, *Negro Educational Review*, 33(1), pp. 4–27.

Horner, B. (1994). Mapping Errors and Expectations for Basic Writing: From the "Frontier Field" to the "Border Country," *English Education*, 16, pp. 29–51.

Howard-Pitney, D. (1990) *The Afro-American Jeremiads: Appeals for Justice in America*. Philadelphia, PA: Temple University Press.

Hubbard, L. (1997) A Gendered Look at the Academic Achievement of Low-income African-American High School Students: Strategies of Success. Paper presented at the Annual Meeting of the American Educational Research Association, March, ERIC document ED 414 287.

Hudley, C. A. (1992) Using Role Models to Improve the Reading Attitudes of Ethnic Minority High School Girls, *Journal of Reading*, 36(3), pp. 182–8.

Hurston, Z. N. (1935) *Mules and Men*. In Gates, H. and Nellie, M. (eds) (1997) *The Norton Anthology of African-American Literature*. New York: W. W. Norton and Company, pp. 1,032–41.

Hymes, D. (1968) The Ethnography of Speaking. In Fishman, J. A. (ed.) *Readings in the Sociology of Language*. Paris/The Hague: Mouton.

Ivanic, R. (1998) *Writing and Identity: The Discourse Construction of Identity in Academic Writing*. Philadelphia, PA: John Benjamins.

Jacobs, H. (1861) *Incidents in the Life of a Slave Girl*. In Gates, H. L. (ed.) (1987) *The Classic Slave Narratives*. New York: Mentor/Penguin Books.

Johnson, G. D. (1929) *Safe*. Federal Theater Project Collection at George Mason University.

Jones, A. L. (1990) *Jane Edna Hunter: A Case Study in Black Leadership, 1910–1950*. Brooklyn, NY: Carlson Publishing.

Jordan, J. (1985) Nobody Mean More to Me than You and the Future Life of Willie Jordan. In *On Call: Political Essays*. Boston, MA: South End Press, pp. 123–40.

Kaestle, C. (1991) *Literacy in the United States: Readers and Reading since 1880*. New Haven, CT: Yale University Press.

Kelley, R. D. G. (1997) *Yo' Mama's Disfunktional!: Fighting the Culture Wars in Urban America*. Boston, MA: Beacon Press.

King, M. L. K. Jr (1968) The Other America, speech given to Local 1199, March 10, 1968, National Union of Hospital and Nursing Home Employees. New York. Foner, M. (ed.) (audio tape).

Knoblauch, C. H. (1990) Literacy and the Politics of Education. In Lunsford, A., Moglen, H., and Slevin, J. (eds) *The Right to Literacy*. New York: MLA.

Knowles-Borishade, A. F. (1991) Paradigm for Classical African Orature: Instrument for a Scientific Revolution, *Journal of Black Studies*, 21(4), pp. 488–500.

Kochman, T. (1981) *Black and White Styles in Conflict*. Chicago: University of Chicago Press.

KRS One (1999) Keynote speech, Hip Hop conference, Cleveland, Ohio, at Cleveland State University, September 12, 1999.

Labov, William. (1972) *Language in the Inner City: Studies in the Black English Vernacular.* Philadelphia, PA: University of Pennsylvania Press.

—— (1985) *The Increasing Divergence of Black and White Vernaculars.* National Science Foundation Research Project, University of Pennsylvania.

—— and Baker, B. Final Report on African-American Literacy and Cultural Project: Linguistic Component, available online at http://www.ling.upenn.edu/~labov/home.html

Ladson-Billings, G. (1994) *The Dream Keepers: Successful Teachers of African-American Children.* San Francisco: Jossey-Bass Publishers.

—— (1995) Toward a Theory of Culturally Relevant Pedagogy, *American Educational Research Journal*, 32(3), pp. 465–91.

Lee, C. D. (1993) *Signifying as a Scaffold to Literacy Interpretation: The Pedagogical Implications of an African-American Discourse Genre.* Urbana, IL: NCTE.

Levernier, J. (1993) Style as Protest in the Poetry of Phillis Wheatley, *Style*, 27(2), pp. 172–93.

Levine, L. W. (1977) *Black Culture and Black Consciousness: Afro-American Folkthought from Slavery to Freedom.* Oxford; New York: Oxford University Press.

Lewis., S. A. (1981) Practical Aspects of Teaching Composition to Biadialectal Students: The Nairobi Method. In Whiteman, M. F. (ed.) *Writing: The Nature, Development, and Teaching of Written Communication*, vol. 1. Hillsdale, NJ: Lawrence Erlbaum Associates.

Locke, A. (ed.) (1968) *The New Negro.* New York, Atheneum.

Logan, S. W. (1999) *"We Are Coming": The Persuasive Discourse of Nineteenth-Century Black Women.* Carbondale and Edwardsville: Southern Illinois University Press.

Macedo, D. P. (1994) *Literacies of Power: What Americans Are Not Allowed to Know.* Boulder, CO: Westview Press.

MacIntosh, P. (1992) White Privilege and Male Privilege: A Personal Account of Coming to See Correspondences through Work in Women's Studies, Wellesley College Center for Research on Women. Working Paper Series 189. Reprinted in Andersen, M. and Collins, P. (eds) *Race, Class, and Gender: An Anthology.* Belmont, CA: Wadworth.

Mahiri, J. (1998) *Shooting for Excellence: African-American and Youth Culture in New Century Schools.* Urbana and New York: NCTE and Teachers College Press.

Major, C. (1994) *Juba to Jive: A Dictionary of African-American Slang.* New York: Penguin. First published in 1970 as the *Dictionary of Afro-American Slang*, International Publishers.

Majors, R. and Billson, J. (1992) *Cool Pose: The Dilemmas of Black Manhood in America.* New York: Touchstone.

Marshall, P. (1997) The Making of a Writer: From Poets in the Kitchen, *The Norton Anthology of African-American Literature.* Henry L. Gates Jr and Nellie McKay (eds). New York and London: W. W. Norton, pp. 2,072–9.

Martin-Jones, M. and Jones, K. (2000) *Multilingual Literacies: Reading and Writing Different Worlds.* Philadelphia, PA, and Amsterdam, The Netherlands: John Benjamins.

McNenny, G. and Fitzgerald, S. (2001) (eds) *Mainstreaming Basic Writers: Politics and Pedagogies of Access.* Mahwah: Lawrence Erlbaum Associates.

Meier, A. (1964) *Negro Thought in America, 1880–1915: Racial Ideologies in the Age of Booker T. Washington.* Ann Arbor, MI: University of Michigan Press.

Mejia, J. (2001) Community and Mexican American Students of Composition: Papeles de Honor. Paper given at Pennsylvania State University.

Mitchell-Kernan, C. (1971) *Language Behavior in a Black Urban Community*. Berkeley, CA: University of California Berkeley, Language Behavior Research Laboratory.

Moody, J. (2001) Enslaved Women as Autobiographical Narrators: The Case of Louisa Picquet, talk given at the Ethnic Rhetorics Conference, Pennsylvania State University, July.

Morgan, J. (2000) *When Chickenheads Come Home to Roost: A Hip Hop Feminist Breaks It Down*. New York: Touchstone.

Morgan, M. (1989) From Down South to Up South: The Language Behavior of Three Generations of Black Women Residing in Chicago (Illinois), unpublished dissertation, University of Pennsylvania.

—— (1993) The Africanness of Counterlanguage among African-Americans. In Mufwene, S. and Condon, N. (eds) *Afro-American Language Varieties*. Athens: University of Georgia Press.

—— (1999) No Woman, No Cry: Claiming African-American Women's Place. In Bucholz, M., Liang, A. C., and Sutton, L. A. (eds) *Reinventing Identities: The Gendered Self in Discourse*. New York and Oxford: Oxford University Press.

—— (2001) "Nuthin' But A G Thang": Grammar and Language Ideology in Hip Hop Identity. In Lanehart, S. (ed.) *Sociocultural and Historical Contexts of African-American English*. Philadelphia and London: John Benjamins Publishing Company, pp. 187–209.

Morrison, T. (1984) Rootedness: The Ancestor as Foundation, an interview with Mari Evans. In Evans, M. (ed.) *Black Women Writers 1950–1980: A Critical Evaluation*. Garden City, NY: Anchor Press/Doubleday, pp. 339–45.

Morrison, T. (1987) *Beloved: A Novel*, first edition, New York: Knopf/Random House.

Moses, W. J. (1998) *Afrotopia: The Roots of African-American Popular History*. Cambridge, UK: Cambridge University Press.

Moss, B. (1994) *Literacy across Communities*. Cresskill, NJ: Hampton Press.

Mufwene, S. (ed.) (1993) *Africanisms in Afro-American Language Varieties*. With assistance from Nancy Condon. Athens: University of Georgia Press.

National Assessment of Educational Progress (NAEP) 1998 Writing: Report Card for the Nation and the States. Washington, DC: US Department of Education, National Center for Education Statistics.

Nehusi, K. (2001) From Medew Netjer to Ebonics. In Crawford, C. (ed.) *Ebonics and Language Education of African Ancestry Students*. New York and London: Sankofa World Publishers, pp. 56–122.

Nieman, D. G. (ed.) (1994) Legal Disfranchisement of the Negro. In *African-Americans and Southern Politics: from Redemption to Disfranchisement*. New York and London: Garland.

Noonan-Wagner, D. A. (1981) Possible Effects of Cultural Differences on the Rhetoric of Black Basic Skills Writers, unpublished master's thesis, Houston, TX: University of Houston.

Ogbu, J. (1992) Understanding Cultural Diversity and Learning, *Educational Researcher*, 21(8) November 24, pp. 5–14.

—— and Simons, H. (1994) Final Report, Cultural Models of School Achievement: A Quantitative Test of Ogbu's Theory. Cultural Models of Literacy: A Comparative Study, Project 12, ERIC document ED 376515.

Orban, K. (1993) Dominant and Submerged Discourses in the Life of Olaudah Equiano (or Gustavus Vassa?), *African American Review*, 27(4), Winter 1993, pp. 655–64.

Perkins, W. (ed.) (1996) *Droppin' Science: Critical Essays on Rap Music and Hip Hop Culture*. Philadelphia, PA: Temple University Press.

Perrow, E. C. (1915) Shuck Corn, *The Journal of American Folk-lore*, 28, p. 139. Lancaster, PA and New York: American Folklore Society.

Pough, G. [forthcoming] Rhetoric that Should Have Moved the People: Rethinking the Black Panther Party. In Richardson, E. and Jackson, R. (eds) *African-American Rhetoric(s): English Studies Perspectives*, Southern Illinois Press, Carbondale, IL.

Prendergast, C. (1998) Race: The Absent Presence in Composition Studies, *Journal of College Composition and Communication*, 50(1), pp. 36–53.

Ramage, J. and Bean, J. (1998) *Writing Arguments*. Needham Heights, MA: Allyn and Bacon.

Raussert, W. (2000) *Negotiating Temporal Differences: Blues, Jazz, and Narrativity in African-American Culture*. Heidelberg, Germany: Universitatsverlag C. Winter.

Redd, T. (1993) An Afrocentric Curriculum in a Composition Classroom: Motivating Students to Read, Write, and Think. Paper presented at the Annual Meeting of the Conference on College Composition and Communication (44th, San Diego, CA, March 31–April 3), ERIC document ED 362898.

—— (1995) Untapped Resources: "Styling" in Black Students' Writing for Black Audiences. In Rubin, D. (ed.) *Composing Social Identity in Written Language*. Hillsdale, NJ: L. Erlbaum, pp. 221–40.

Reed, C. (1973) Adapting TESL Approaches to the Teaching of Written Standard English as a Second Dialect to Speakers of American Black English Vernacular, *TESOL Quarterly*, 7(3), pp. 289–307.

—— (1996) Personal communication, March 11.

Rickford, J. (1980) Variation in a Creole Continuum: Quantitative and Implicational Approaches, dissertation. University of Pennsylvania, 1979, Ann Arbor, MI: University Microfilm.

—— (1998) Using the Vernacular to Teach the Standard. In Rickford, J. *African American Vernacular English: Features, Evolution, Educational Implications*. Malden, MA, and Oxford, UK: Blackwell Publishers.

—— and Rickford, A. (1995) Dialect Readers Revisited, *Linguistics and Education*, 7(2), pp. 107–28.

—— and Rickford, R. (2000) *Spoken Soul: The Story of Black English*. New York: John Wiley and Sons.

Roberts, J. W. (1989) *From Trickster to Badman: The Black Folk Hero in Slavery and Freedom*. Philadelphia, PA: University of Pennsylvania Press.

Robertson, C. (1996) Africa into the Americas?: Slavery and Women, the Family, and the Gender Division of Labor. In Hine, D. C. and Gaspar, B. D. (eds) *Black Women and Slavery in the Americas: More than Chattel*. Bloomington and Indianapolis, IN: Indiana University Press, pp. 3–40.

Rose, M. (1990) *Lives on the Boundary: A Moving Account of the Struggles and Achievements of America's Educational Underclass*. New York: Free Press, 1989, New York: Penguin.

Rose, T. (1991) "Fear of a Black Planet": Rap Music and Black Cultural Politics of the 1990s, *Journal of Negro Education*, 60(3), pp. 276–90.

—— (1994a) A Style Nobody Can Deal With: Politics, Style and the Post-industrial City in Hip Hop. In Rose, T. and Ross, A. (eds) *Microphone Fiends: Youth Music and Youth Culture*. New York and London: Routledge, pp. 71–88.

—— (1994b) *Black Noise: Rap Music and Black Culture in Contemporary America*. Hanover, NH: University Press of New England.

Rowan, C. T. (1993) *Dream Makers, Dream Breakers: The World of Justice Thurgood Marshall*. Boston, MA: Little, Brown and Company.

Royster, J. J. (1990) Perspectives on the Intellectual Tradition of Black Women Writers. In Lunsford, A., Moglen, H., and Slevin, J. (eds) *The Right to Literacy*. New York: MLA.
—— (1996) When the First Voice You Hear Is not Your Own, *CCC*, 47(1), pp. 29–40.
—— (ed.) (1997) *Southern Horrors and Other Writings: The Anti Lynching Campaign of Ida B. Wells*. Boston, MA: Bedford Books.
—— (2000) *Traces of a Stream: Literacy and Social Change among African-American Women*. Pittsburgh, PA: University of Pittsburgh Press.
Saville-Troike, M. (1982) *The Ethnography of Communication: An Introduction*. Baltimore, MD: University Park Press.
Schweizer, T. (1998) Epistemology: The Nature and Validation of Anthropological Knowledge. In Bernard, H. R. (ed.) *Handbook of Methods in Cultural Anthropology*. Walnut Creek, CA: Altamira Press, pp. 39–87.
Scott, J. (1993) Accommodating Nonmainstream Language in the Composition Classroom. In Glowka, A. W. and Lance, D. (eds) *Language Variation in North American English: Research and Teaching*. New York: Modern Language Association, pp. 331–45.
Severino, C., Guerra, J., and Butler, J. (eds) (1997) *Writing in Multicultural Settings*. New York: MLA.
Shaughnessy, M. P. (1977) *Errors and Expectations: A Guide for the Teacher of Basic Writing*. New York: Oxford University Press.
—— (1987) Basic Writing. In Tate, G. (ed.) *Teaching Composition*, Fort Worth, TX: Fort Worth University Press.
Shields, J. C. (ed.) (1988) *The Collected Works of Phillis Wheatley*. New York and Oxford: The Oxford University Press. The Schomburg Library of Nineteenth-Century Black Woman Writers Series.
Shor, I. (1996) *When Students Have Power: Negotiating Authority in a Critical Pedagogy*. Chicago and London: University of Chicago Press.
Simpkins, C., Simpkins, G., and Holt, G. (1977) *Bridge, a Cross-culture Reading Program: Study Book*. Boston, MA: Houghton Mifflin.
Smitherman, G. (1969) A Comparison of the Oral and Written Styles of a Group of Inner City Black Students, PhD dissertation, Ann Arbor, MI: University of Michigan.
—— (1977/1986) *Talkin and Testifyin: The Language of Black America*. Boston, MA: Houghton Mifflin; reissued, with revisions, Detroit, MI: Wayne State University Press.
—— (1992) Black English, Diverging or Converging?: The View from the National Assessment of Educational Progress, *Language and Education*, 6(1), pp. 47–61.
—— (1994) The Blacker the Berry, the Sweeter the Juice: African-American Student Writers. In Dyson, A. H. and Genishi, C. (eds) *The Need for Story: Cultural Diversity in Classroom and Community*. Urbana, IL: National Council of Teachers of English, pp. 80–101.
—— (1997a) Black Language and the Education of Black Children: One Mo' Once, *Black Scholar*, 27(1), pp. 28–35.
—— (1997b) "The Chain Remain the Same": Communicative Practices in the Hip Hop Nation, *Journal of Black Studies*, 28(1), pp. 3–25.
—— (2000) *Talkin' that Talk: Language, Culture, and Education in African America*. New York: Routledge.
—— (2001) Meditations on Language, Pedagogy, and a Life of Struggle. Paper presented at the Pennsylvania State University Rhetoric Conference, July, p. 12.
—— *et al.* CCCC's Language Knowledge and Awareness Survey. Available online: http://www.ncte.org/cccc/langsurvey.pdf. Accessed October 29, 2001.

REFERENCES

Souljah, S. (1994) *No Disrespect*. New York: Times Books.

Spencer, M. B., Noll, E., Stoltzfus, J., and Harpalani, V. (2001) Identity and School Adjustment: Revisiting the "Acting White" Assumption, *Educational Psychologist*, 36(1), pp. 21–30.

Spencer, J. M. (1997) *The New Negroes and Their Music: The Success of the Harlem Renaissance*. Knoxville: University of Tennessee Press.

Stanback, M. H. (1983) Code-Switching in Black Women's Speech, unpublished doctoral dissertation, University of Massachusetts.

—— (1985) Language and Black Women's Place: Evidence from the Black Middle Class. In Treichler, P., Kramarae, C., and Stafford, B. (eds) *For Alma Mater: Theory and Practice in Feminist Scholarship*. Urbana, IL: University of Illinois Press, pp. 177–93.

Steele, C. and Aronson, J. (1995) Stereotype Threat and the Intellectual Test Performance of African-Americans, *Journal of Personality and Social Psychology*, 69(5), p. 797.

Stevenson, B. (1996) Gender, Convention, Ideals, and Identity among Antebellum Virginia Slave Women. In Hine, D. C. and Gaspar, B. D. (eds) *Black Women and Slavery in the Americas: More than Chattel*. Bloomington and Indianapolis, IN: Indiana University Press, pp. 169–90.

Straker, D. (1985) Reading Material. In Brooks, C., Cobb Scott, J. *et al.* (eds) *Tapping Potential*. Urbana, IL: NCTE.

Street, B. (ed.) (1993) *Cross-Cultural Approaches to Literacy*. New York: Cambridge University Press.

—— (2000) Literacy Events and Literacy Practices: Theory and Practice in the New Literacy Studies. In Martin-Jones, M. and Jones, K. (eds) *Multilingual Literacies: Reading and Writing Different Worlds*. Philadelphia and Amsterdam: John Benjamins.

Stuckey, J. E. (1991) *The Violence of Literacy*. Portsmouth, NH: Boynton/Cook Publishers.

Taylor, H. (1991) *Standard English, Black English and Bi-dialectalism: A Controversy*. New York: Peter Lang.

Troutman, D. (1995) The Tongue or the Sword: Which is Master? In Smitherman, G. (ed.) *African-American Women Speak Out on Anita Hill-Clarence Thomas*. Detroit, MI: Wayne State University Press.

—— (2001) African-American Women: Talking that Talk. In Lanehart, S. (ed.) *Sociocultural and Historical Contexts of African-American Vernacular English*. Philadelphia: John Benjamins.

Troutman-Robinson, D. (1987) Oral and Written Discourse: A Study of Feature Transfer, unpublished doctoral disssertation, Michigan State University.

Truth, S. (1853) New York City Anti-Slavery Meeting, *New York Tribune*, September 5, p. 5. In Fitch, Suzanne Pullon, and Mandziuk, Roseann M. (eds) (1997) *Sojourner Truth as Orator: Wit, Story, and Song*. Westport, CN: Greenwood Press.

Turner, J. (ed.) (1993) *David Walker's Appeal to the Coloured Citizens of the World, but in Particular, and Very Expressly, to Those of the United States of America*. Baltimore, MD: Black Classic Press.

Turner, L. D. (1949) *Africanisms in the Gullah Dialect*. Chicago, IL: University of Chicago Press.

US Department of Education, Office of Educational Research and Improvement. National Center for Education Statistics (1995) *Findings from the Condition of Education 1994: The Educational Progress of Black Students*.

Villanueva, V. (1999) On the Rhetoric and Precedents of Racism, *CCC*, 50(4), pp. 645–61.

—— (1993) *Bootstraps: From an American Academic of Color.* Urbana, IL: National Council of Teachers of English.

Visor, J. (1987) The Impact of American Black English Oral Tradition Features on Decontextualization Skills in College Writing, dissertation, Illinois State University.

Walker, A. (1998) In Search of Our Mother's Gardens. In Liggins-Hill, P., Bell, B. *et al.* (eds) *Call and Response: The Riverside Anthology of the African-American Literary Tradition.* Boston, MA: Houghton Mifflin, pp. 1,802–7.

Watson, C. and Smitherman, G. (1996) *Educating Black Males: Detroit's Malcolm X Academy Solution.* Chicago, IL: Third World Press.

West, C. (1993) The New Cultural Politics of Difference. In Thompson, B. and Tyagi, S. (eds) *Beyond a Dream Deferred: Multicultural Education and the Politics of Excellence.* Minneapolis, MN: University of Minnesota Press, pp. 18–40.

Wideman, J. (1976) Frame and Dialect: The Evolution of the Black Voice in American Literature, *American Poetry Review*, 5(5) pp. 34–7.

Williams, P. (1991) The Alchemy of Race and Rights. Cambridge, MA: Harvard University Press.

Williamson Nelson, L. (1990) Code-switching in the Oral Life Narratives of African-American Women: Challenges to Linguistic Hegemony, Journal of Education, 172(3), pp. 142–55.

Wintz, C. D. (1996) Black Culture and the Harlem Renaissance. College State, TX: Texas A. and M. University Press.

Wolfram, W. (1991) Dialects and American English. Englewood Cliffs, NJ: Prentice-Hall Regents.

Woodley, C. L. (1999) The Pseudomasculine Identity and the African-American Male. In The Crisis of the Young African-American Male in the Inner Cities. A Consultation of the United States Commission on Civil Rights, Washington, DC, pp. 152–60.

Woodson, C. G. (1919) The Education of the Negro Prior to 1861. Washington DC: Associated Publishers; first edition, Brooklyn, NY: A. and B. Publishers.

—— (1990) The Miseducation of the Negro. Trenton, NJ: Africa New World Press; original work published 1933.

Yasin, J. (1999) Rap in the African-American Music Tradition: Cultural Assertion and Continuity. In Spears, A. K. (ed.) *Race and Ideology: Language, Symbolism, and Popular Culture.* Detroit, MI: Wayne State University Press.

Zaluda, S. (1998) Lost Voices of the Harlem Renaissance: Writing Assigned at Howard University, 1919–1931, Journal of the Conference on College Composition and Communication, 50(2), pp. 232–57.

Index

abolition of slavery 51–2
Abraham, Roger 34
access 90–1; literacies for 64–8
African American-centered approach;
    literature used in course 120–5;
    research study 97–113, 154 9;
    theory overview 95–7; theory and
    practice 116–20; in traditional
    curriculum 141–9; writing produced
    125–39
African American culture 11–14, 26–8,
    30, 31–72; access, equality, civil rights
    and Black power 64–8; enslavement
    36–52; Hip Hop 68–72; post-
    Reconstruction and Harlem Renais-
    sance 55–64; Reconstruction era 52–5
African American female literacies 73–94;
    defining 76–8; female strengths and
    education 89–92; literacy practices
    82–9; racism and classism 78–82;
    teaching strategies 92–4
African American students: composition
    and 19–26, 28–30; devoicing and
    disempowerment 2; female 89–92,
    literacy underachievement 3–4, 6–11,
    150–1; retention in higher education
    148; survival literacies 16–17
African American Vernacular English
    (AAVE) 11–18, 33–4, 75; programs
    14–16; research on 28–30; research
    study on rhetoric and composition
    course 97–113, 154–9; sociolinguistic
    ideas 18–19; syntax usage 101–10, 126,
    128, 130, 132
Afrocentricity 29, 116–17
Alexander, Alice 53–5
amendments to the Constitution 52, 66
Ampadu, L. 30

"Ann Arbor King School 'Black English'
    Case" 13–14
Aronson, J. 99
Asante, M. 116
assertiveness 86
assimilation 48–9
Association for the Study of Negro Life
    and History 58
authentic voice 22
autonomy 81

"bad nigger" 69
badman 69–70
Baker, Houston 118–19
Baker, Josephine 65
Ball, A. 28, 30
basic writing 12–13, 98–9
Baxter, M. 14–15
Berlin, J. 22, 26
Berry, Fannie 80
biadialectal approach 28–9
biracial identity 144–5
Black artful teaching style 89, 92
Black Atlantic languages 36–7, 151–2
Black discourse 123; in students' texts
    105–7, 108–10, 135–9, 155–7
Black Liberation Movement 8
Black Panther Party for Self-defense 64,
    67
Black Power Movement 67–8
blues matrix 119
borderlands rhetoric 24–5
Bormann, E. G. 109
Bowser, B. P. 140
Bridge Program 15
Brooks, Gwendolyn 64, 65–6
Brotherhood of Sleeping Car Partners 64
Brown, James 65, 67